IMAGES
of America

CHATTANOOGA

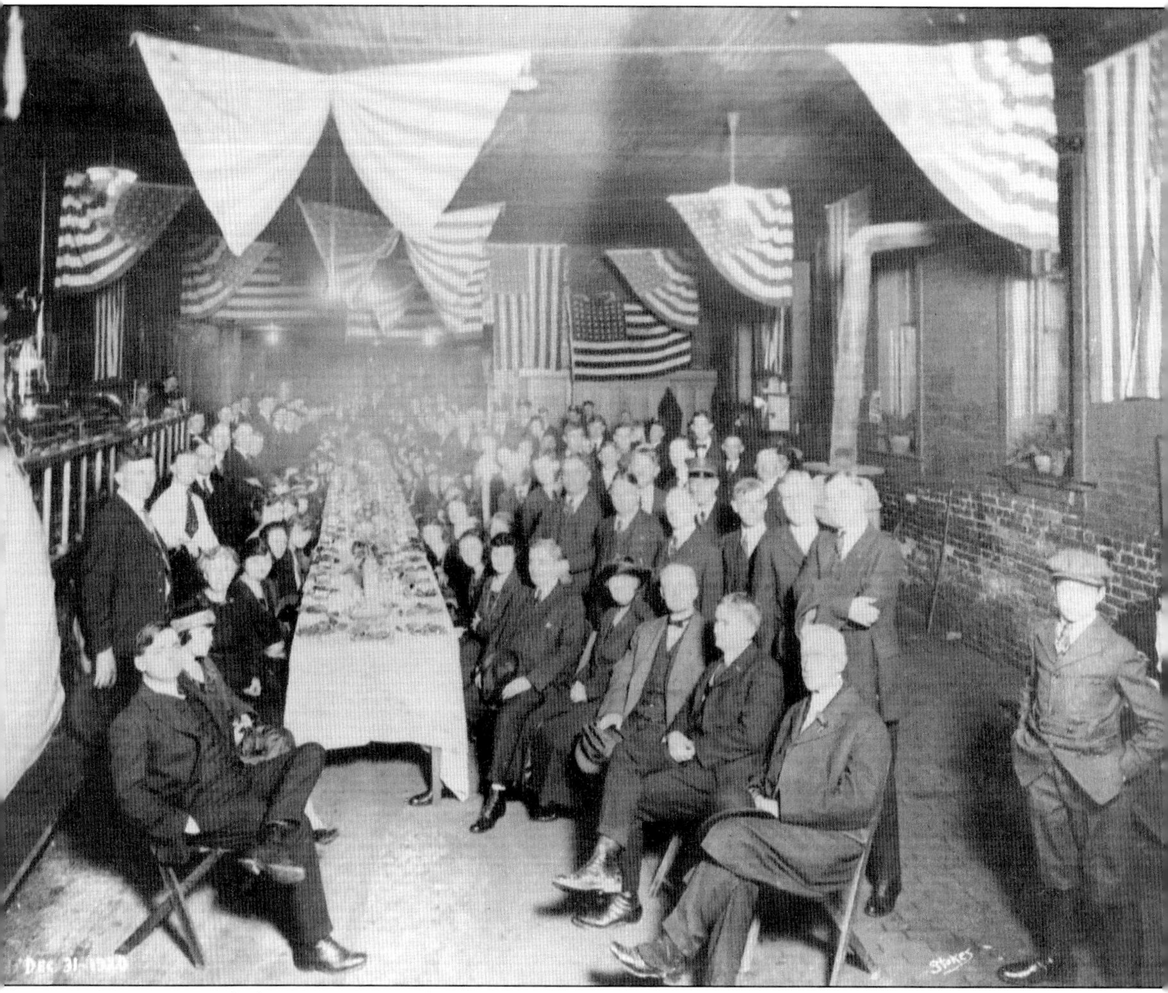

Firemen and their wives crowd into a fire hall on New Year's Eve in 1920. On the left, a fire truck can be seen covered with canvas. In 1920 the population of Chattanooga reached 57,895; but an even greater period of territorial expansion and population growth was being ushered in with the new year on this night.

Cover Photograph: Twelve unknown women and one boy pose on Umbrella Rock at the Point of Lookout Mountain in a photograph taken by George T. Linn in 1910. The Point is part of the Chickamauga and Chattanooga National Military Park, dedicated in 1895. The roof of Point Hotel can be seen just below the Point, and in the distance, the Tennessee River winds past Moccasin Bend.

IMAGES
of America

CHATTANOOGA

Jerry R. Desmond

ARCADIA
PUBLISHING

ISBN 978-0-7385-8999-2

Published by Arcadia Publishing
Charleston, South Carolina

Printed in the United States of America

For all general information contact Arcadia Publishing at:
Telephone 843-853-2070
Fax 843-853-0044
E-mail sales@arcadiapublishing.com
For customer service and orders:
Toll-Free 1-888-313-2665

Visit us on the Internet at www.arcadiapublishing.com

This book is dedicated to all of the members and friends of the Chattanooga Regional History Museum and to my mother, Mabel J. Desmond.

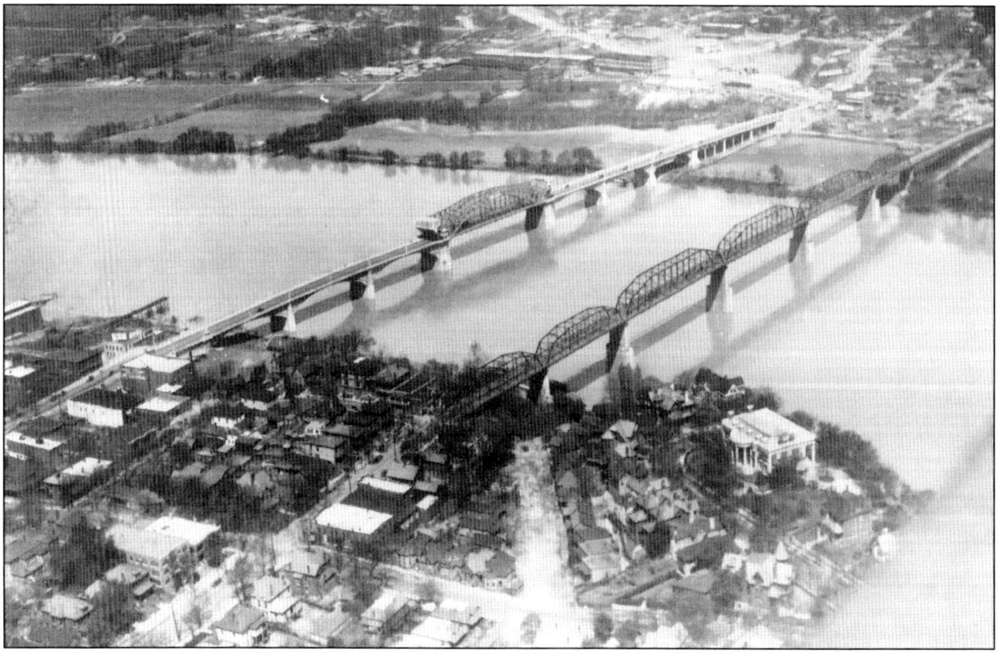

This aerial view of the Tennessee River at Chattanooga shows both the Market Street (John Ross) and the Walnut Street Bridges in the 1930s. At the right, the Bluff View Mansion dominates the other buildings in its neighborhood. Built for Ross S. Faxon, a successful banker, the mansion later passed into the hands of George T. Hunter, an early executive with the Coca-Cola Bottling Company. Today, the building is the home of the Hunter Museum of Art.

Contents

Introduction 7

1. Scenic Beauty 9

2. Civil War and Remembrance 25

3. City Streets and Scenes 43

4. The Business of Chattanooga Is Business 59

5. People 73

6. People at Work 87

7. Edification 101

8. Sports and Leisure 113

Acknowledgments and Bibliography 128

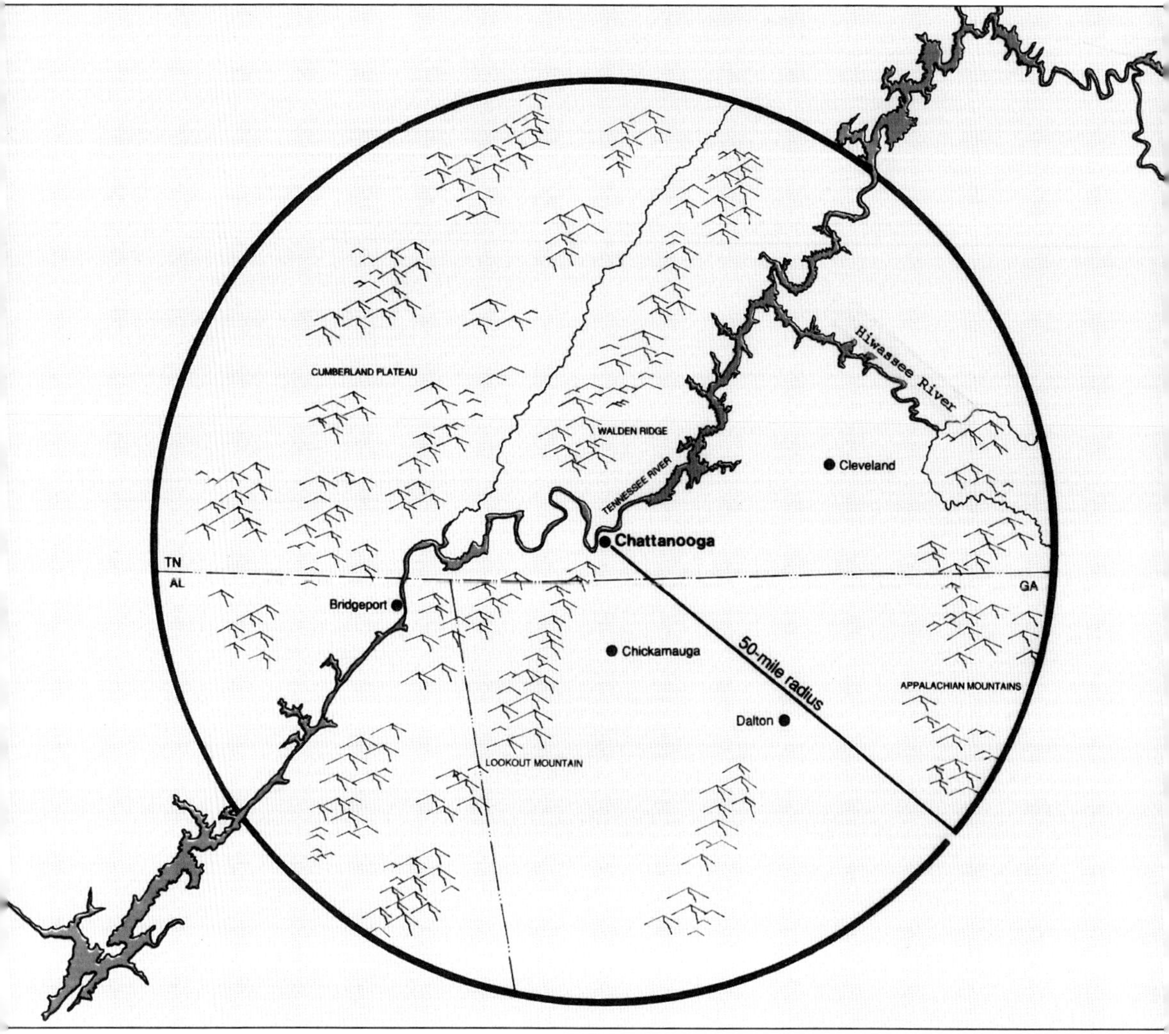

Chattanooga is located in Hamilton County, in the southeastern section of Tennessee. Around 120 miles from both Nashville, TN, and Atlanta, GA, Chattanooga is beautifully situated on the Tennessee River between the Cumberland Plateau and the Great Smoky Mountains. The Chattanooga Regional History Museum, established in 1978, seeks to portray and interpret events in the history of the region within a 50-mile radius of Chattanooga, as shown above.

Introduction

On a summer's day in 1838 a meeting was called for the residents of Ross's Landing, a small community in Hamilton County. With the recent removal of the Cherokee Indians from the area, it was expected that the white population of the town, comprising more than fifty households at this time, would grow. A surveyor had recently plated the area and streets had been laid out (with numbered streets running perpendicular to those named for trees). Lots had been reserved for schools and churches and new deeds had been issued.

The only item of business remaining was the naming of the new community. Since any part of the shoreline of the Tennessee River could be called a landing, a more distinctive title than Ross's Landing was necessary, one which would attract potential settlers. One citizen, noting the white cliffs of Walden's Ridge, suggested Albion; another recommended Lookout City. Still a third thought Montevideo had a nice ring to it.

Finally, John P. Long, town commissioner and postmaster, apparently returned the discussion to an even earlier proposal, an ancient Indian word which, literally translated, meant "mountains looking at each other." "The name might sound outlandish and strange to some ears," Long noted, "but if our city was a success, it would become familiar and pleasant, and there would not be another name like it in the world." Enough of those present were swayed by this argument that the proposal was accepted. The post office adopted it in November 1838 and the Tennessee Legislature approved it in 1839. The town of Chattanooga was born.

It has been a success. Today the city of Chattanooga has a population of 152,000 and Hamilton County another 133,000. Chattanooga is the state's fourth largest city. The redevelopment of the downtown area and the construction of several major attractions such as the Tennessee Aquarium, the Imax Theater, and the Creative Discovery Museum have rejuvenated the city and boosted tourism dramatically. Such developments reflect an extremely healthy business environment, which results in high levels of employment. Although the city has its share of the usual modern day problems, one thing is certain: Chattanooga is booming.

It has not, of course, always been this good. Chattanooga and Hamilton County have experienced economic crises, and man-made and natural disasters. One of the few cities in the country to suffer a wartime siege, Chattanooga has also been struck by disastrous floods in 1867, 1875, 1886, and 1917. Fires have occasionally swept through the downtown, including blockbusters in 1871, 1887, and 1888. Add on a cholera epidemic in 1873 and a yellow fever epidemic in 1878, and one wonders how the city managed to survive. However, three watershed events shaped the future of the city and ensured its success: the arrival of the railroads in the 1850s; the Civil War and its aftermath in the 1860s and 1870s; and the taming of the Tennessee River by the Tennessee Valley Authority (TVA) in the 1930s.

Early Chattanooga was a river town. A geographic twist of fate made it a convenient place for Indian canoes, keelboats, and other river traffic to stop before reaching a dangerous series of rapids further down the river. When the first train of the Western and Atlantic Railroad arrived in 1849, the future of the community was assured. It was now cheaper to ship the products of eastern Tennessee to Chattanooga and on to the Atlantic Ocean by rail than to move cargo all the way to New Orleans by river, and this development in communications boosted industrial and other businesses in the region. Additional railroads soon connected Chattanooga to Nashville, Knoxville, Memphis, and thus, to the rest of the country.

However, there was a downside to these developments: as an important crossroads, the city found itself one of the key focal points of the Civil War. The bloody battles of Chickamauga, Lookout Mountain, and Missionary Ridge were fought in 1863 to determine strategic ownership of the railroad crossing; they also played a part in deciding the fate of the nation. The countryside was ravaged, the city denuded of trees, buildings were destroyed, and the population declined dramatically. Yet, the war had a positive and lasting effect on the city.

Many of the Union soldiers who fought in the region during the war were struck by the scenic beauty of the area and saw its economic potential. The city was rebuilt by these men, their families, and returning natives. Indeed, Chattanooga soon became a leading manufacturing and business center in the South. Companies such as the Wheland Foundry, Chattanooga Medicine Company (today called Chattem), the Chattanooga Brewery, and the Provident Life and Accident Insurance Company flourished at the turn of the century. The first Coca-Cola bottling plant was franchised in Chattanooga in 1899. The establishment of the Chickamauga and Chattanooga National Military Park in 1895, the development of the Ruby Falls and Rock City attractions in the 1930s, and the opening of the Dixie Highway contributed greatly to the growth of tourism.

The development that can be said to have been the final ingredient in the Chattanooga success story occurred in the 1930s. At last, the mighty Tennessee River was tamed by the TVA. The completion of the Chickamauga Dam in 1940 not only assured that the city would be relatively flood free but also meant cheap electrical power which in turn stimulated additional economic growth. Growth did not come without its environmental downside, however. By the mid-twentieth century, Chattanooga was not a particularly nice place to visit. Air and water pollution had taken its toll on the urban landscape, and it has required a concerted effort over the past thirty years to reverse that trend. Today, Chattanooga is known as the environmental city, an exciting model for renewal.

The photographs and drawings in this book come entirely from the collection of the Chattanooga Regional History Museum. They are not presented in chronological order, nor is this book intended as a conventional history of Chattanooga and Hamilton County. It is, however, a photographic history of the region: a history based upon the visual records of the century or so between the birth of photography and the 1960s. The main focus is on the people of the region: people at work, people at play, civic-minded citizens, the prominent, and the unknown. In addition, two chapters present images which show how the physical appearance of the community has changed over the past 150 years: Chapter One, "Scenic Beauty," concentrates on the natural environment; Chapter Three, "City Streets and Scenes," centers on structural changes.

The Chattanooga Regional History Museum is housed in a 1910 school building two blocks from the Tennessee River in downtown Chattanooga. Through exhibits, education, and outreach projects, the museum, which was founded in 1978, seeks to present events in the history of southeast Tennessee, northwest Georgia, and northeast Alabama, from prehistory to the present by collecting, preserving, researching, interpreting, and displaying its written, spoken, pictorial, and artifactual records.

The story of these events and the people of the region is told in the museum's award-winning permanent exhibit, a three-dimensional, interactive experience entitled *Chattanooga Country: Its Land, Rivers, and People*. Temporary exhibits are constantly being changed in the museum's other galleries. In addition, the museum has outstanding collections of artifacts related to prehistoric Chattanooga, the Civil War, nineteenth- and early twentieth-century business and industry, and the history of tourism in the region.

Perhaps the largest and fastest growing of the museum's collections is its extensive photographic archive. Several thousand original photographs have been collected concerning every aspect of the history of Chattanooga and its environs. The photographs selected for this book represent the best of that collection, and many of them are being published for the very first time.

One

Scenic Beauty

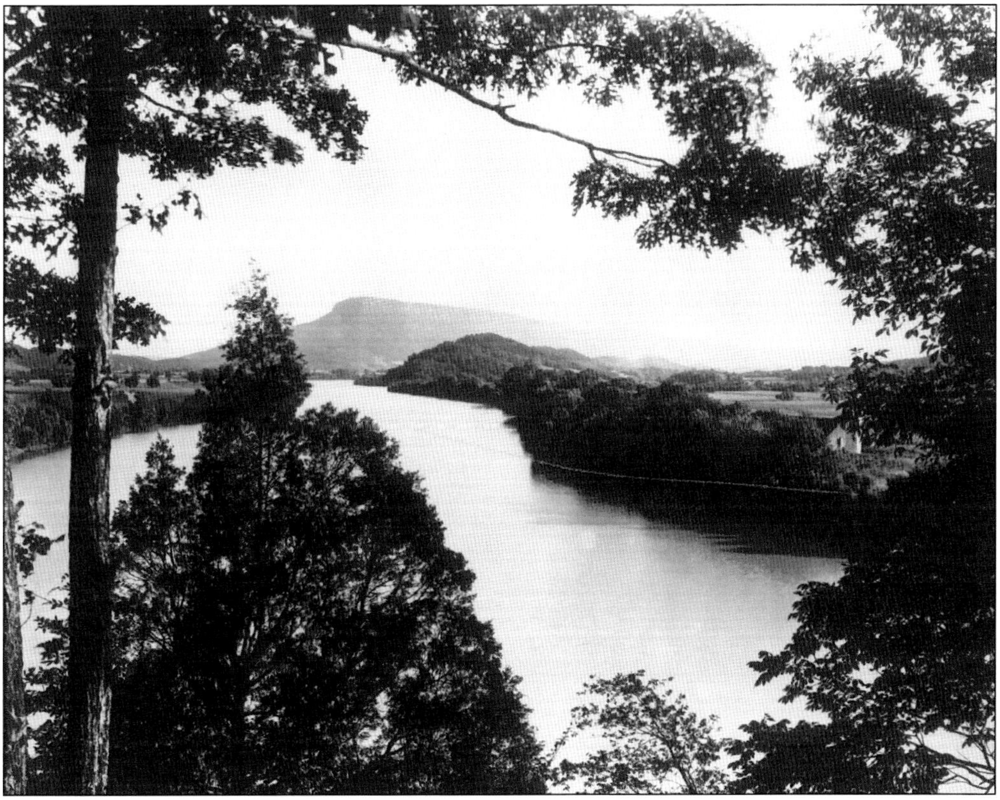

"We have nothing in Europe comparable to this," noted Prince Henry of Prussia while taking in the panoramic view from Lookout Mountain. The prince had been escorted to the top of the mountain by Chattanooga dignitaries during his 1902 tour of the United States. While he may have conveniently forgotten the Bavarian Alps of his homeland, his sentiments are shared by thousands of tourists each year. The scenic beauty of the Chattanooga region is unmatched. This photograph, with Lookout Mountain in the background, was taken from Williams Island on the Tennessee River.

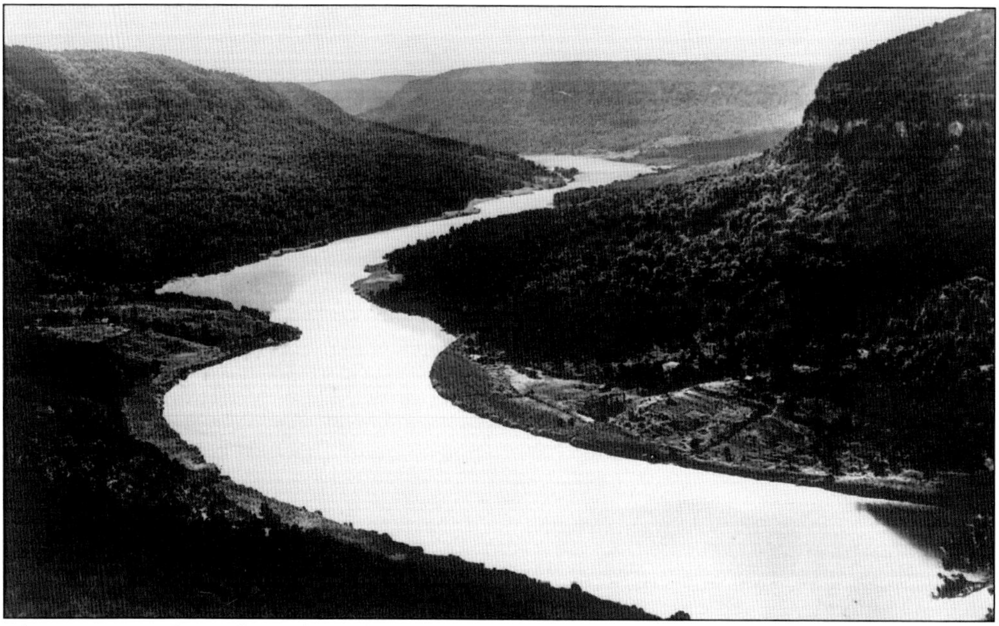

The Tennessee River flows through an area known as the "Grand Canyon of the Tennessee." Here the Unaka Mountains (known by most people as the Great Smoky Mountains) meet the Cumberland Plateau. In the early days, it was necessary for those traveling by water to stop upstream before attempting the swift currents and rapids of this section of the river.

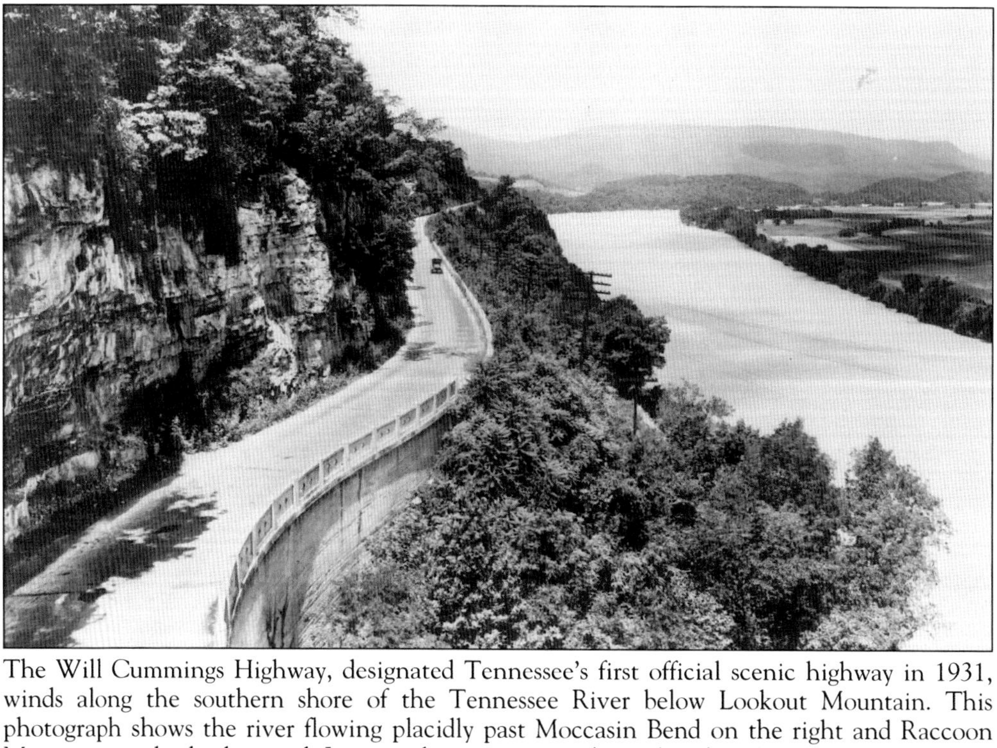

The Will Cummings Highway, designated Tennessee's first official scenic highway in 1931, winds along the southern shore of the Tennessee River below Lookout Mountain. This photograph shows the river flowing placidly past Moccasin Bend on the right and Raccoon Mountain in the background. Just a mile upstream, early settlers found a convenient spot to locate a river community.

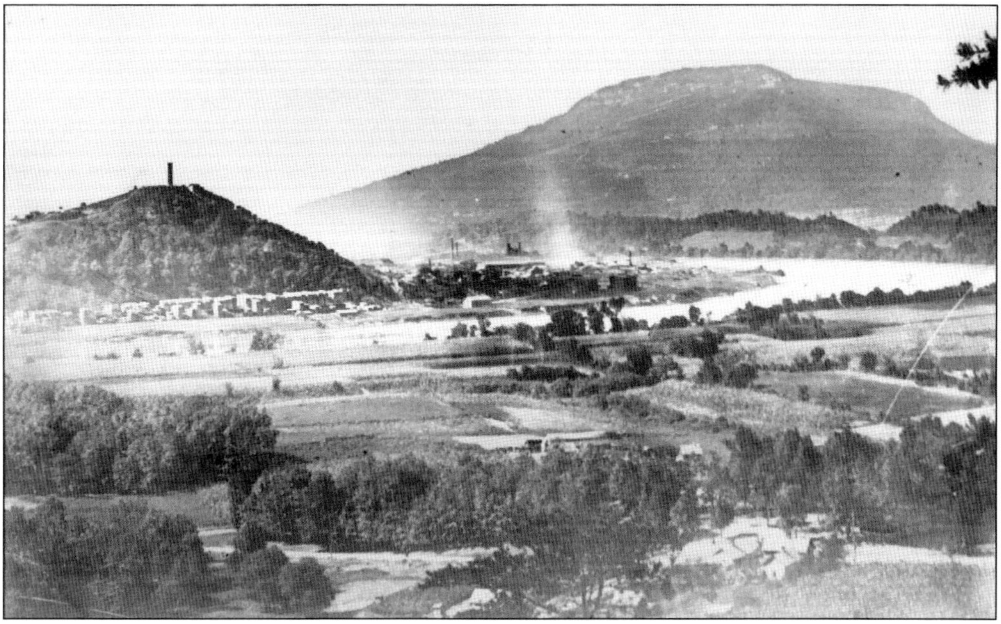

Chattanooga's fate has always been tied to the Tennessee River. This photograph, taken in 1898, shows the Loomis and Hart Lumber Yard at the base of Cameron Hill. The hill was named for James Cameron, an artist who lived there for a few years while painting landscapes of the region.

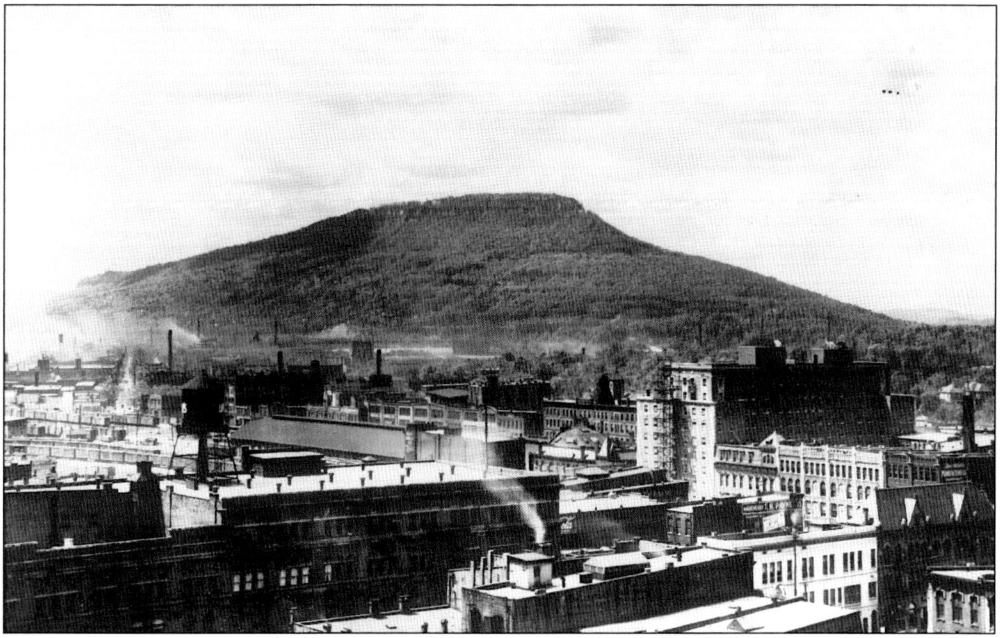

This rooftop view of Chattanooga was probably taken in the 1930s. Rising to a height of slightly less than 2,000 feet above sea level in Tennessee, Lookout Mountain actually extends south into Georgia for 83 miles, varying in width from 1 to 10 miles. The 240 million-year-old sandstone cap of the mountain, known at the Point as the "Palisades," is clearly visible in this photograph.

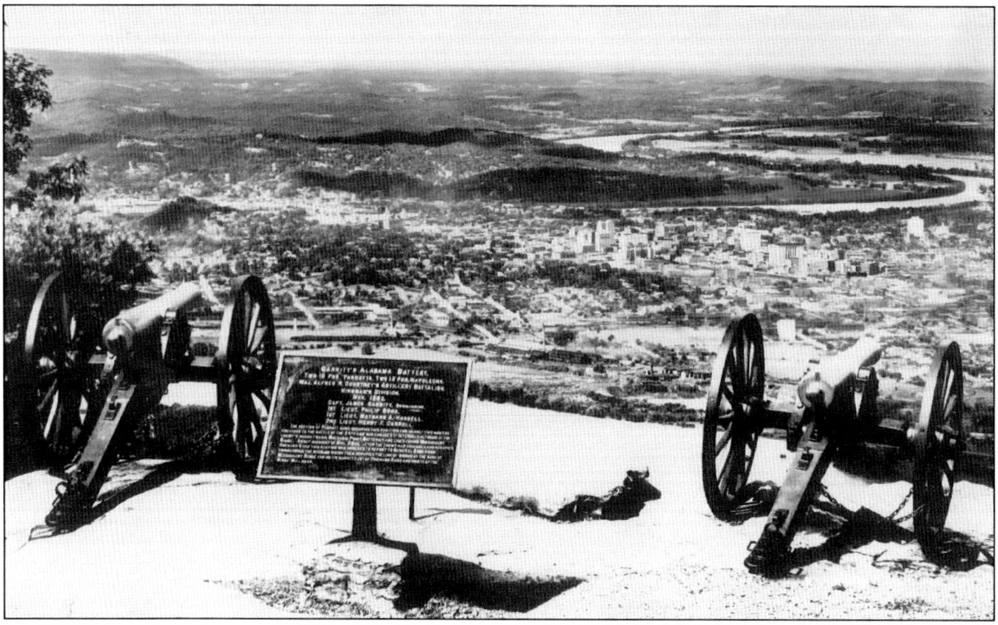

The cannon of Garrity's Alabama Battery point down at the city from Point Park. Purchased at a cost of $35,000, the 16.5 acres of the Point were added to the Chickamauga and Chattanooga National Military Park three years after the 1895 dedication of the park. It has become a perfect place to shoot: today excellent photographs of the city are shot far more frequently than the cannon. Over nine hundred thousand visitors explore the park each year.

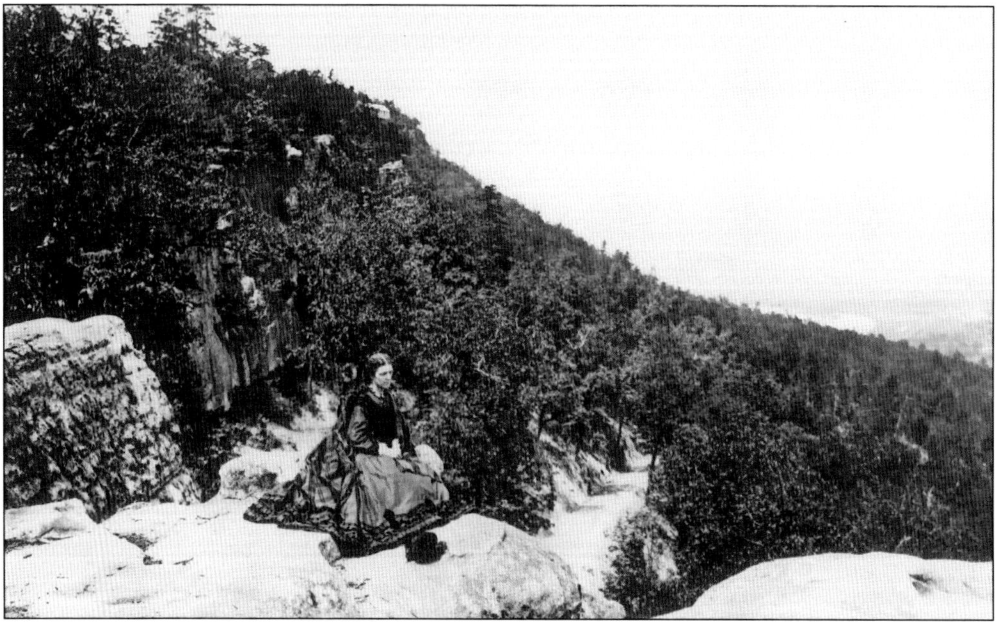

Mrs. H.C. Cook, the wife of Captain Cook of the United States Regular Army, is shown sitting on an escarpment of Lookout Mountain in this 1864 photograph. She and her husband had taken a home on the mountain following the Civil War battles for Chattanooga in 1863. The Whiteside Turnpike, the only road up the mountain for many years, is clearly visible below Mrs. Cook.

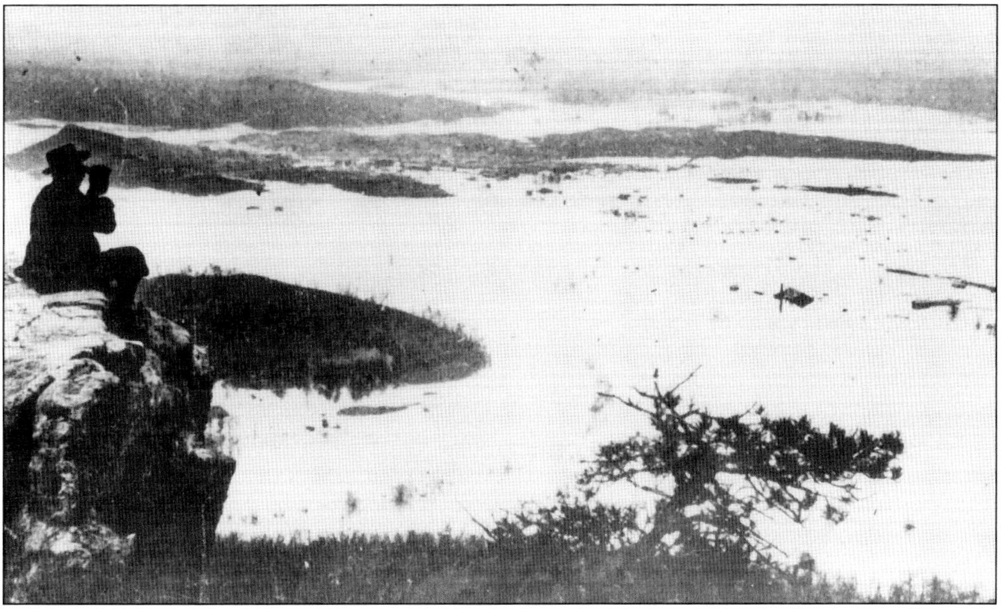

In 1867, the Tennessee River crested 58 feet above its normal level (the highest mark reached in the recorded history of the river), flooding most of the downtown area and sweeping away the three-year-old military bridge. One lucky Chattanooga man had his house washed away only to have a better one come to rest on the spot. Another house floated to Chestnut Street. When it remained unclaimed, it was sold to provide funds for flood relief. Floods in 1875, 1886, and 1917 also caused considerable damage in Chattanooga.

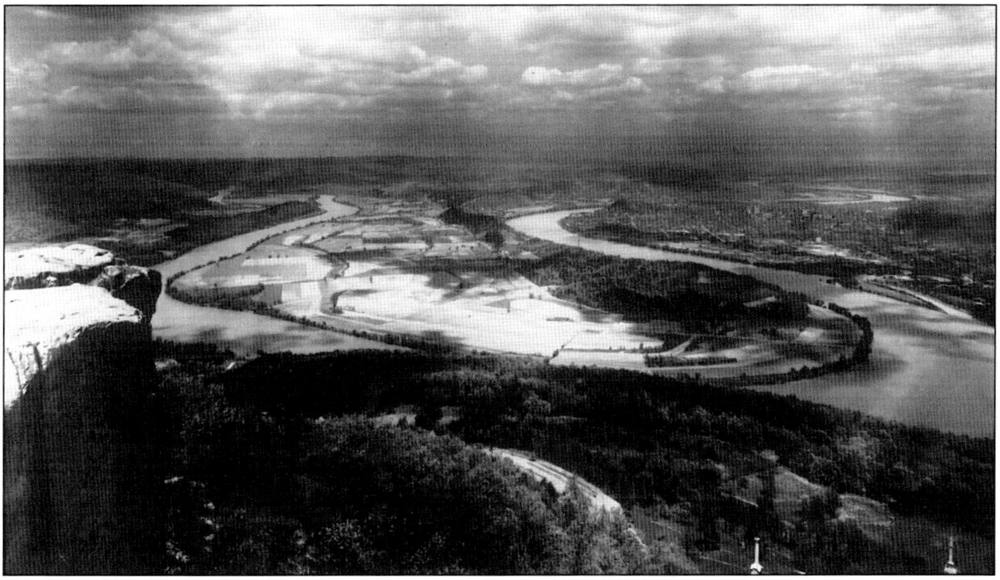

This image, taken from Lookout Point, shows the distinctive shape of Moccasin Bend and, in the lower right-hand corner, the Iowa and New York Civil War monuments. More plans have been made for Moccasin Bend than for any other piece of real estate in Hamilton County. In 1961, it was purchased by the city and county. Since then, discussions about its development and about the possible preservation of important archaeological and Civil War sites have continued.

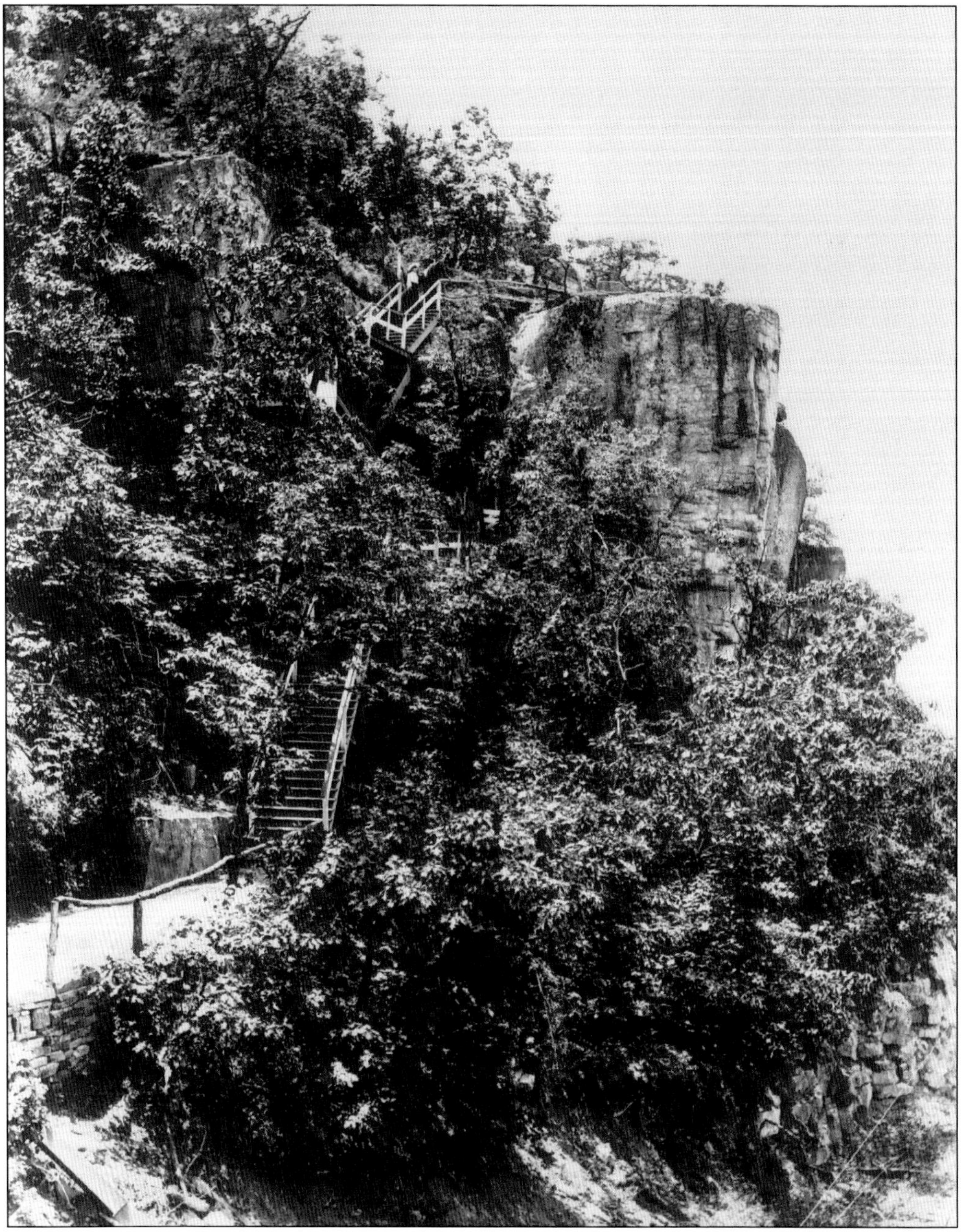

Visitors to Lookout Mountain climbing wooden stairs up to Roper Rock (also known as Roper's Rock) on the west brow of the mountain at the turn of the century. Situated a few yards from the point of the mountain, the rock was named for Corporal Roper of the Union army who accidentally fell 60 or 70 feet to his death from this spot on March 17, 1864. The view from the rock is spectacular, as Lookout Valley and Sand Mountain seem to stretch endlessly west and south into Georgia.

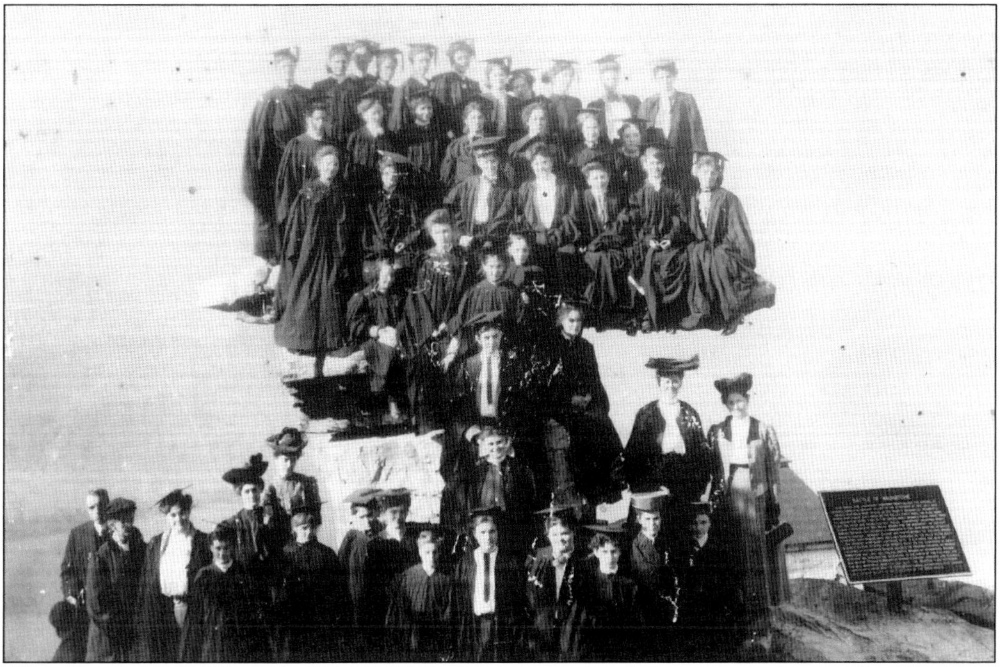

Umbrella Rock was a popular attraction at Point Park for many years. Thousands have had their picture taken on or near the rock, including General Ulysses Grant. Shown here are the young ladies of the 1907 graduating class of Centenary College with several faculty members. Today, this unusual formation still stands but it is closed to the public due to its immediate proximity to dangerous ledges.

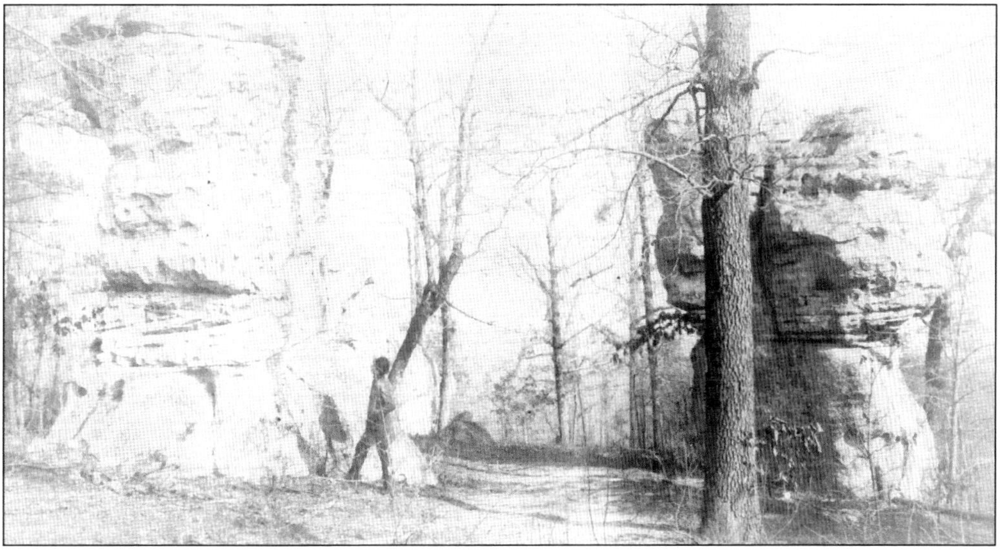

Strange rock formations dot the top and sides of Lookout Mountain. The rock on the left is known as the "Old Man of the Mountain" and is located near "Rock City," a popular tourist attraction. The rocks looked so much like gnomes and other mythical creatures to settlers that this section of the mountain was called "Fairyland." This image was taken by Hardie Brothers Photographers, a popular photographic studio that was located on the side of the mountain in the late nineteenth century.

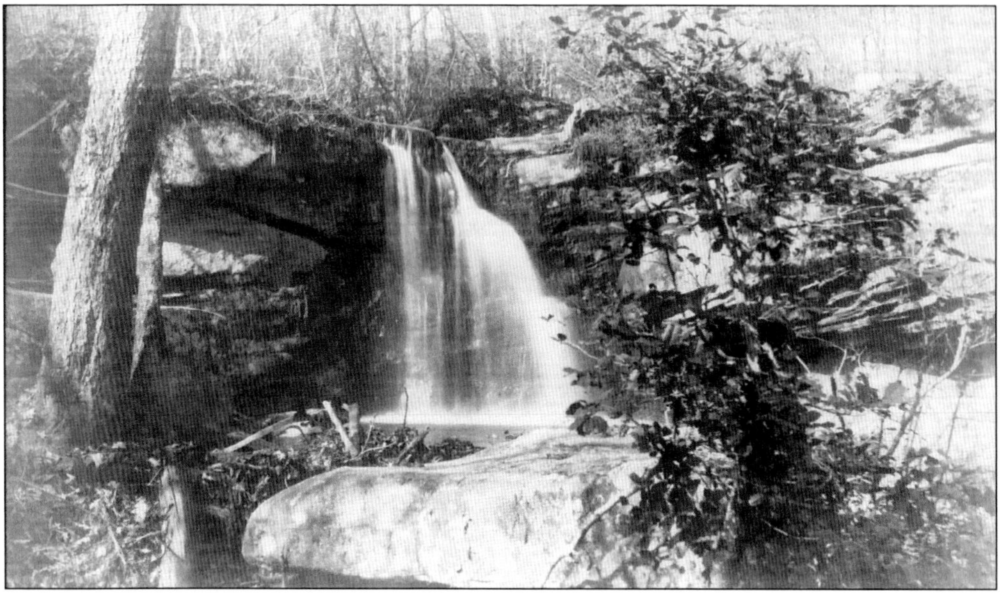

A small waterfall and the body of water above it on Lookout Mountain were named for Princess Telulah of the Cherokee Indians. According to legend, Princess Telulah plunged to her death over the falls when her father refused to let her marry her lover. Over time, the name was shortened to Lulah, and then, to Lula Falls and Lula Lake.

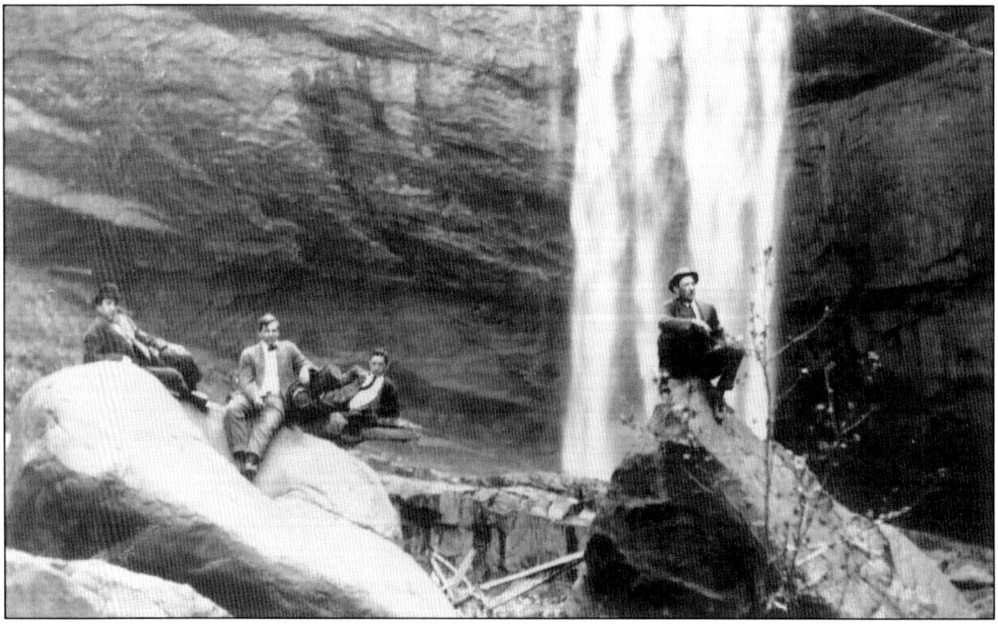

For a time after the Civil War, there was an attempt to change the name of Lula Falls to Seclusion Falls but the name did not stick. In the 1890s, grandiose plans were made to turn the area into a resort town, complete with a spa and luxury hotel. No ideas were ever taken past the planning stage, however, and the area remains fairly undeveloped.

Sunset Rock extends out from the west brow of Lookout Mountain. In October 1863 Confederate Generals Bragg and Longstreet met here to plan a counterattack against the Federal army. The Battle of Wauhatchie, fought around midnight on the day of their meeting, was a Union victory. Today, the area near Sunset Rock is a popular spot for rock climbers.

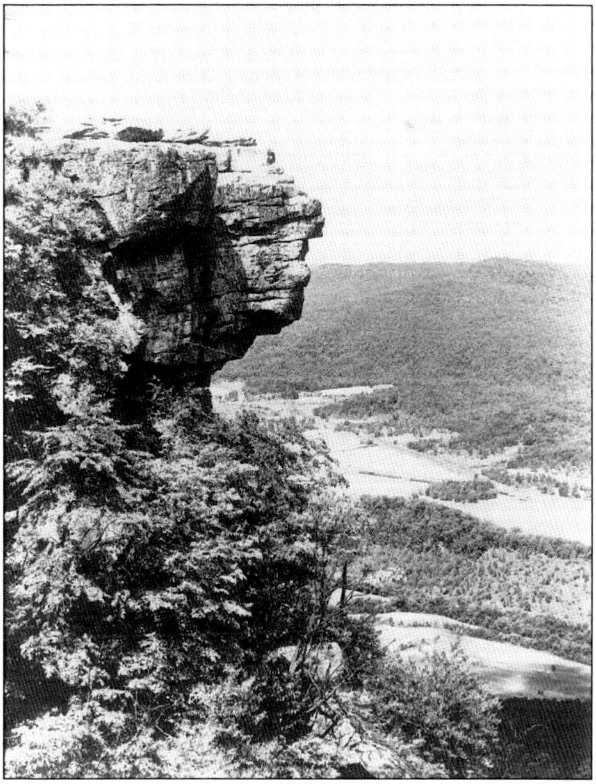

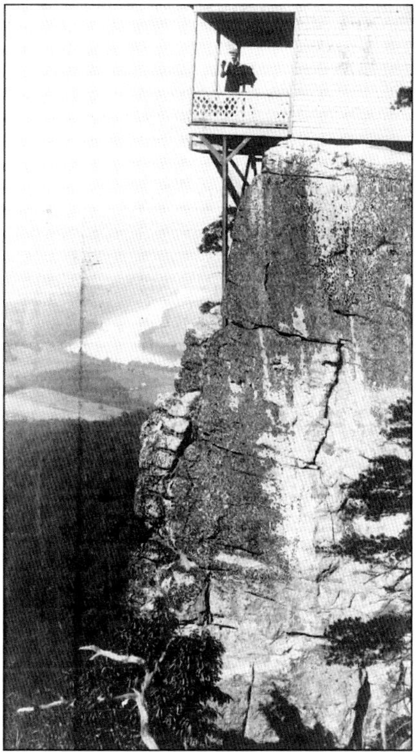

Robert M. Linn came to Chattanooga from Ohio in 1863, after the Battle of Missionary Ridge. He built a photographic studio at Lookout Point, and soon had a thriving business taking souvenir pictures for soldiers and other sightseers. When the lease to the studio was sold to the Hardie brothers of Michigan, Linn's son, George T. Linn, built the studio at Sunset Rock shown in this photograph. He eventually moved back to the Point in 1900 and stayed there until 1939, when the Ochs Observatory and Museum was built on the site.

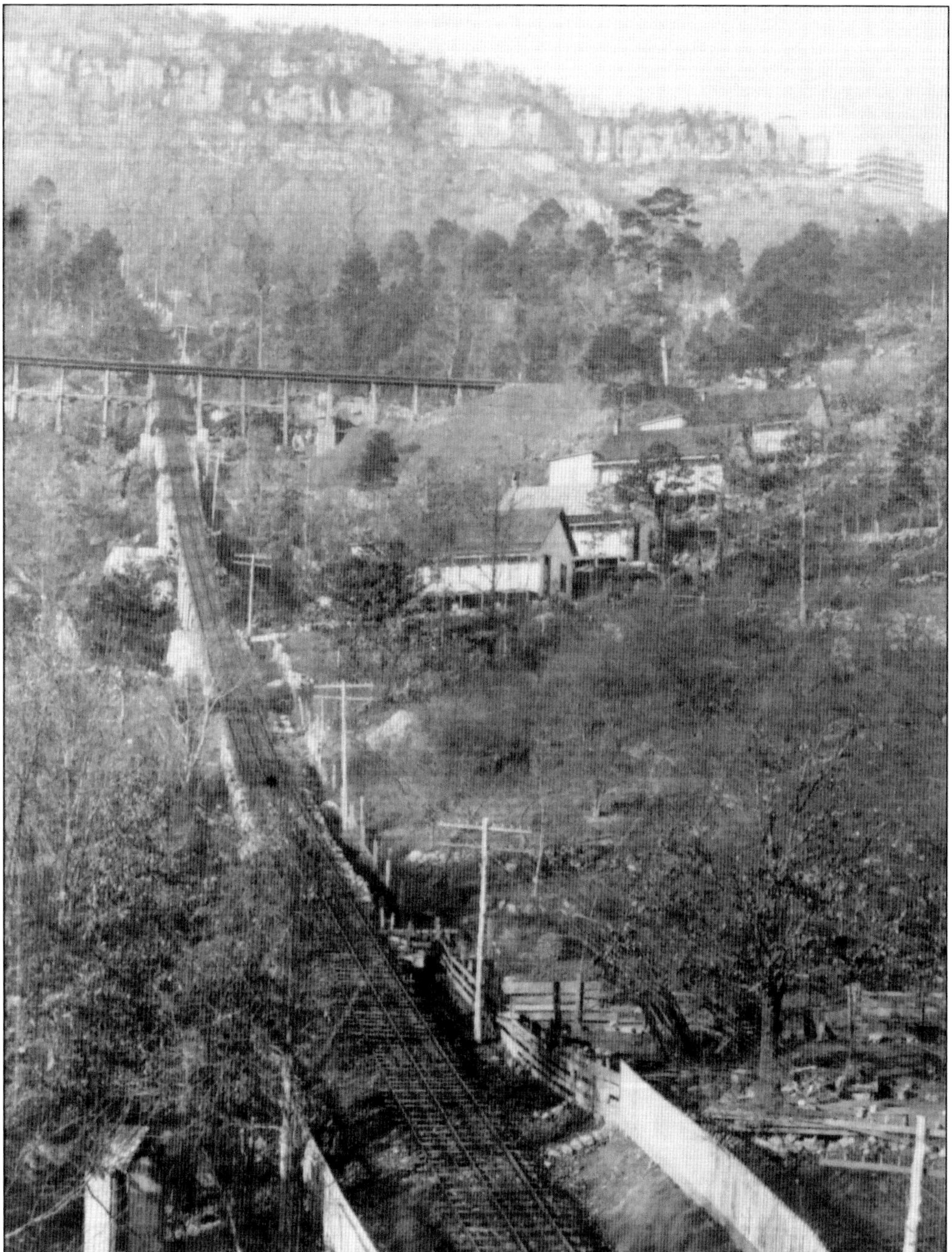

Following the deadly yellow fever epidemic in 1878, various attempts were made to improve access to the more healthful environment of Lookout Mountain. Several hotels, railroads, and inclines were built between 1880 and 1900. Incline #2 was completed in 1895 in time for the dedication ceremonies for the National Military Park. At one point climbing at a gradient of 72.7%, the incline was thought to be the steepest passenger incline in the world. This early Hardie Brothers photograph of Incline #2 also shows Point Hotel in the upper right-hand corner.

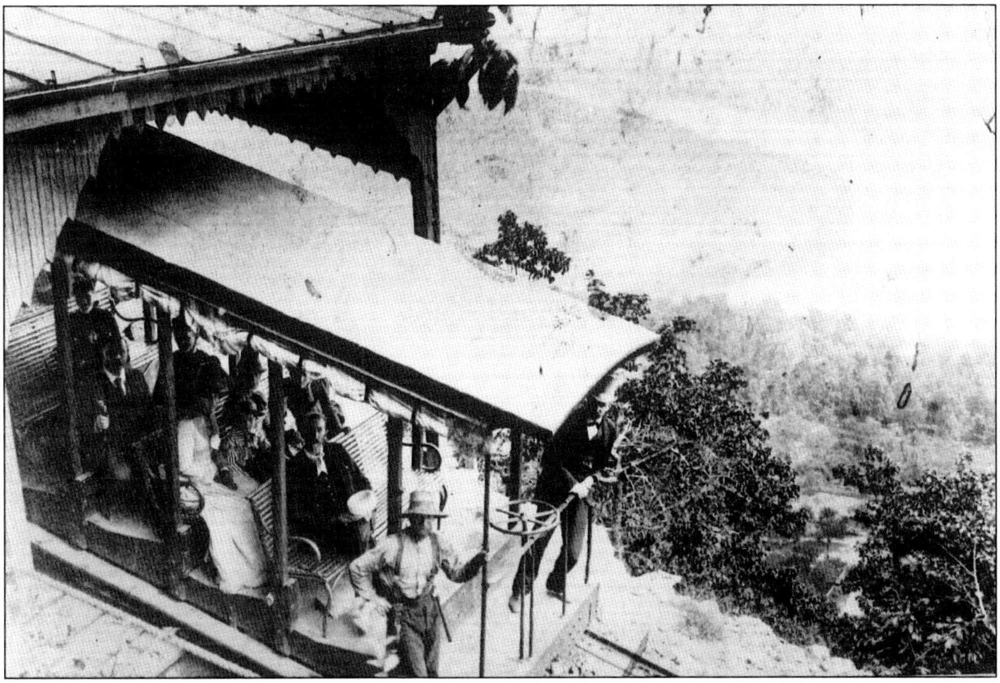

An Incline #1 car is shown here entering the depot at the Point. Incline #1 was completed in 1885 and passenger service began in 1887. Although the steepest grade on Incline #1 was 33%, it was considered quite an engineering feat for its time. Each car could hold 35 passengers and the round trip ticket cost 50¢. In 1888, Point Hotel was constructed near the depot.

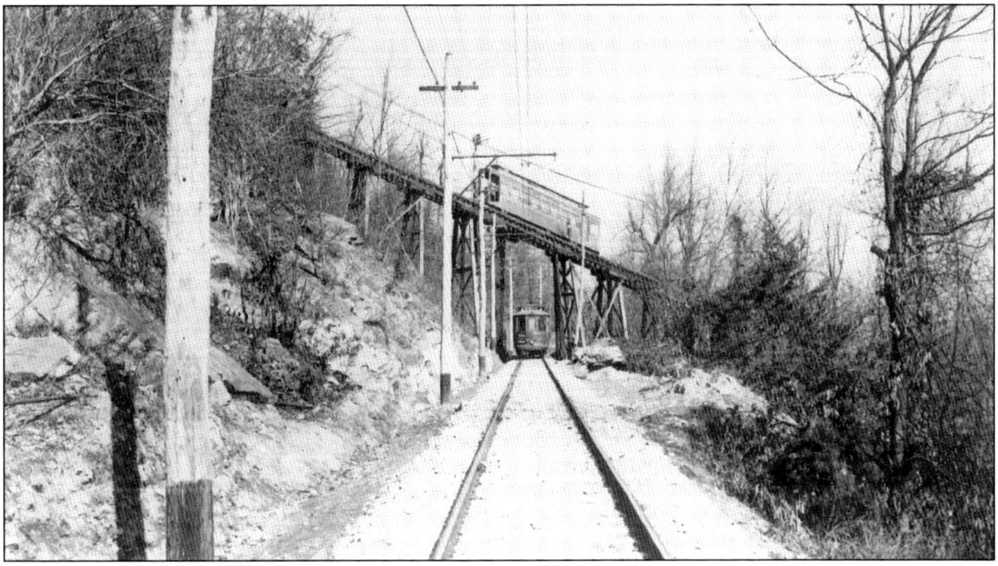

Built to compete with Incline #1, the Broad Gauge Railroad eventually reached the top of Lookout Mountain in 1889. That year, the magnificent Lookout Inn was begun near the mountain railroad terminus. The Broad Gauge Railroad and Incline #1 soon fell on hard times due to competition from Incline #2 and by 1899, both were out of business. For a while, between 1913 and 1920, an attempt was made to run an electric streetcar line on the old Broad Gauge tracks. This photograph shows the streetcar running under Incline #2.

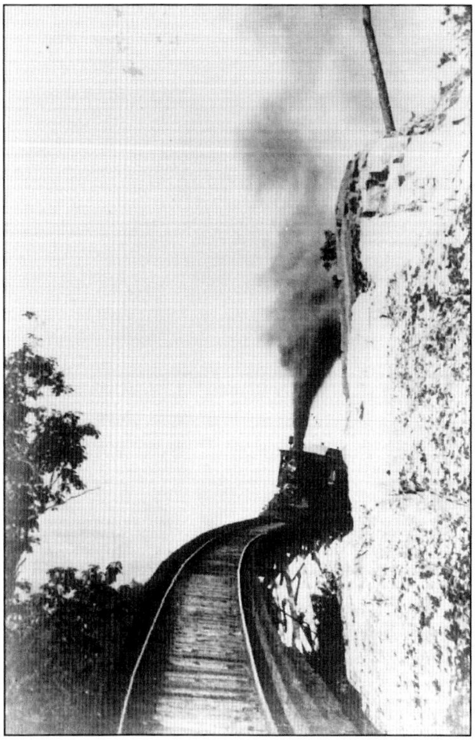

The Narrow Gauge Railroad was built from the Point Hotel around the west brow of Lookout Mountain to Sunset Rock and was eventually extended to the Natural Bridge. This photograph shows an engine on the Narrow Gauge track rounding a bend blasted from solid rock. Today, hiking trails that follow the bed of the old tracks have replaced the railroads on the mountainside.

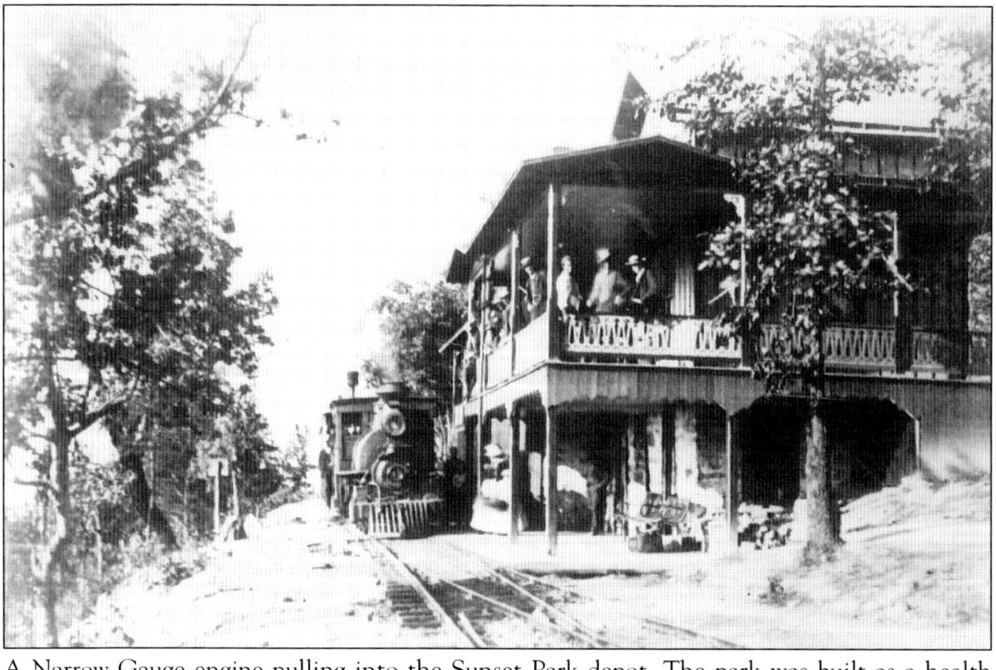

A Narrow Gauge engine pulling into the Sunset Park depot. The park was built as a health haven and plans were made to build a model sanitarium on the site. Passengers on the Narrow Gauge could also stop at this station to visit the "Garden of the Gods," a wild section of the mountain featuring unusual rock formations. These included "Damon" and "Pythias," a pair of large boulders connected by a swinging bridge.

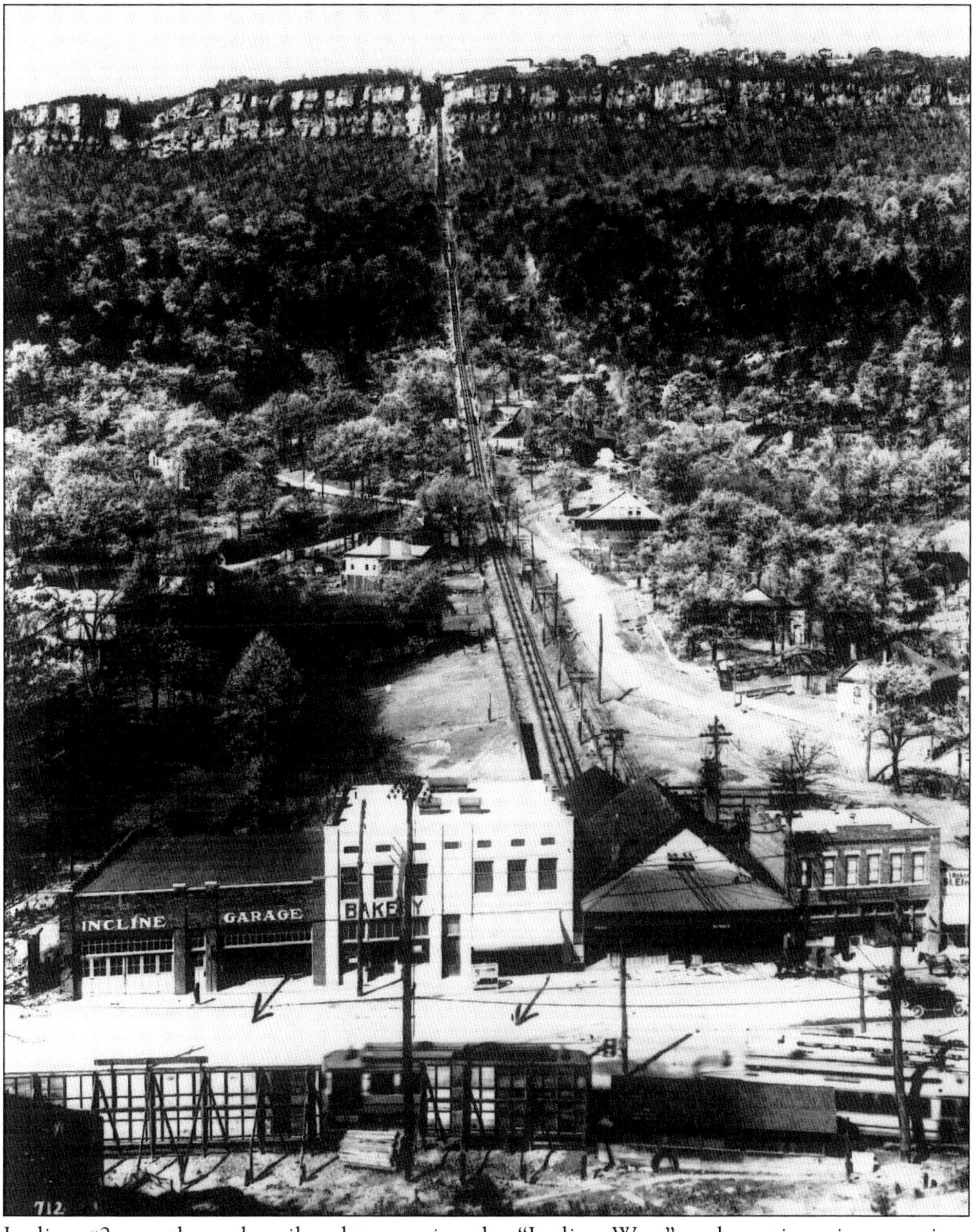

Incline #2 was the only railroad to survive the "Incline Wars" and continue in operation. This photograph from 1910 shows the lower incline station in the suburban community of St. Elmo. Across the street, trolley cars run next to billboards owned by the Stoops Billposting and Advertising Company. Today, Incline #2 is still advertised as "America's Most Amazing Mile."

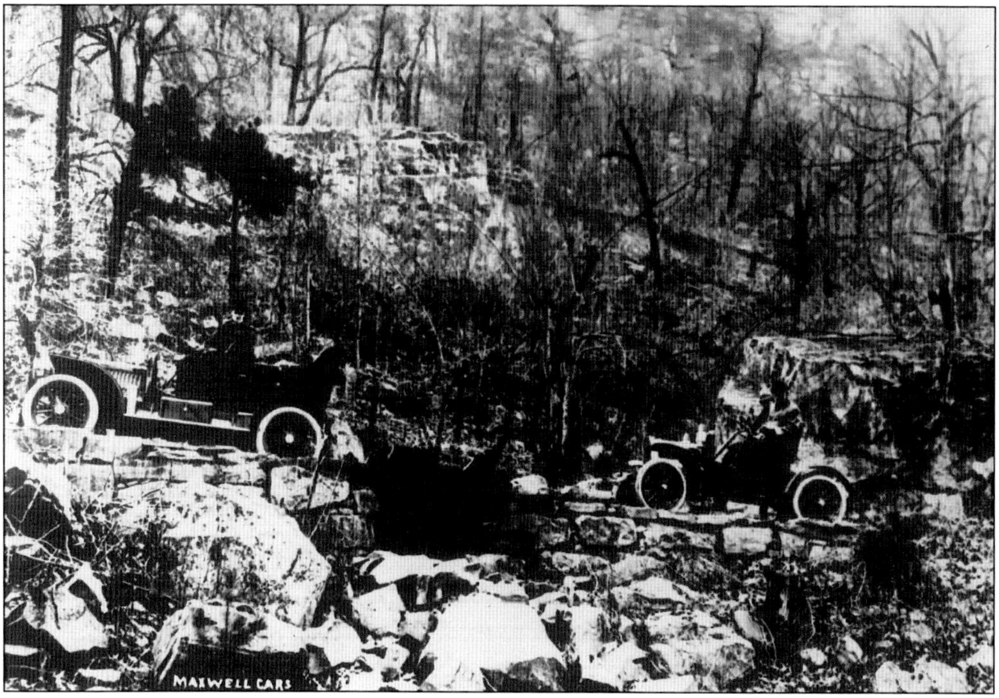

In 1909 an automobile race was held from St. Elmo to the summit of Lookout Mountain on the newly completed Lookout Mountain Boulevard. Over fifty thousand spectators, some from as far away as New Orleans, came to watch the "Lookout Mountain Automobile Climb." Louis Chevrolet had the best time of the day, an incredible 6 1/2 minutes. In 1927, the first paved road up the mountain, the Lookout Mountain Scenic Highway, was opened.

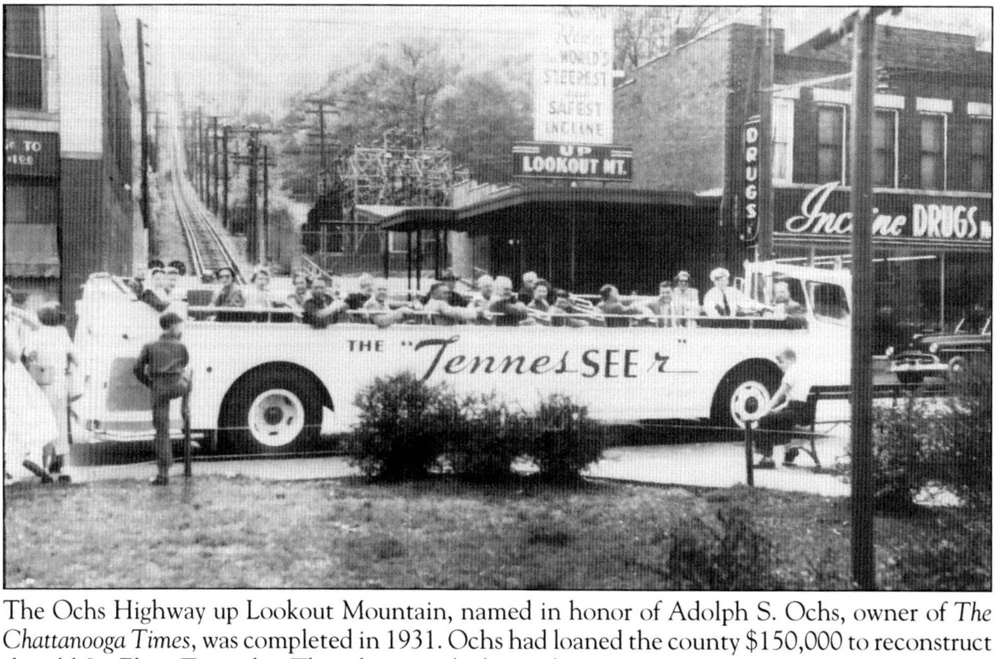

The Ochs Highway up Lookout Mountain, named in honor of Adolph S. Ochs, owner of *The Chattanooga Times*, was completed in 1931. Ochs had loaned the county $150,000 to reconstruct the old St. Elmo Turnpike. This photograph shows the "TennesSEEr," an open-air tourist ride popular in the late 1950s.

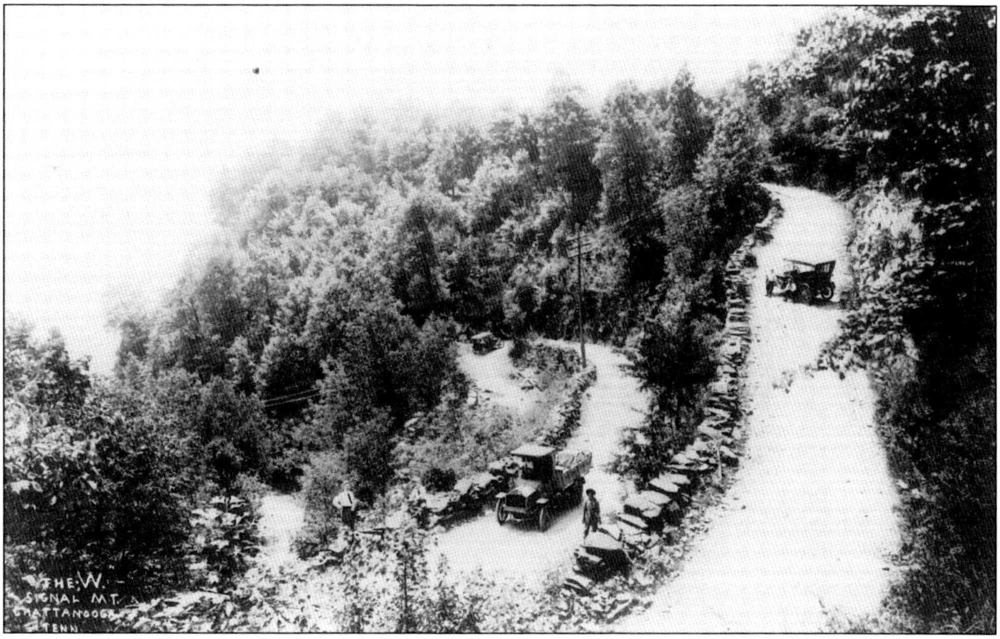

Railroad and road development was also taking place on other mountains in the region. On Signal Mountain, the "W" road was completed in 1893. It was built on what had once been called the "Old Corduroy Road," a log road used during the Civil War as part of the Anderson Pike. The most spectacular part of the construction process involved the blasting of Hanging Rock, a large boulder which extended over the road.

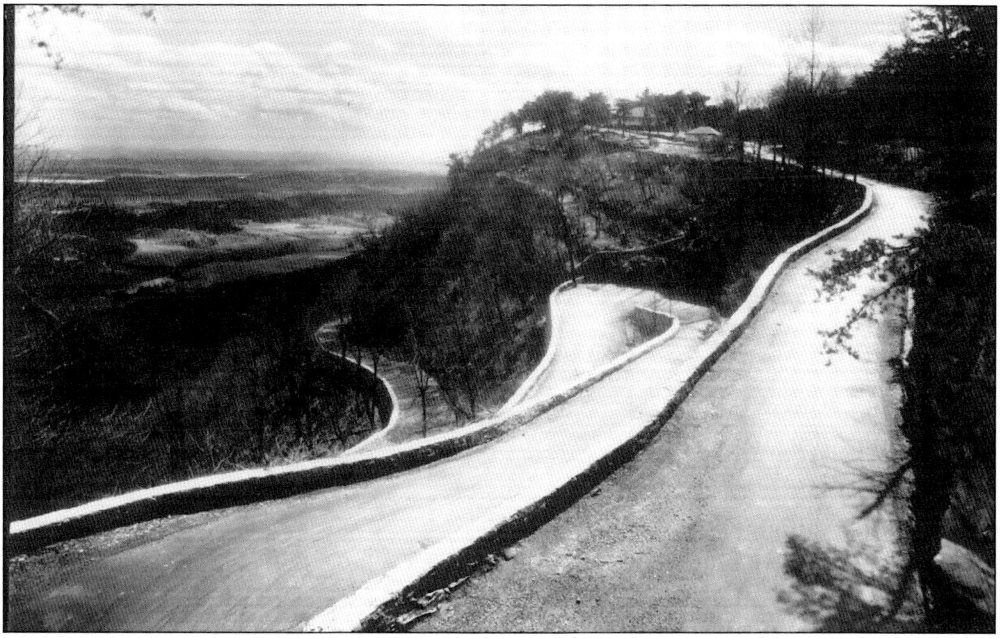

In 1912 the "W" road had a surface of crushed rock and walls made of loose stone without mortar. In 1927, the county rebuilt part of the road, paved and widened it, and built new retaining walls, as shown in this photograph. One of the most scenic roads in the county, it is still very popular today.

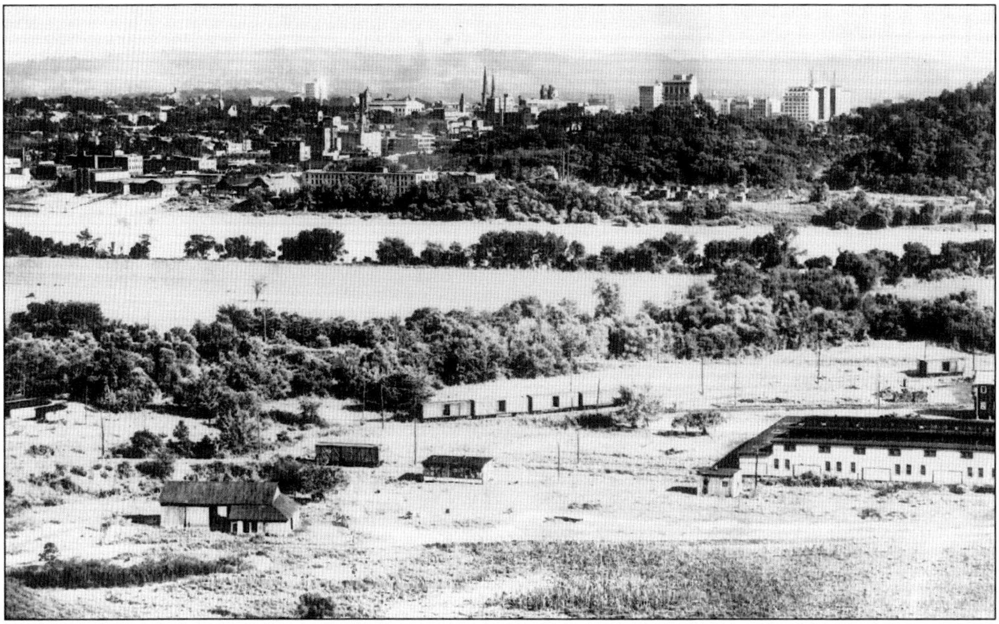

This photograph, taken from the north shore of the Tennessee River in the 1950s, shows a more modern Chattanooga skyline. In the background, Missionary Ridge, scene of one of the most heroic charges of the Civil War, stretches behind the city. Much of the area in the foreground of the picture has now been developed with new structures such as the Olgiati Bridge, built in 1959.

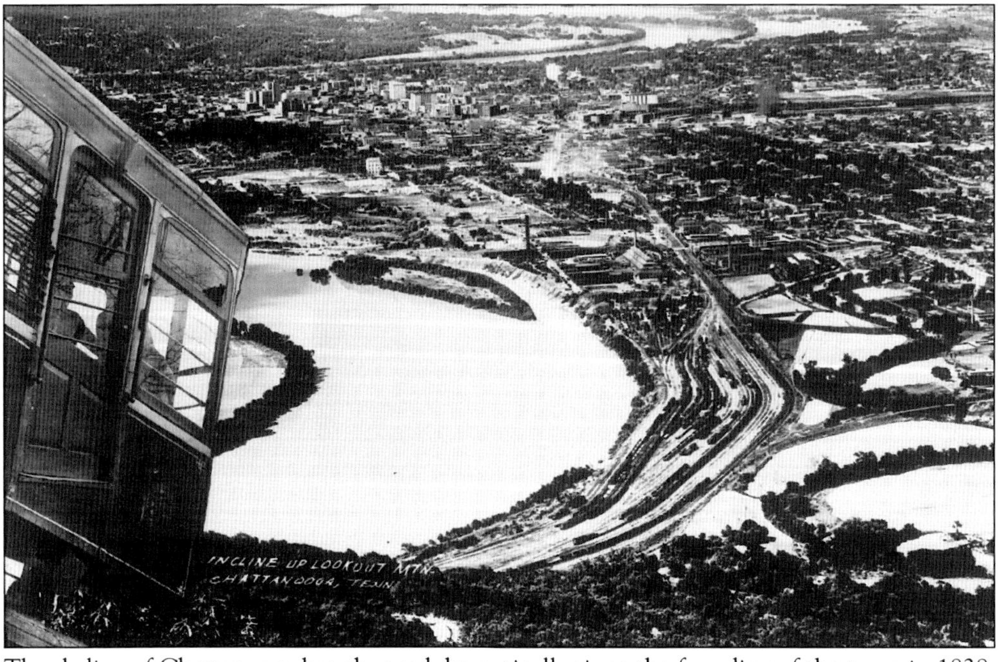

The skyline of Chattanooga has changed dramatically since the founding of the town in 1838. Today, the city covers 118 square miles and is home to over 150,000 residents. However, as this photograph, taken from the steepest part of Incline #2 testifies, it can still justifiably claim to be "America's Most Scenic City."

Two

Civil War and Remembrance

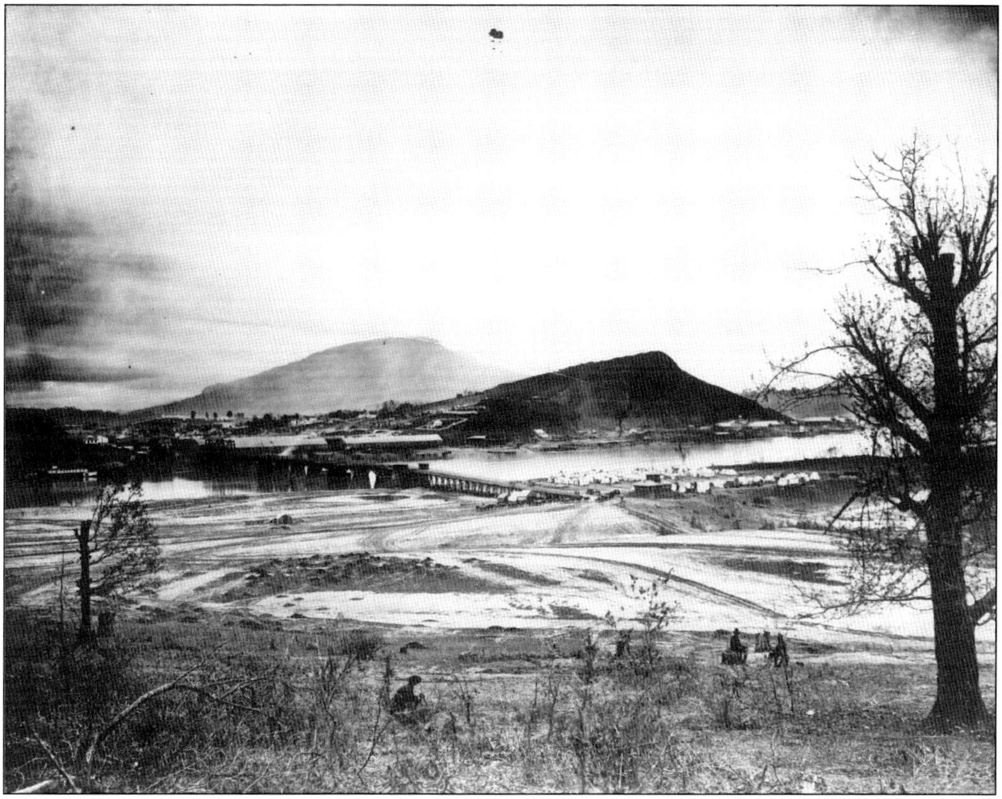

During his visit to Chattanooga, Prince Henry of Prussia was not only impressed by scenic beauty: he was well aware of, and impressed by, the city's military history. In fact, he mentioned that every ten-year-old school boy in Germany could pass an examination upon the Chattanooga campaign of the American Civil War. An impressive feat, if true, as it has been estimated that over six hundred battles, engagements, and skirmishes took place during the time that Chattanooga was the objective of both the Union and Confederate armies. This photograph, taken from the north shore of the Tennessee River, shows the newly completed Meigs Military Bridge in 1864.

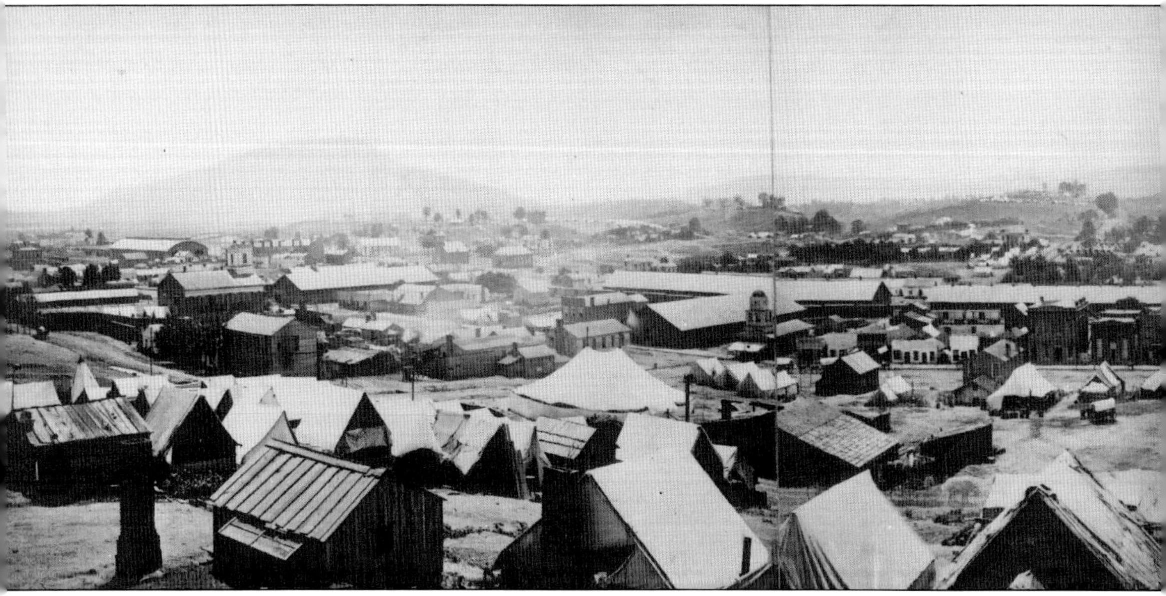

This amazing panoramic view of Chattanooga was taken by Robert M. Linn or by one of Matthew Brady's photographers who traveled the South during the Civil War. Although it is often difficult to date images such as this, the date that this photograph was taken can be narrowed down to one of the three days that Union General James B. McPherson's body lay in state at the Kennedy/Nottingham house (shown in the left center of the photograph). General McPherson had been killed during the siege of Atlanta on July 22, 1864, and his body had

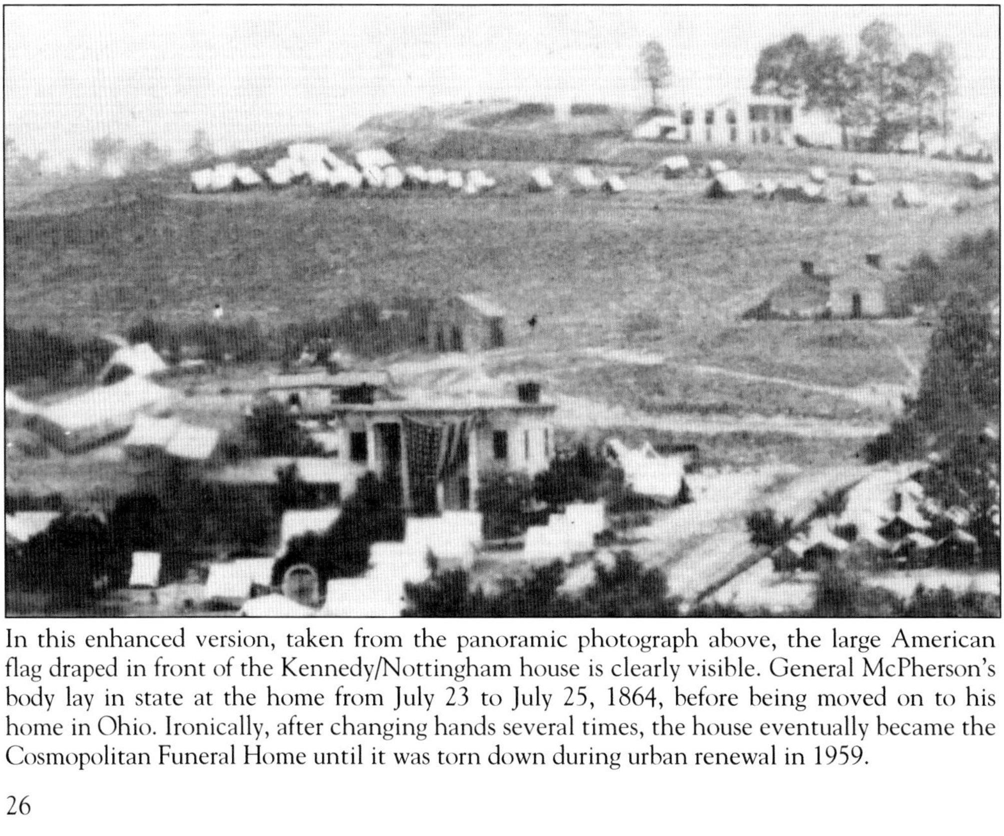

In this enhanced version, taken from the panoramic photograph above, the large American flag draped in front of the Kennedy/Nottingham house is clearly visible. General McPherson's body lay in state at the home from July 23 to July 25, 1864, before being moved on to his home in Ohio. Ironically, after changing hands several times, the house eventually became the Cosmopolitan Funeral Home until it was torn down during urban renewal in 1959.

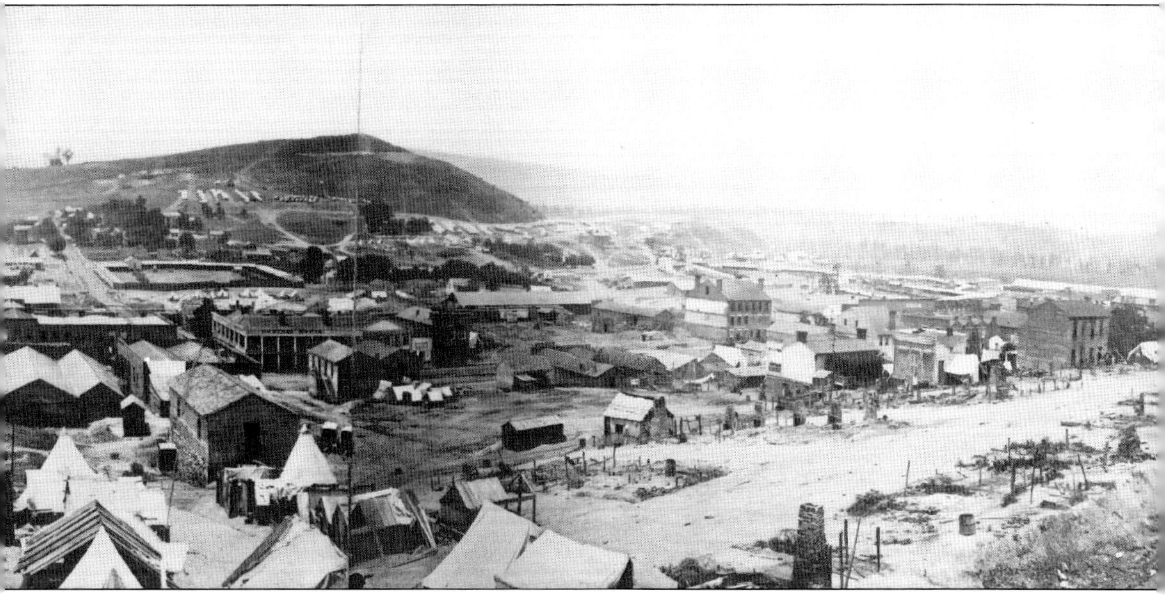

been moved by rail to Chattanooga. The entire length of Market Street, from the Western and Atlantic passenger depot on the left to the Tennessee River bank on the right, can be seen in this image. On Cameron Hill (at right center) are the tents of the First Heavy Artillery, U.S. Colored Troops, stationed in Chattanooga to guard the important rail "lifeline" of General Sherman's army. Various other tents and wooden shacks belonging to the Federal troops can be seen in the foreground of the picture.

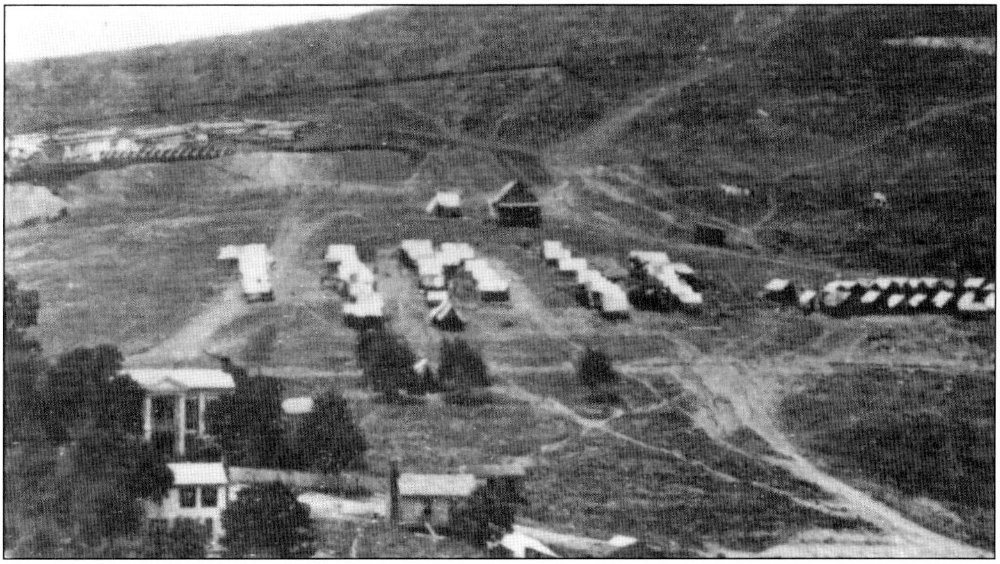

This enhanced photograph, taken from the panorama above, shows the camp of the 1st Heavy Artillery, USCT, on the side of Cameron Hill. The regiment was organized in February of 1864 and completed most of its service in Chattanooga, mustering out on March 31, 1866, in the city. The colonel of the regiment, J.E. MacGowan, stayed on in the community as a lawyer and journalist for *The Chattanooga Times*. MacGowan had a strong paternalistic attitude toward blacks. He publically deplored "the white man who maltreats a decent colored man merely to exploit his superiority or display his brutal prejudice."

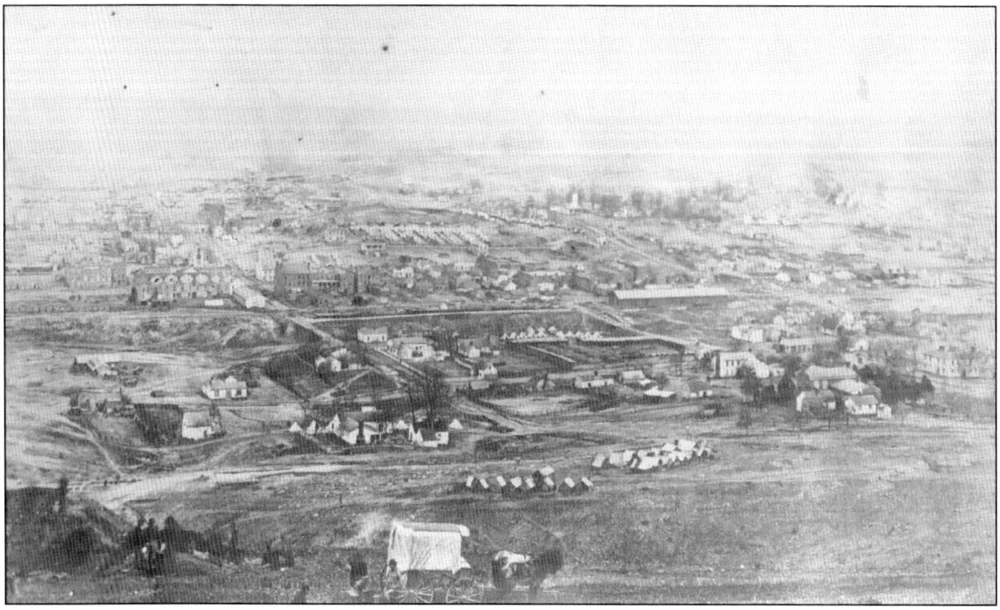

This is the first time that this photograph of Chattanooga, taken in 1863, has been published or seen in print. The warehouses along Railroad Street (eventually renamed Broad Street) are clearly visible. Missionary Ridge stretches across the background. Very few trees in the town survived the Confederate siege of Chattanooga: in the foreground, workers on the water pumping station rest on a completely denuded Cameron Hill.

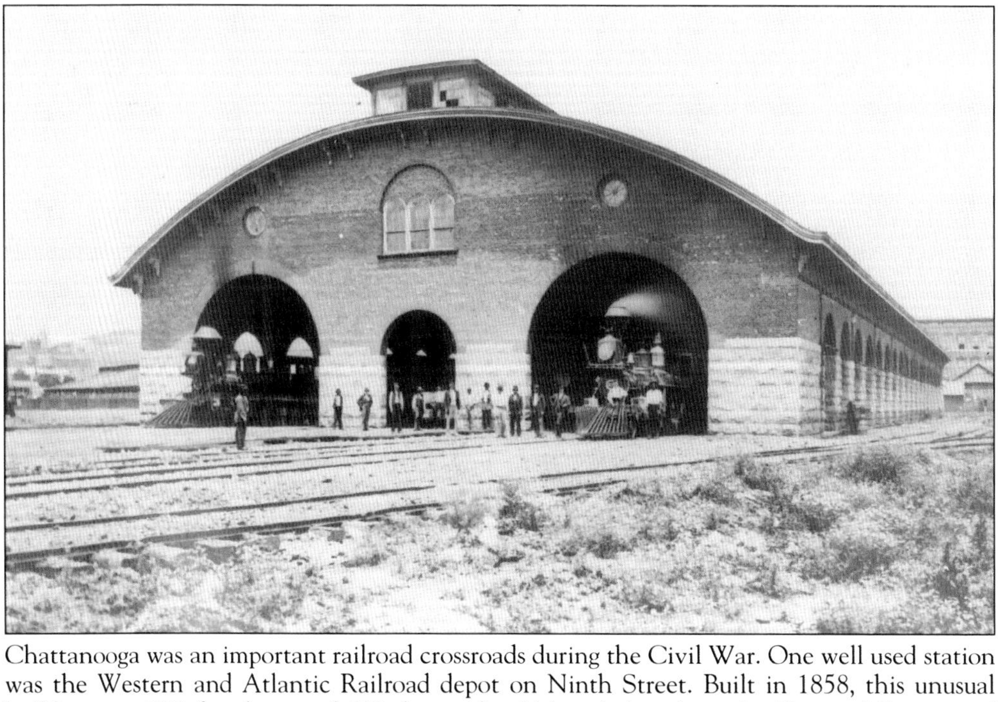

Chattanooga was an important railroad crossroads during the Civil War. One well used station was the Western and Atlantic Railroad depot on Ninth Street. Built in 1858, this unusual building was 300 feet long and 100 feet wide. Although listed on the National Register of Historic Places, the depot was demolished in 1973. The Krystal Building and the Chattanooga-Hamilton County Bicentennial Library now stand on the site.

An attempt to sabotage the railroad from Chattanooga to Atlanta was made in April 1862. A group of Federal raiders, led by James Andrews, hijacked the Confederate train, the "General" (shown here as a model), and led southern authorities on a mad chase across northern Georgia. Although several of the raiders escaped, Andrews and seven others went to the gallows. They are buried in the National Cemetery in Chattanooga.

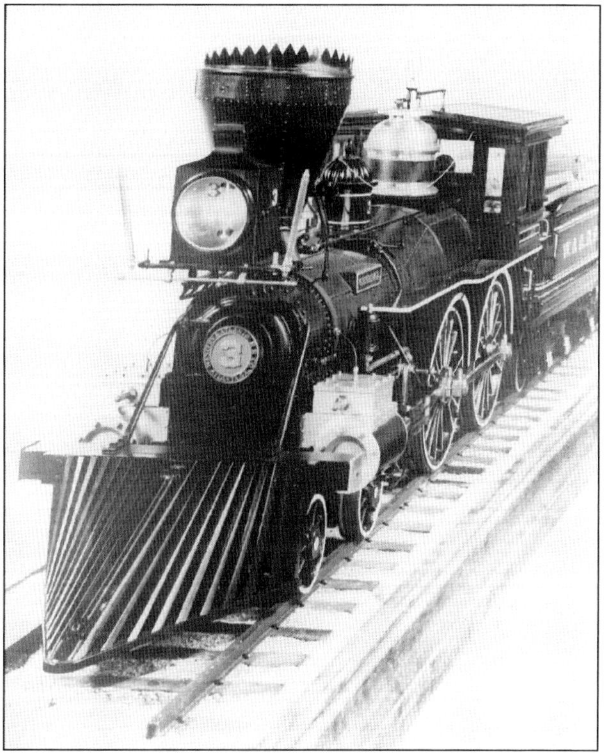

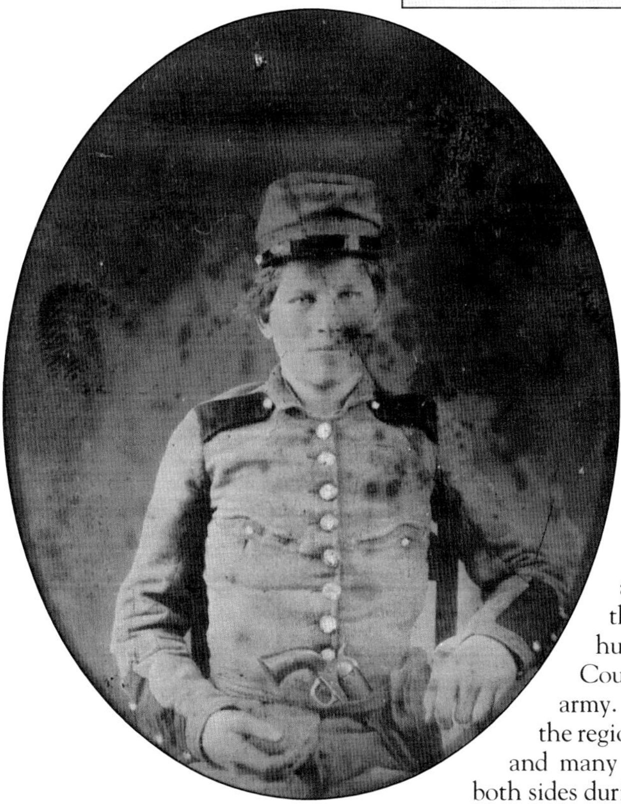

B.J. Roan of Signal Mountain in an ambrotype (an early type of photograph, consisting of a glass negative backed by a dark surface so as to appear positive). Shown in a gray uniform with a Colt pistol at the ready in his belt, B.J. was one of hundreds of young men in Hamilton County who joined the Confederate army. However, a majority of citizens in the region retained strong Union sentiments and many families had members fighting on both sides during the war.

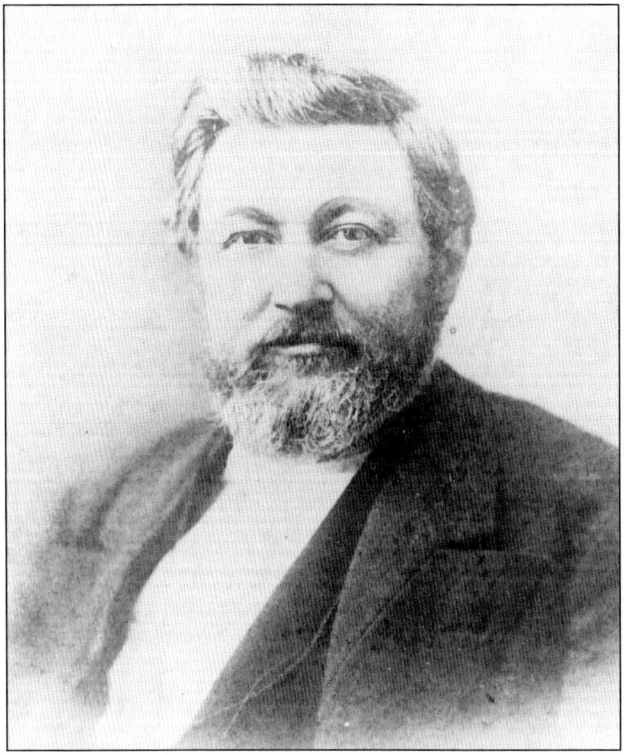

Tom Crutchfield, Jr., the owner and operator of the Crutchfield House, the largest hotel in Chattanooga, found himself deeply involved in the Civil War, although he was exempt from military service due to physical disabilities. Even before the war started, he had to restrain his hot-headed brother, William, from fighting a duel with Jefferson Davis after an argument in the hotel lobby. During the early assaults on Missionary Ridge in November 1863, his farm in Amnicola was overrun by Union troops.

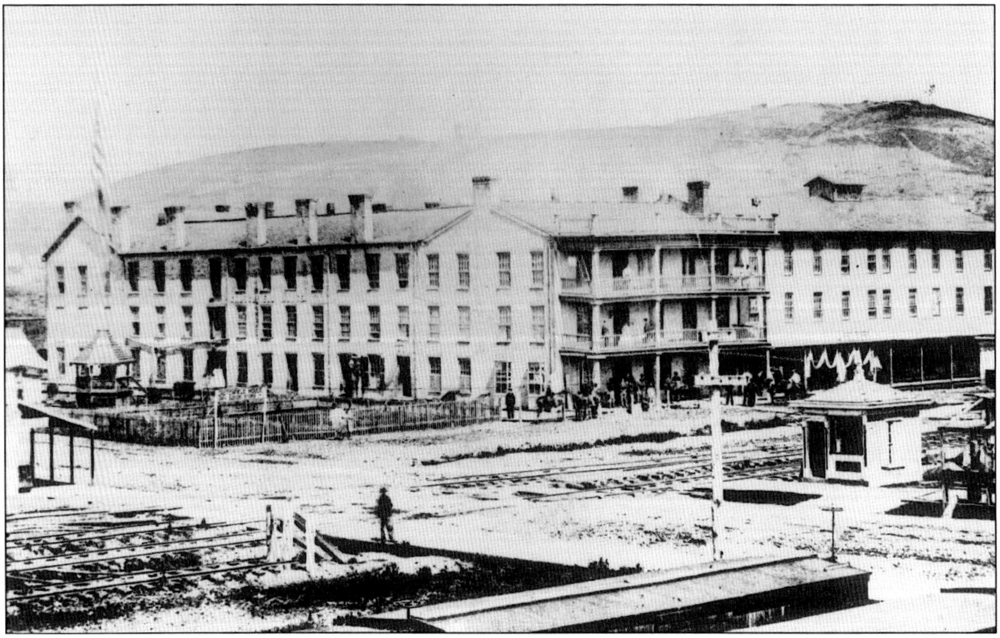

The Crutchfield House was located opposite the railroad depot at Ninth and Broad Streets. Built by Tom Crutchfield, Sr., in 1847, the hotel soon became the social and political center of the town. During the war, the hotel was used as a hospital and recovery area. It was destroyed by a fire in 1867 and was replaced by the Read House.

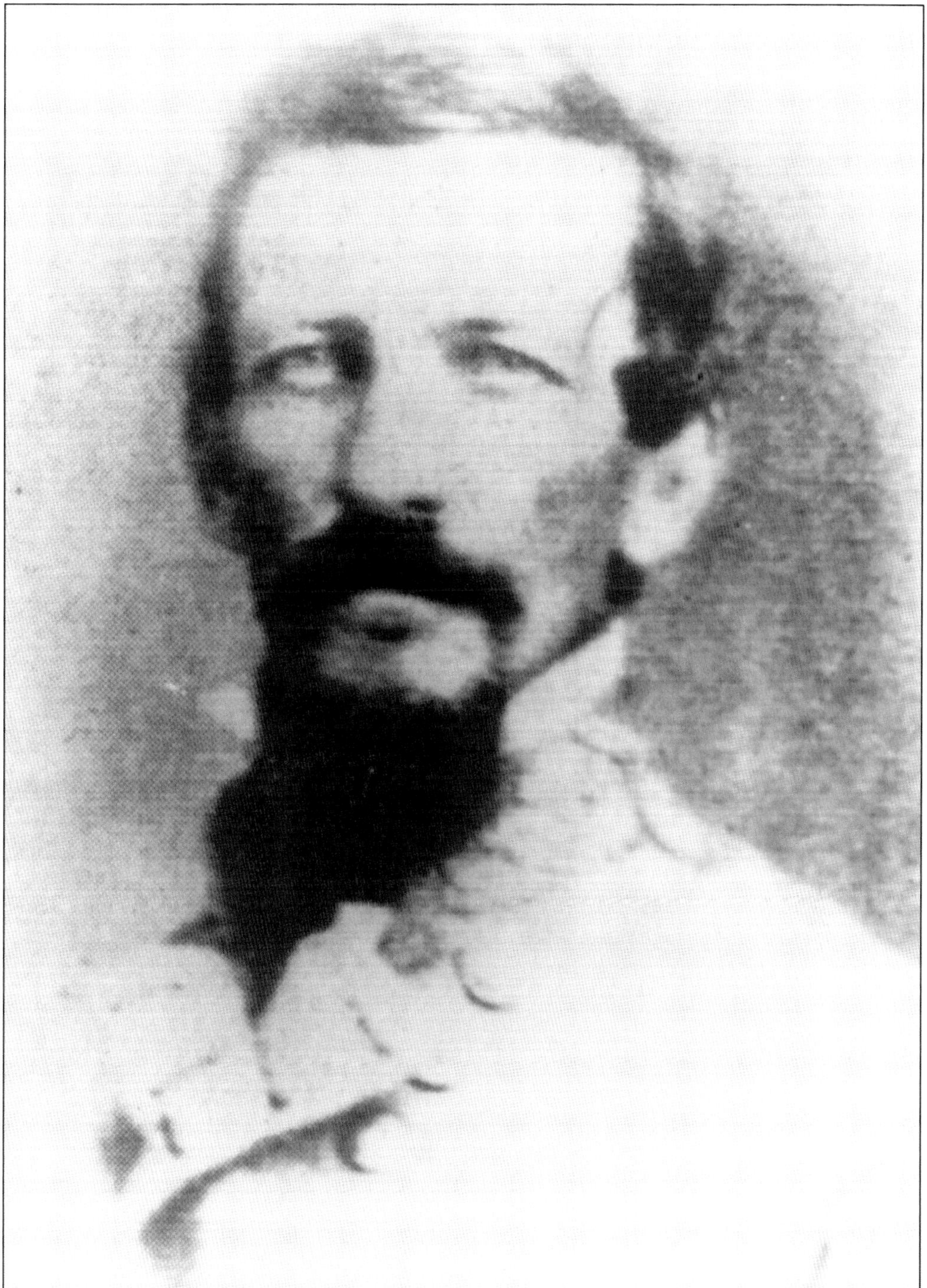

General Alexander Peter Stewart's division unsuccessfully defended a section of Missionary Ridge during the Federal assaults on November 25, 1863. Following the war, Stewart served as chancellor of the University of Mississippi and was one of the first commissioners of the Chickamauga and Chattanooga National Military Park.

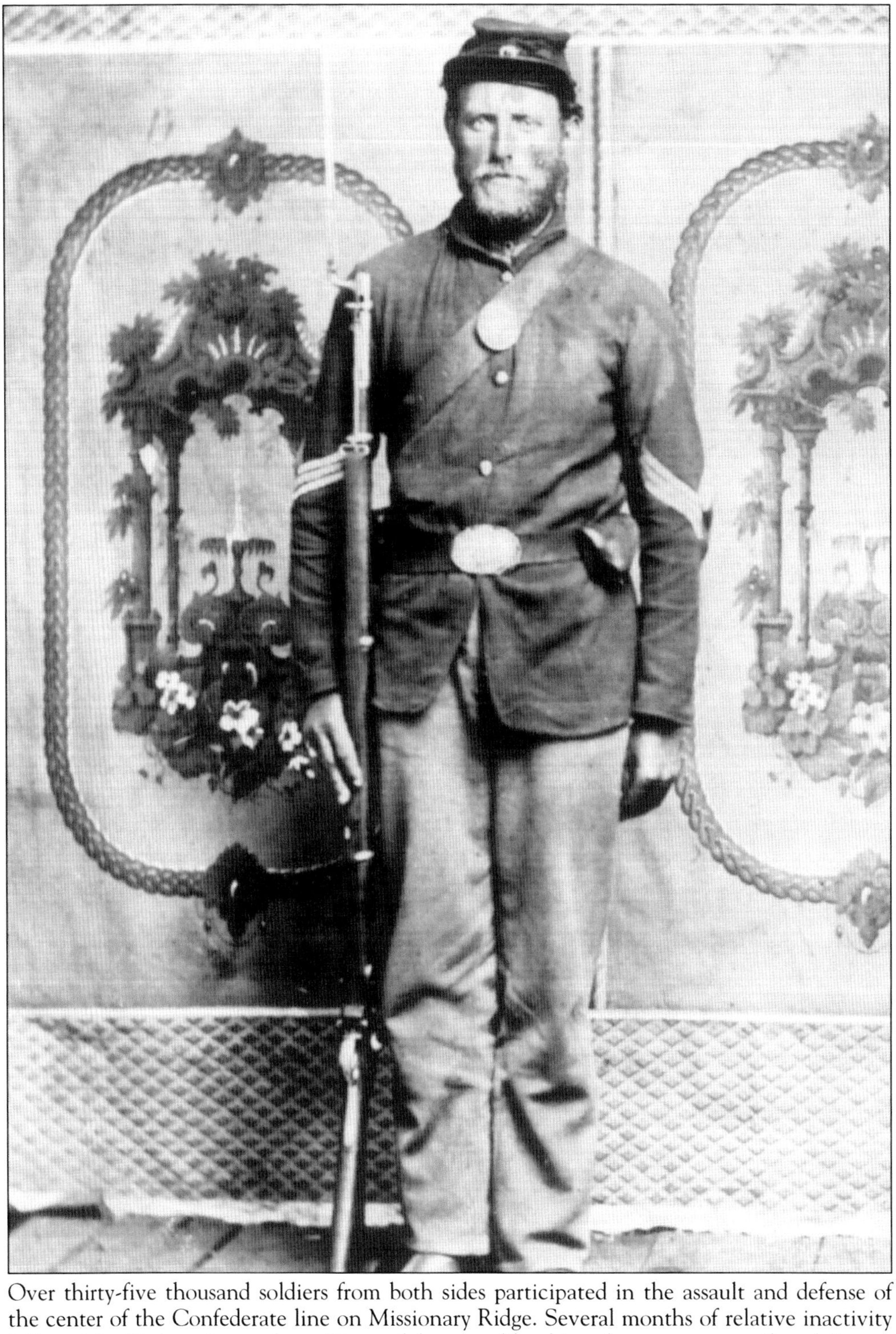

Over thirty-five thousand soldiers from both sides participated in the assault and defense of the center of the Confederate line on Missionary Ridge. Several months of relative inactivity followed the Union victory there. Many of the men, like this unknown sergeant, found time to have their picture taken by one of the photographers who swarmed the town after the battles.

"I wish I was a young lady. I hate boarders. I cannot bear the idea of those Yankee women coming here. I know I will have to keep my teeth clinched all the while." Kate Foster, a fifteen-year-old girl living on Lookout Mountain in 1864, kept a fascinating diary of events in the Union-occupied town. The Foster family hosted boarders—including the wives of Union soldiers—at their home on the east brow of the mountain. Although unimpressed by the exigencies of the war when she wrote the entry quoted above, Kate's views soon changed: young army men came calling and her life was filled with dances, elegant balls, and presents from admirers. She eventually settled on Lieutenant Frederick Ferdinand Wiehl and they were married in 1869. After the war Wiehl became a prominent businessman in Chattanooga. Kate (Foster) Wiehl's diary is now on display at the Chattanooga Regional History Museum.

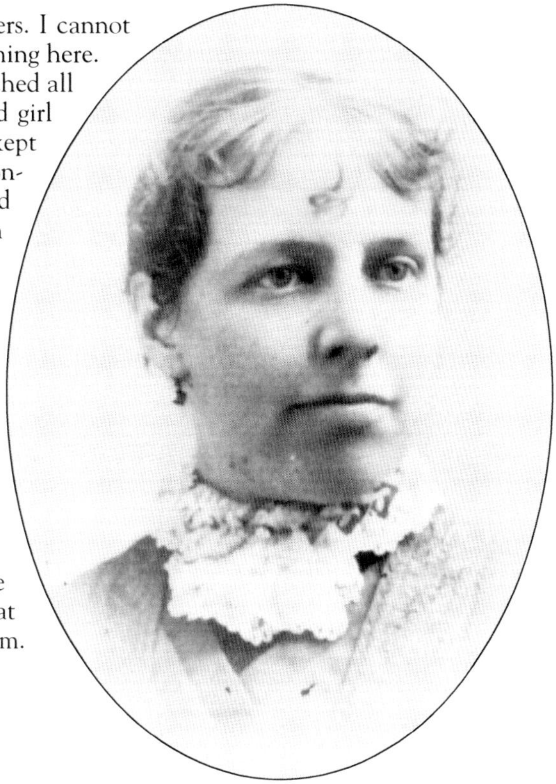

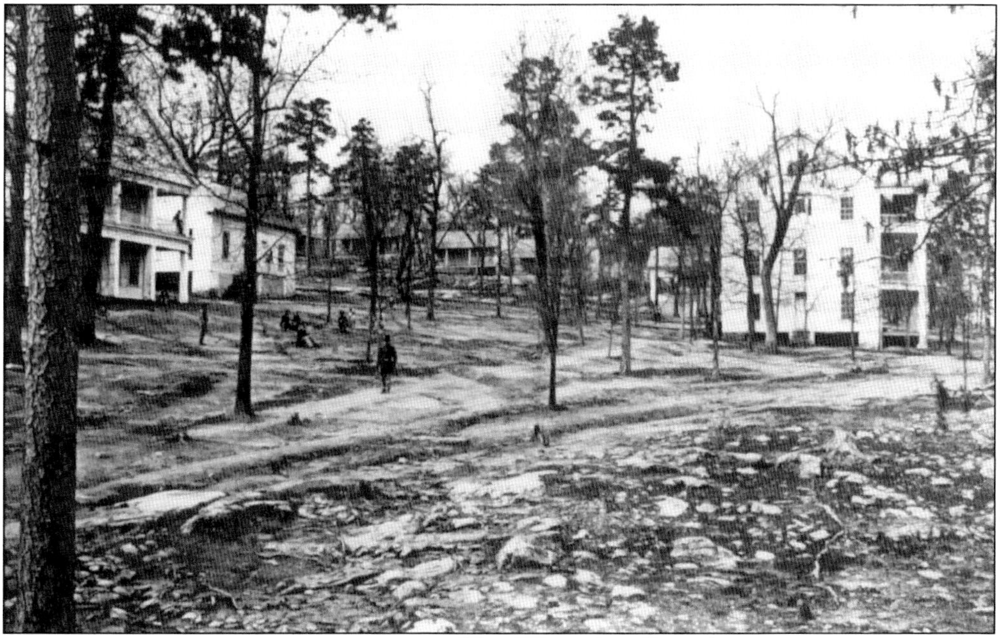

Lookout Mountain became a popular rest area for Union soldiers during the war. General Joseph Hooker kept his headquarters there after the "Battle Above the Clouds." This photograph shows the compound at the Summertown Hotel. A Federal soldier stands at attention in the foreground as others lounge on the ground and the hotel balcony.

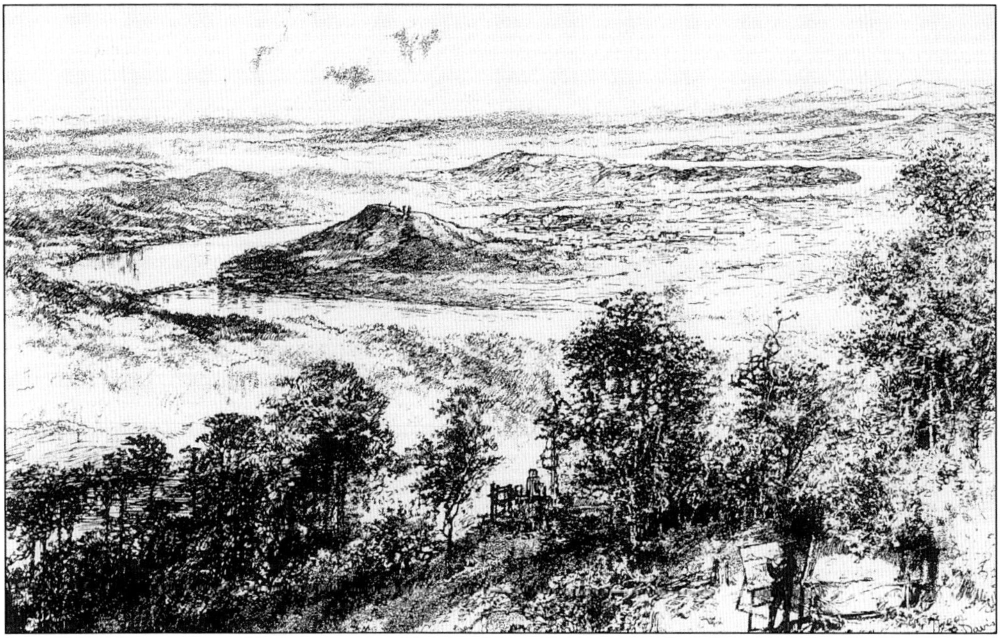

Theodore R. Davis was a young man of twenty-four when *Harper's Weekly* sent him to Chattanooga on assignment in 1863. A veteran artist/correspondent who had already covered the secession crisis in the South and the Vicksburg campaign, he was to document the events of the Civil War in Chattanooga through drawings. Twenty-four of Davis' pen and ink drawings are now part of the Chattanooga Regional History Museum's collection. This drawing shows the artist himself sketching the view from Lookout Mountain.

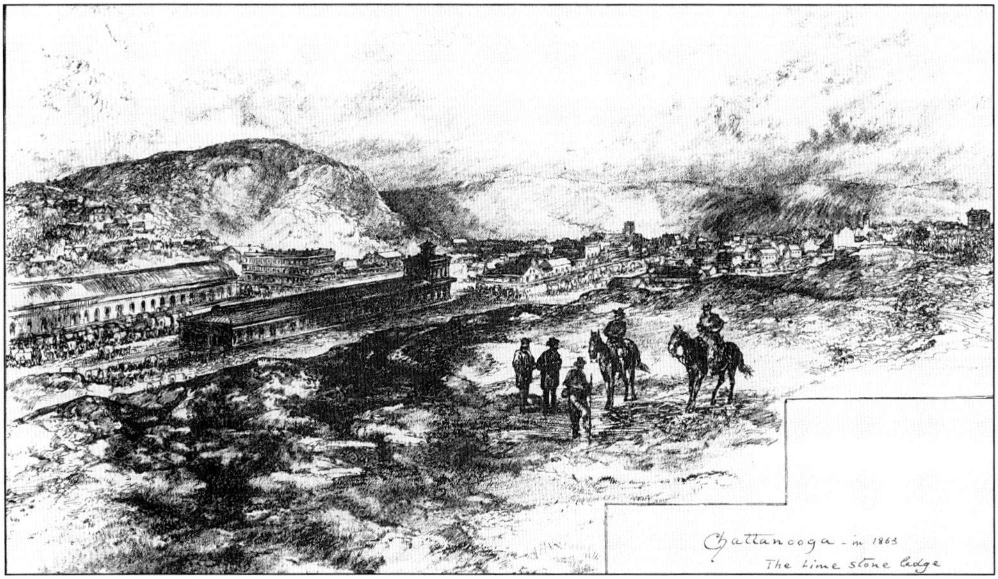

This Davis drawing shows the view from a rocky high point near the site where the Patten Towers stand today. The Western and Atlantic Railroad passenger and freight depots can be seen at left center. The Crutchfield House is also prominently featured. Cameron Hill and Stringer's Ridge seem to surround the northern part of the town. The Tennessee River actually separates the two hills, as shown in the previous drawing.

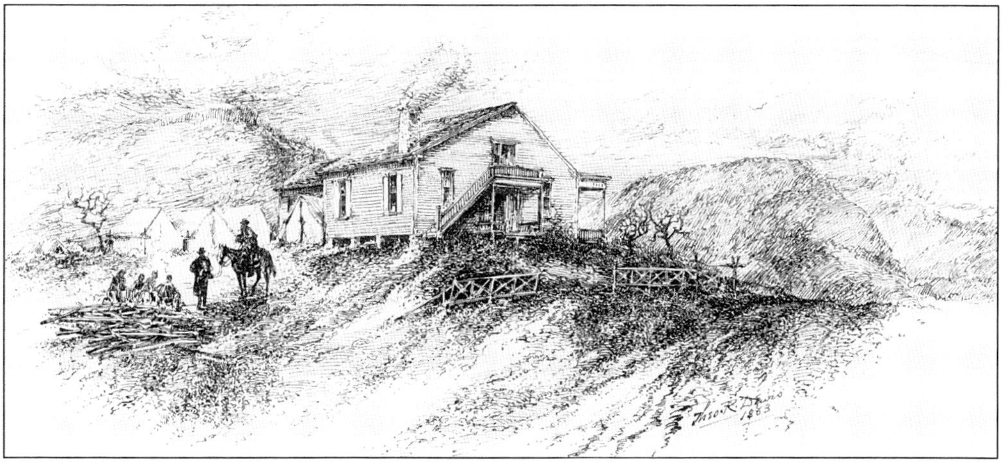

The house that was used as General Ulysses S. Grant's headquarters was a famous landmark in Chattanooga for many years. The building, on First Street between Cherry and Walnut Streets, had been owned by Thomas Jefferson Lattner, a local merchant, in the years before the war. Unfortunately, efforts to save the house were unsuccessful and it was eventually condemned by the Better Housing Commission. It was torn down in 1966.

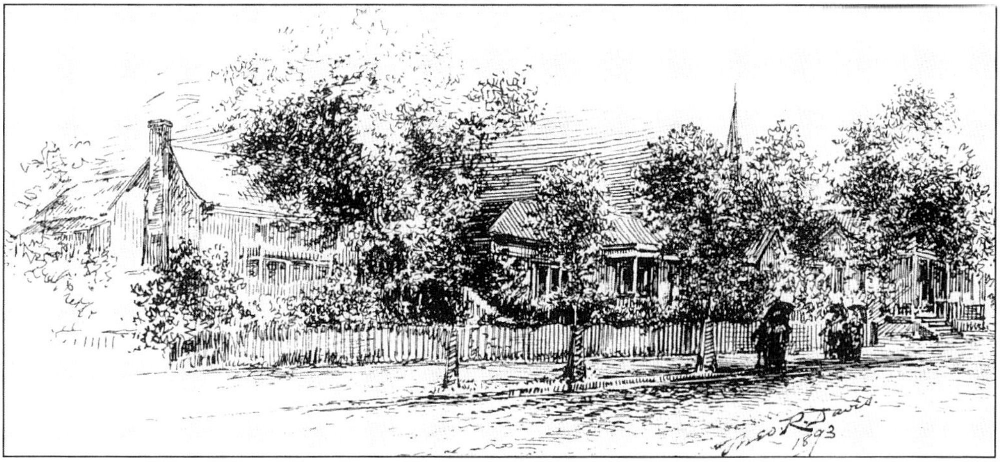

Returning to Chattanooga in 1893, Davis made this sketch of the headquarters of Major General George H. Thomas. During the Battles for Chattanooga, Thomas was in command of the Army of the Cumberland. In 1863, this site was filled with soldiers and cannon; by the 1890s, it was a quiet street in a residential neighborhood.

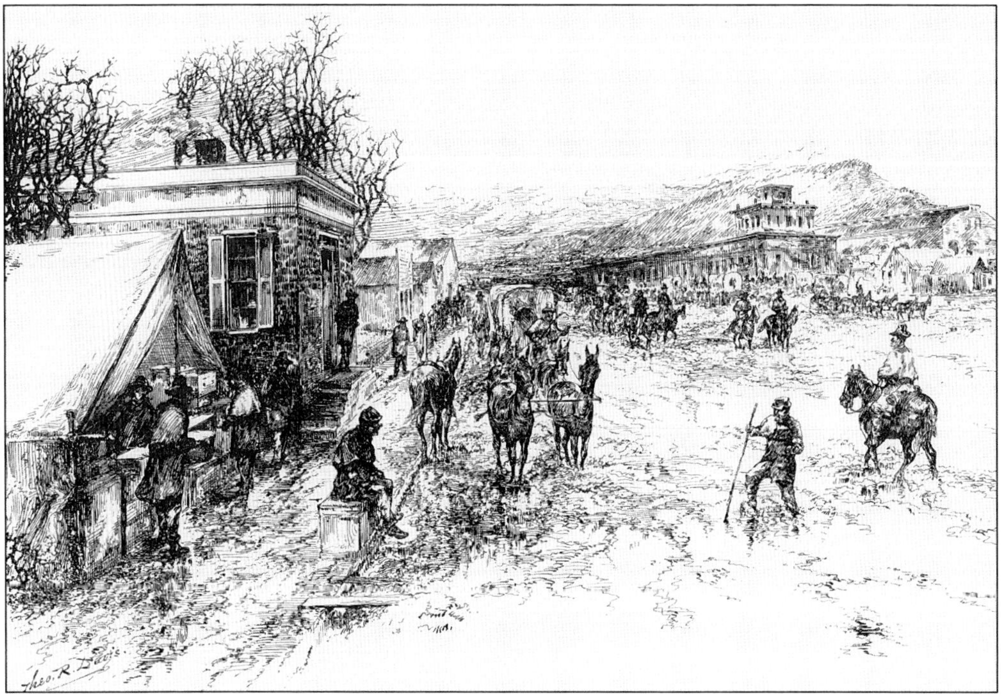

Chattanooga had about 2,500 residents in 1860. During the war more than 100,000 Union soldiers made it their temporary home. In this drawing the artist has captured the noise and confusion of the scene near the Provost Marshall's Office on Market Street. The W & A freight depot is on the right.

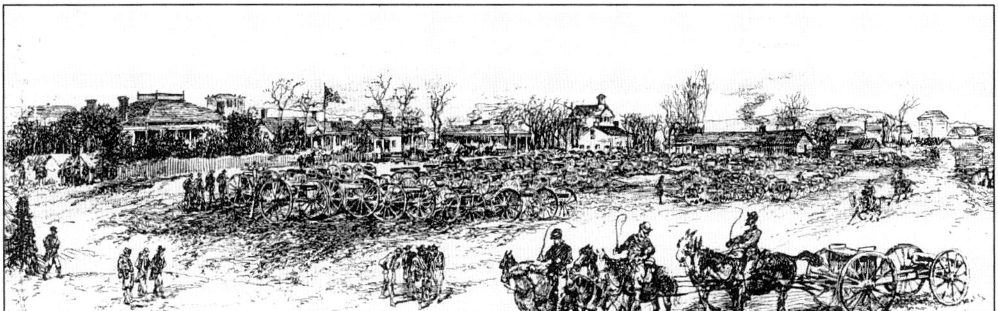

Confederate cannon captured at Missionary Ridge were stored in the field in front of General Thomas' headquarters near Walnut Street between Third and Fourth Streets. As General William Sherman's march to Atlanta commenced in the spring of 1864, Chattanooga became a major supply depot.

This untitled image shows a scene that was probably typical of Civil War camp life, complete with smoky fires, tobacco, and hours of boredom. However, as preparations for the Atlanta campaign began, engineers and quartermasters turned the town into a hive of activity. Machine shops, boat docks, warehouses, barracks, corrals, and wagon shops were all built with incredible speed in the winter and spring of 1864.

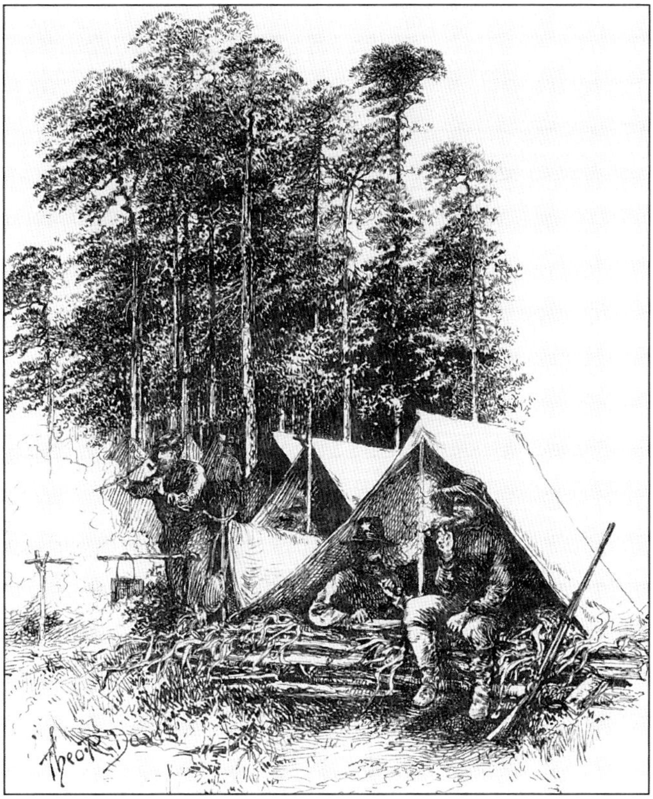

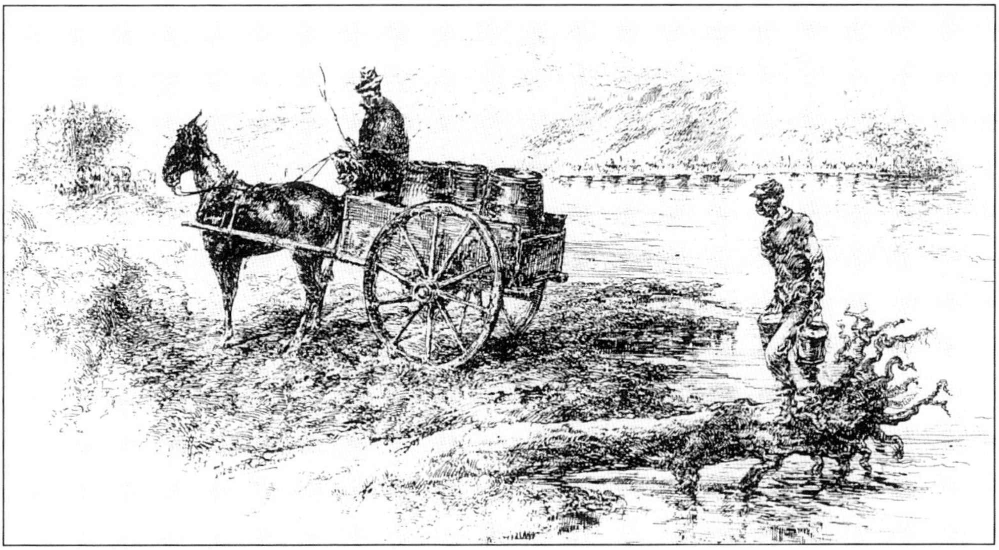

With a touch of humor, Davis entitled this drawing *The Chattanooga Water Works 1863*. These men hauled water by the barrel from a spot on the Tennessee River near the army's pontoon bridge. By 1864, the Union army had built a real waterworks that piped water into town via a reservoir on the side of Cameron Hill.

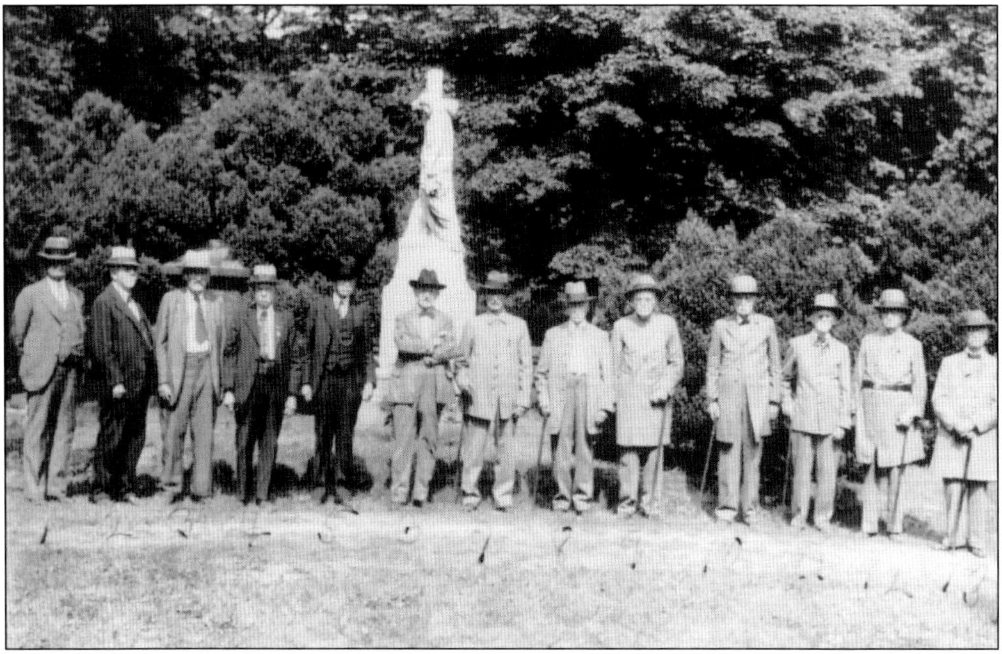

After the War Between the States, Chattanooga naturally became a gathering place for veterans from both sides to honor the living and to remember fallen friends. This photograph shows members of the Nathan B. Forrest Camp, U.C.V., assembled at the Silverdale Cemetery on July 15, 1937. Colonel W.M. Nixon (second from the left) had been a prime mover in the establishment of the cemetery and the re-interment of 160 unknown Confederate soldiers.

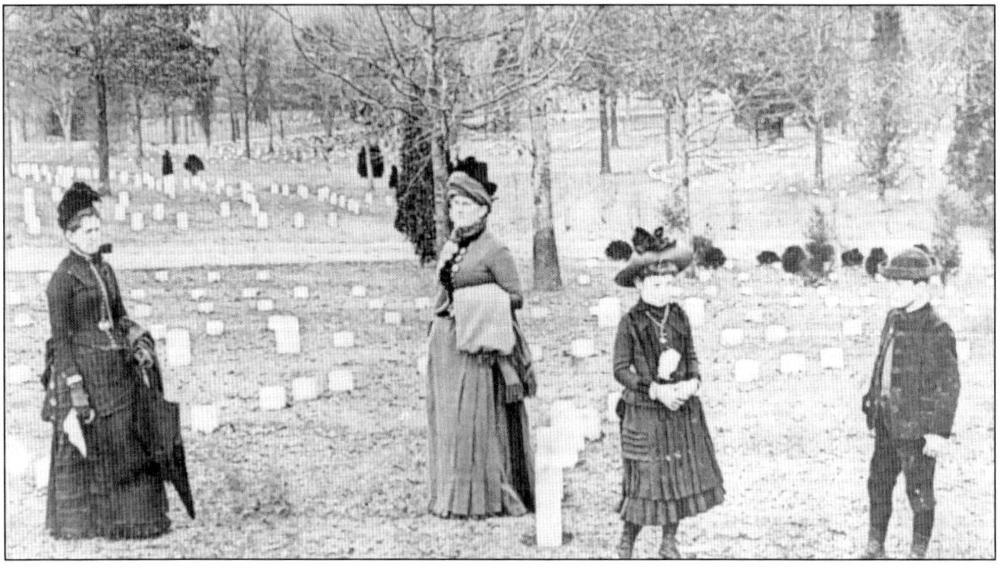

In December 1864, by order of General Thomas, a national cemetery was established on a 75-acre site beyond the W & A Railroad, "in commemoration of the battles of Chattanooga . . . to provide a proper resting-place for the remains of the brave men who fell." By 1865, more than twelve thousand bodies (including five thousand unknowns) had been buried there. General Thomas insisted that none of the honored dead be placed by states, making it a truly "national" cemetery.

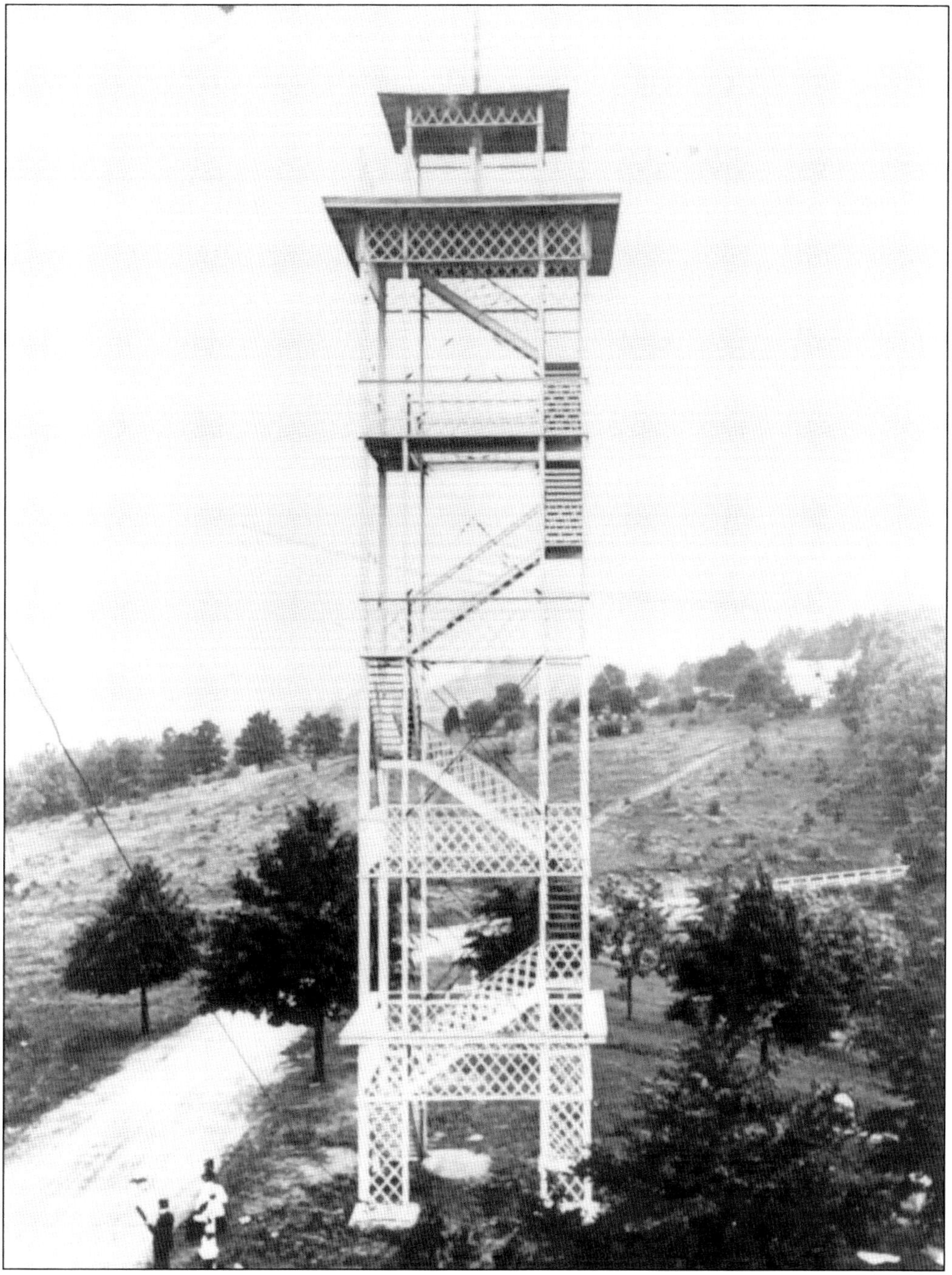

Missionary Ridge, to the east of Chattanooga, runs south from the Tennessee River for about 20 miles. The ridge, at a height of about 400 feet above the city, was heavily fortified by the Confederates and yet it fell to the Army of the Cumberland in one incredible charge. Several areas of the ridge are reserved by the National Park Service and are open to the public. The Bragg reservation, shown here, marks the site of Confederate General Bragg's headquarters. The observation tower was torn down years ago.

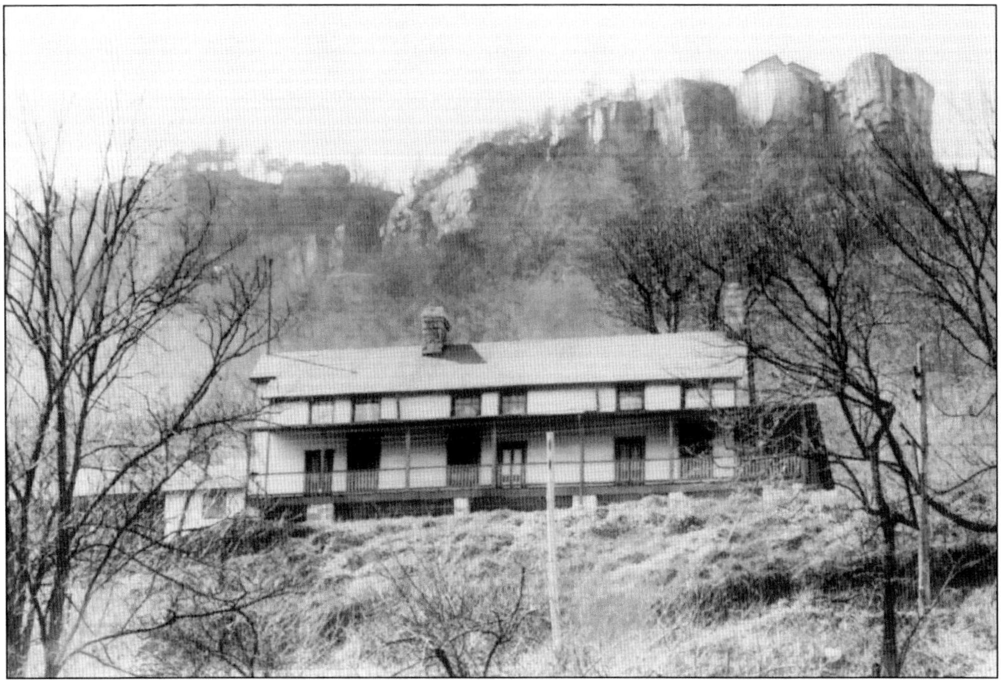

The Cravens House is one of the few buildings from the Civil War era still standing in Chattanooga. Built by Robert Cravens, the owner of the Bluff Furnace, the building became the focal point of the "Battle Above the Clouds" on November 23, 1863. Demolished in the battle, the home was rebuilt and eventually restored by the Association for the Preservation of Tennessee Antiquities. It is now operated by the National Park Service.

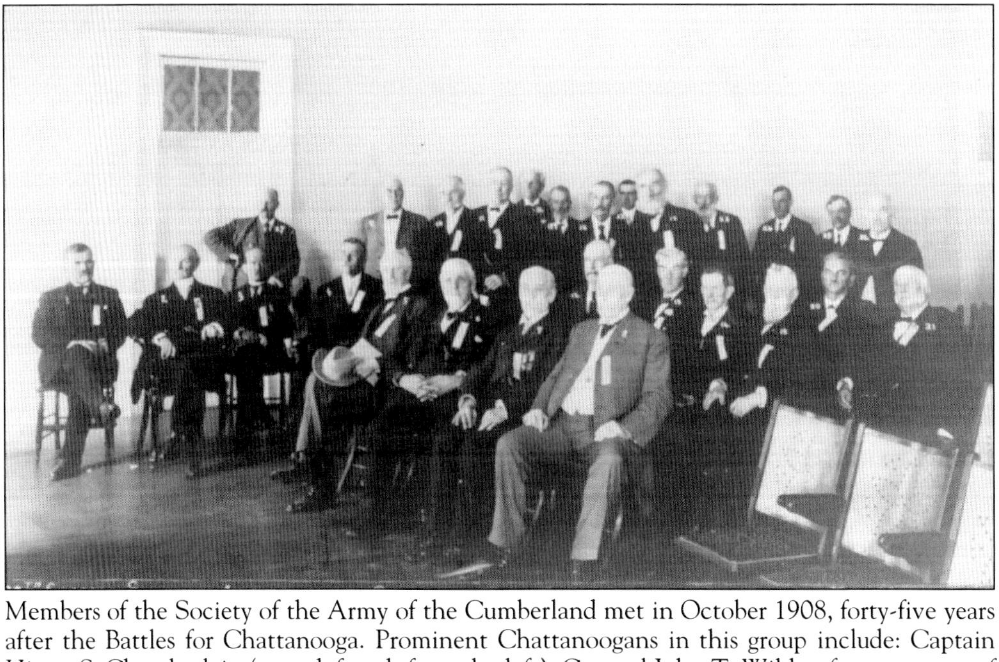

Members of the Society of the Army of the Cumberland met in October 1908, forty-five years after the Battles for Chattanooga. Prominent Chattanoogans in this group include: Captain Hiram S. Chamberlain (seated, fourth from the left); General John T. Wilder, former mayor of the city (seated, sixth from the left); and Zeboim C. Patten (standing, second from the left).

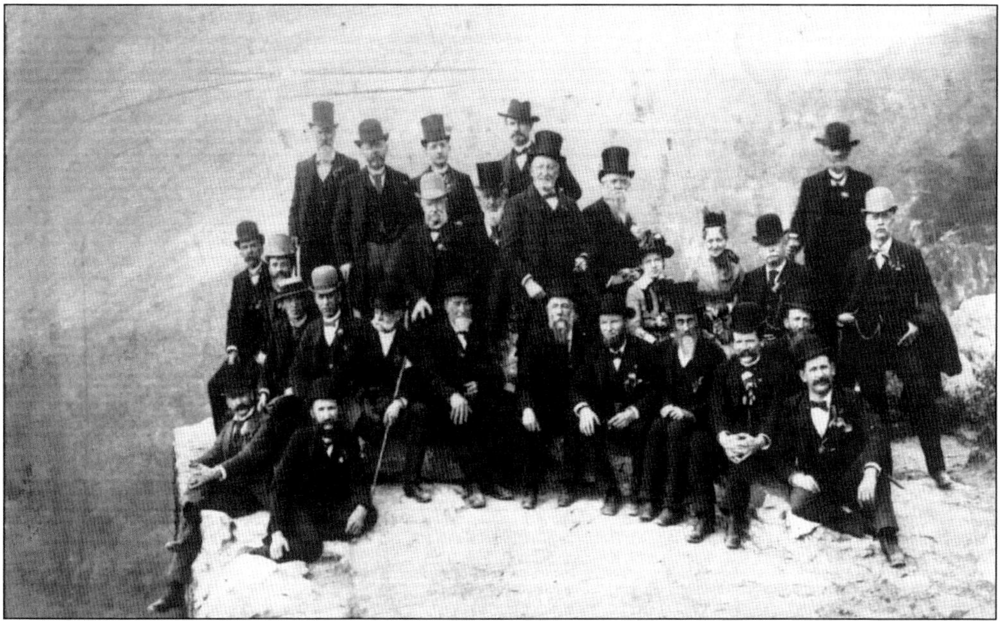

General William S. Rosecrans (in the center, wearing a top hat) poses with members of his staff at Lookout Point. Rosecrans, the "liberator" of Chattanooga, was replaced by General Grant after the Confederate victory at the Battle of Chickamauga. In 1888, General H.V. Boynton and Ferdinand Van Derveer began developing support for the idea of establishing a national military park in the area. President Benjamin Harrison signed the bill creating the Chickamauga and Chattanooga National Military Park in 1890.

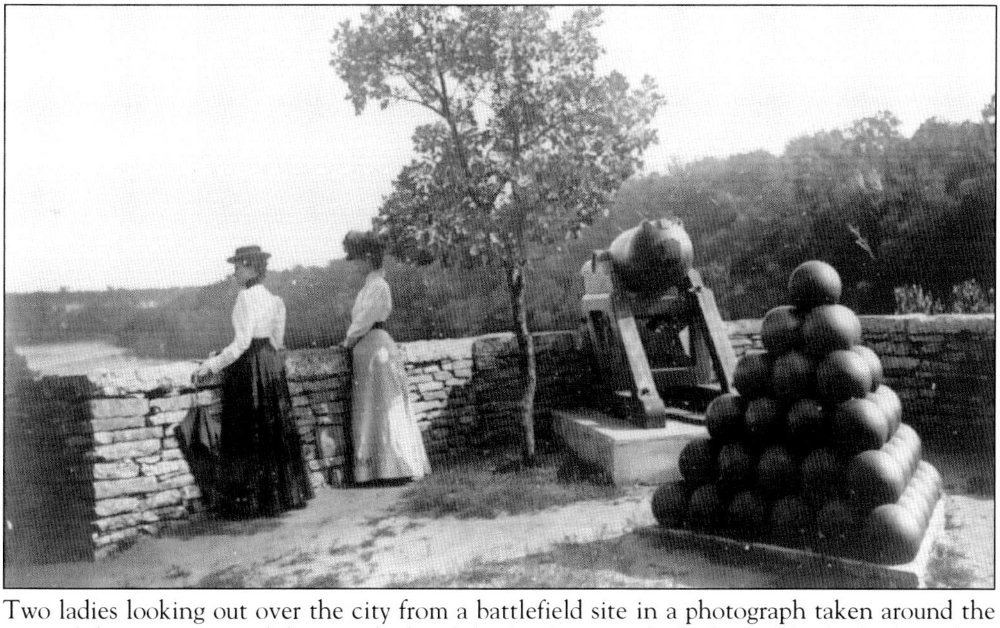

Two ladies looking out over the city from a battlefield site in a photograph taken around the turn of the century. Luckily, very little of the land upon which the battles had taken place was developed during the twenty-five years between the Civil War and the creation of the national park. Officially dedicated in September 1895, the park contains approximately 1,400 monuments and markers, many of which were placed by veterans committees.

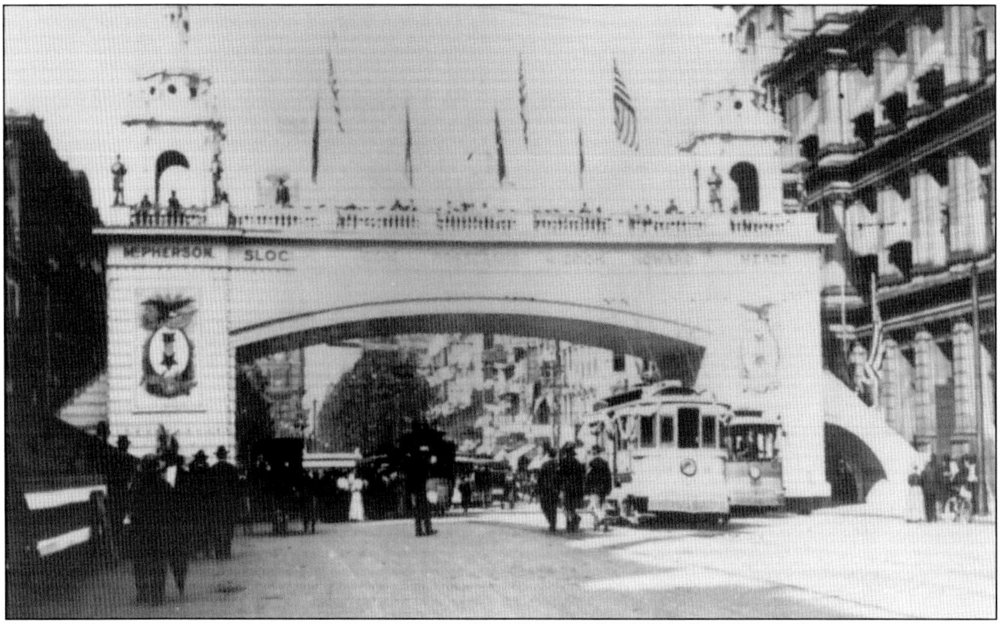

This temporary ceremonial arch, erected for the fiftieth anniversary of the Battles for Chattanooga in 1913, honored some of the famous Union generals of the Civil War. The names McPherson, Slocum, Cox, Rosecrans, McCook, Howard, and Meade stretch across the arch. Underneath, veterans, some in their old uniforms, walk next to the downtown trolley cars.

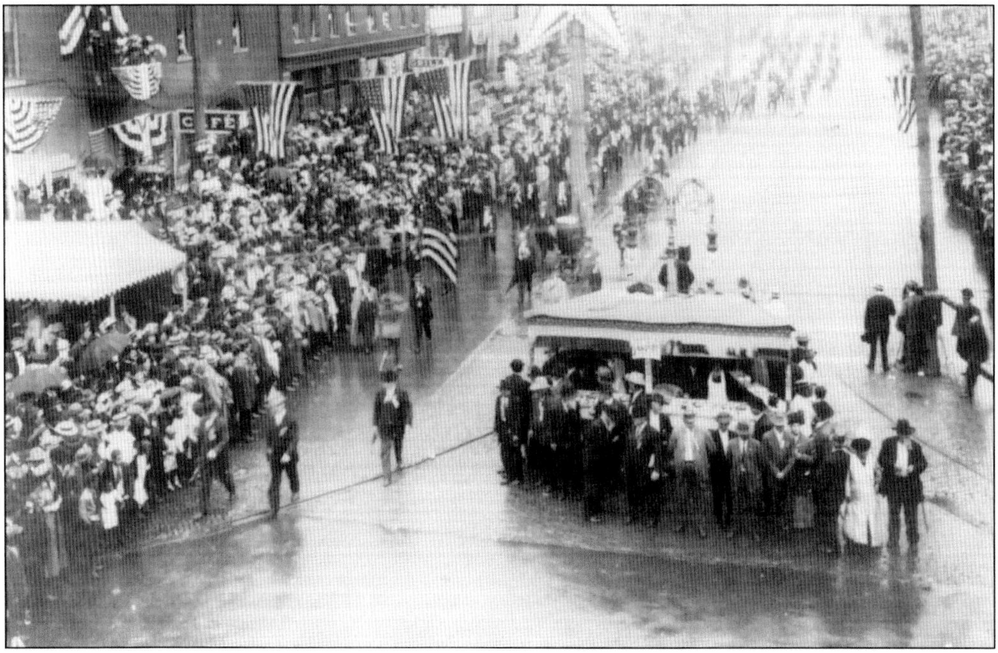

Civil War veterans walk in the rainy 1913 Encampment Parade under the "Welcome GAR" (Grand Army of the Republic) sign. It was the fiftieth anniversary of the Battle of Chickamauga. Next to the double lamp in the middle of Broad Street vendors sell Coca-Cola in a bottle for 5¢. To the left, local dignitaries wave from a Read House hotel balcony.

Three

City Streets and Scenes

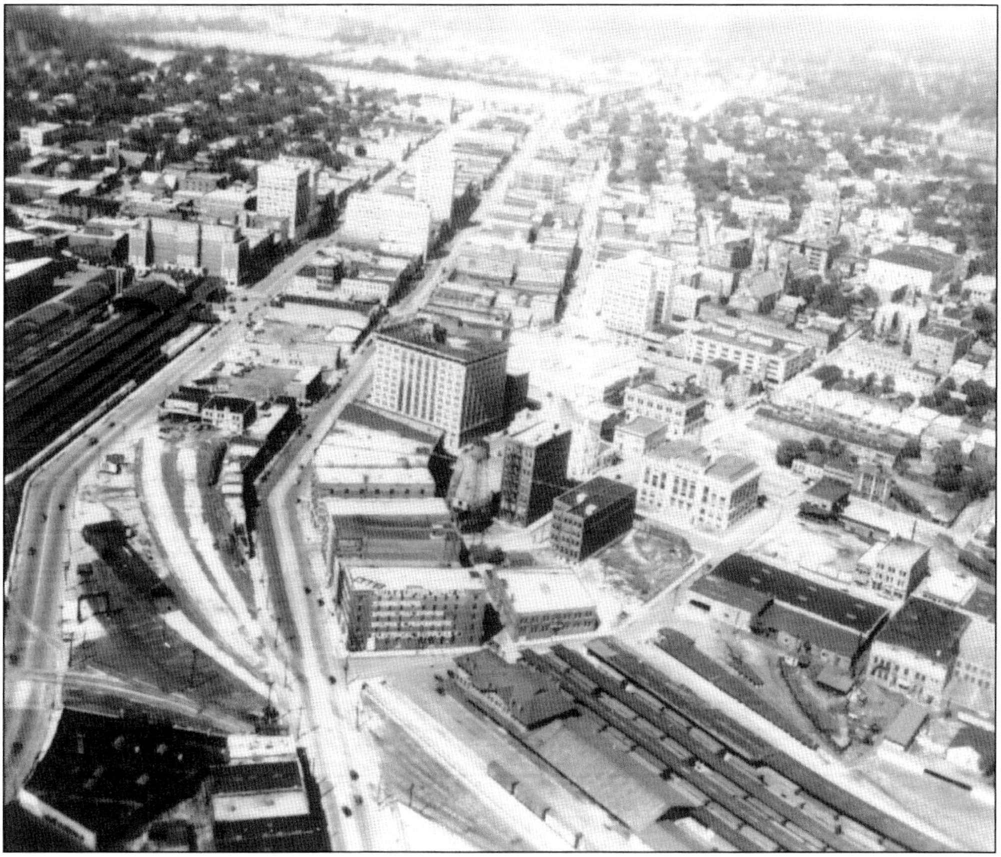

Like most American cities, Chattanooga has undergone dramatic changes during the twentieth century, most of them due to the influence of the automobile. Chattanooga expanded rapidly in the first three decades of the century: the population of the city increased from 30,000 in 1900 to more than 120,000 by the time this photograph was taken in 1934. Although population growth has slowed since that time (it currently stands at about 152,000), the city's streets and buildings continue to change.

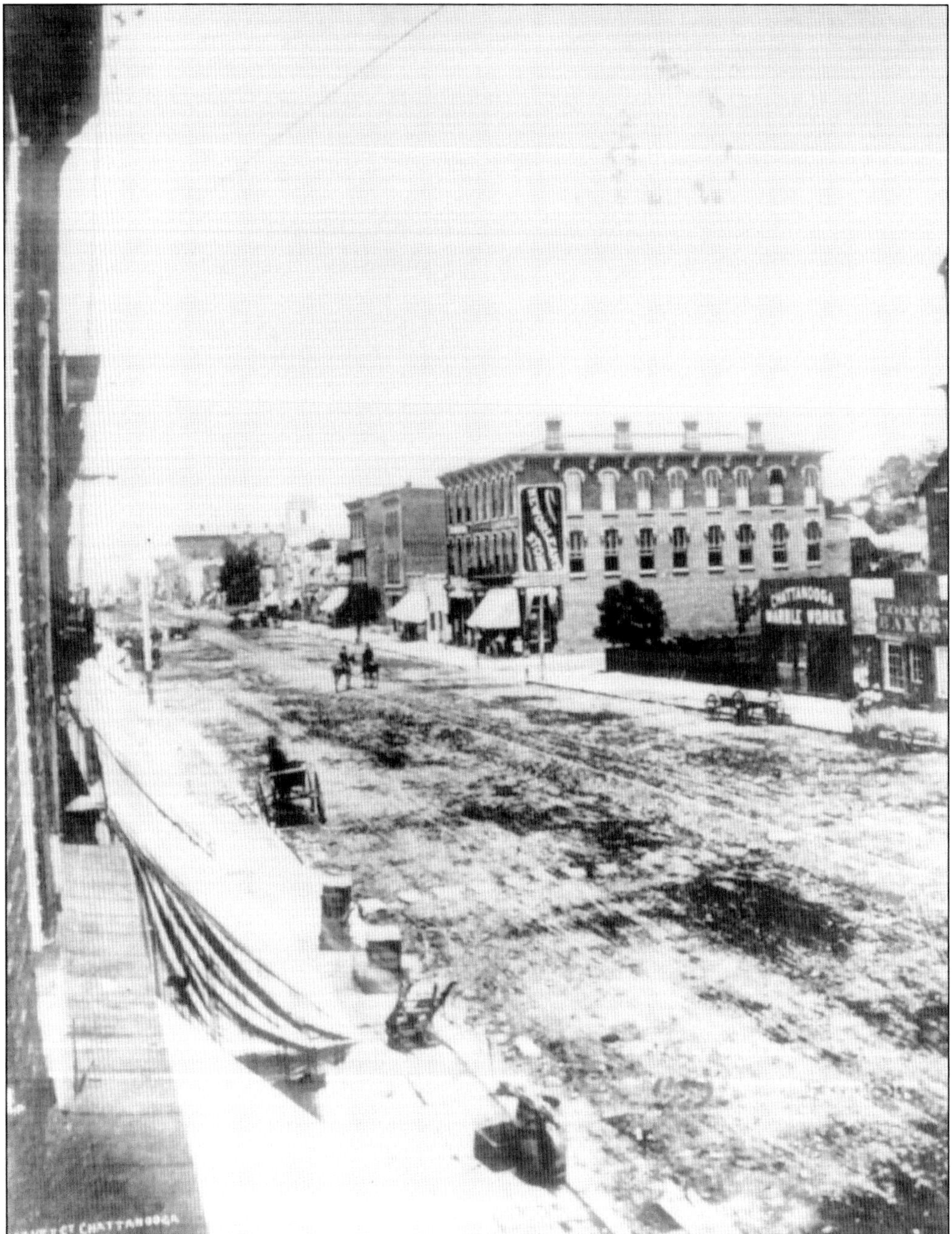

When the streets of Chattanooga were first laid out, Market Street was intended to be the commercial center of the town. In 1875, it was still an unpaved dirt road with stepping stones laid down for the rainy season. The New Orleans Store at the northeast corner of Eighth and Market Streets was the forerunner of Loveman's department store. D.B. Loveman bought the store at about the time this photograph was taken.

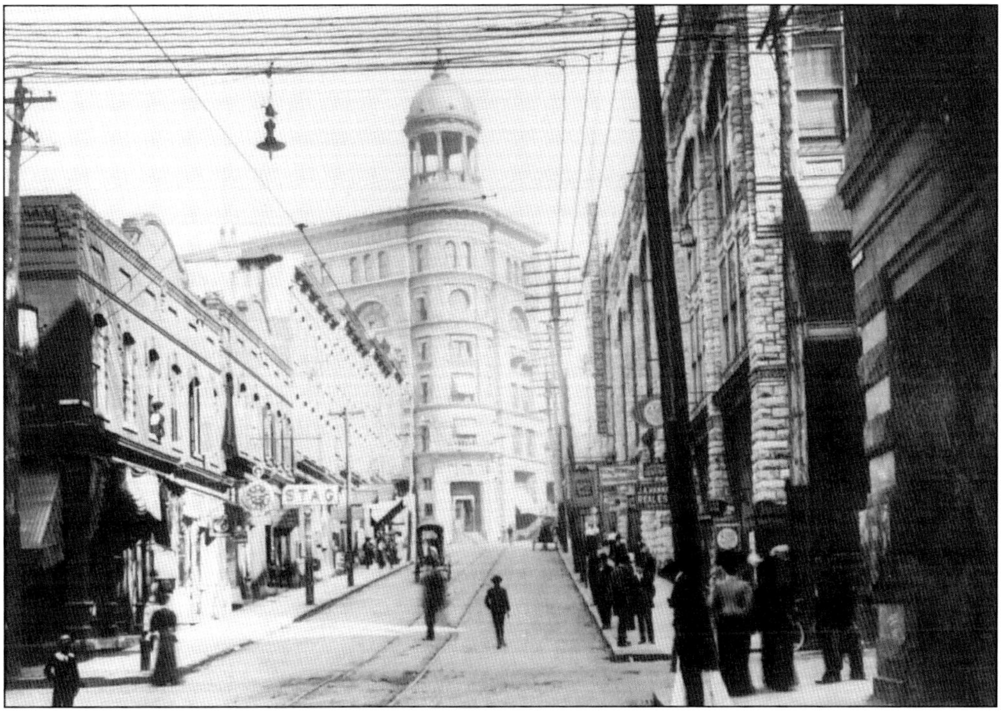

A streetcar line bisects Eighth Street in this photograph taken looking east toward *The Chattanooga Times* building. The building, topped by a golden dome, was completed in 1892. It is still a prominent city landmark. On the left, a woman looks out from a window above the watch repair shop. Will H. Stokes, a well-known Chattanooga photographer, took many of these early street scenes.

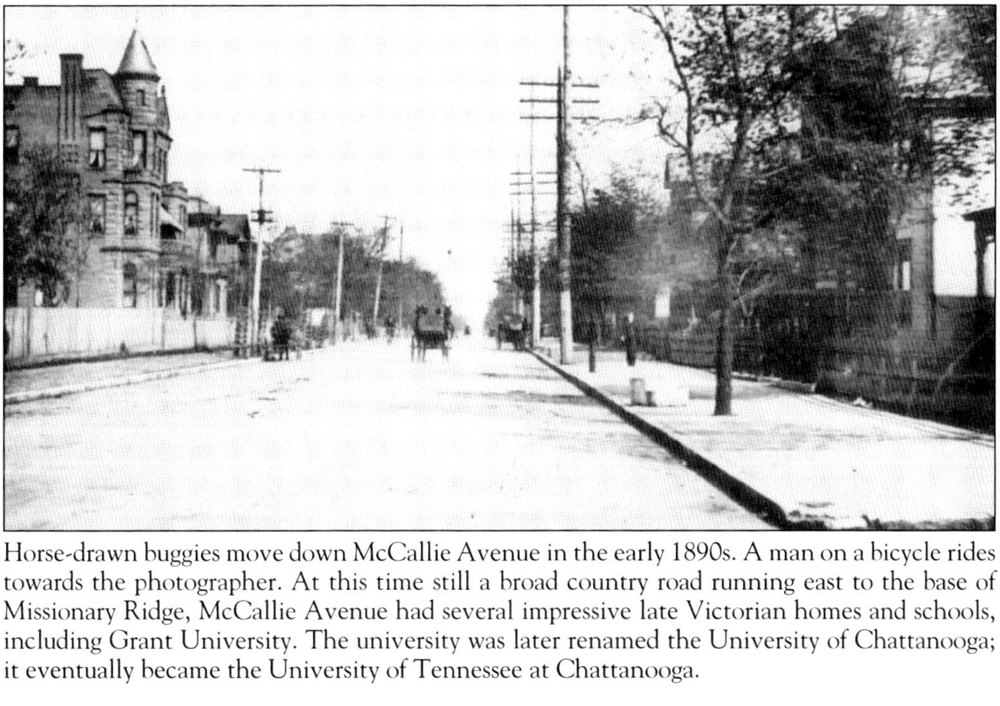

Horse-drawn buggies move down McCallie Avenue in the early 1890s. A man on a bicycle rides towards the photographer. At this time still a broad country road running east to the base of Missionary Ridge, McCallie Avenue had several impressive late Victorian homes and schools, including Grant University. The university was later renamed the University of Chattanooga; it eventually became the University of Tennessee at Chattanooga.

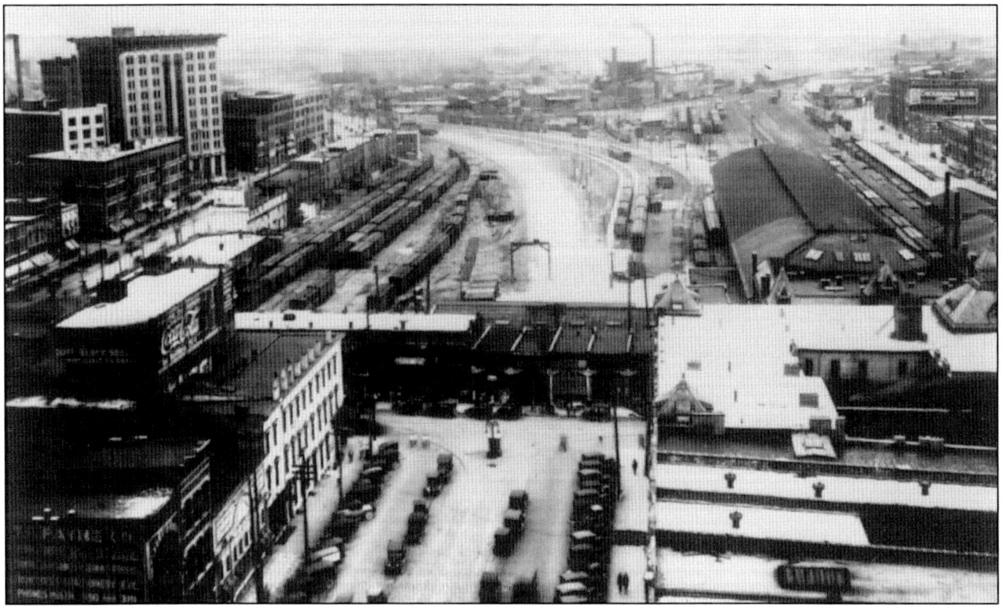

The south end of Broad Street was once separated from the Union Station site by buildings containing small businesses and an automobile shop. This obstruction to Broad Street traffic was removed in 1926. The last regularly scheduled passenger train left Chattanooga in May 1971. Soon after, the State of Georgia sold the station site for development. The large building on the left is the Hotel Patten.

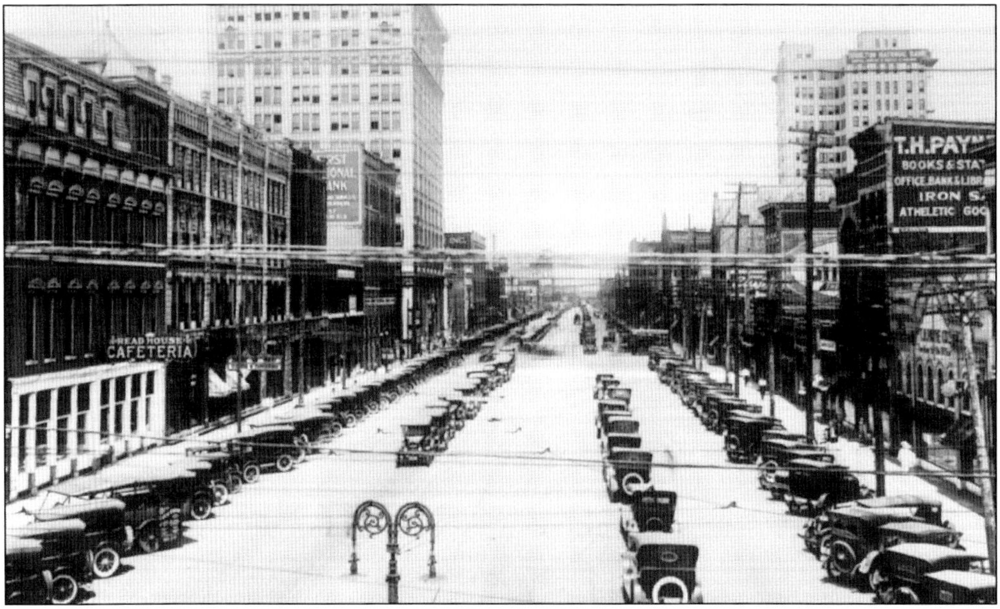

Dating from about the same time as the photograph above (the 1920s), this picture of Broad Street was taken looking north towards the river. The James Building on the left, with its twelve stories, was at one time the city's tallest structure. Its builders claimed that it had a thousand windows and seven hundred doors. The Hamilton National Bank building which seems to be across the street is actually on Market Street. The T.H. Payne Company (which sells office supplies) has been in business since 1865.

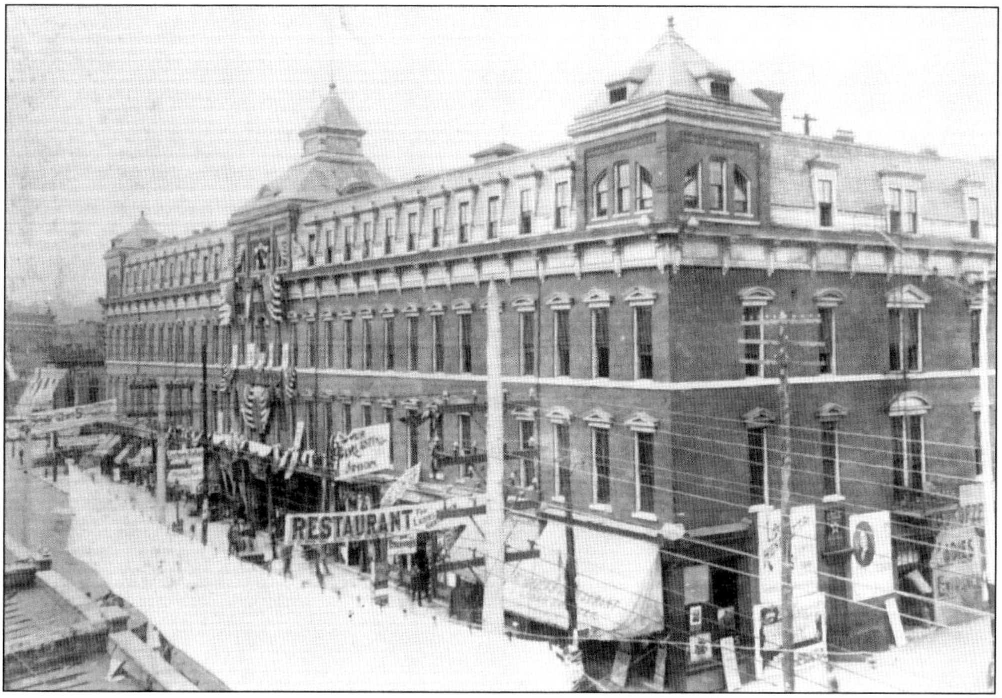

When the Crutchfield House was razed in 1867, several Chattanooga investors wanted to erect an office building on the site. Dr. John Thomas Read convinced them to build a hotel instead, and the Read House, pictured here, opened for business in 1872. Dr. Read often acted as the resident physician. His son, Sam Read, had most of the old building taken down in 1926 and the present Read House, ten stories high, built in its place.

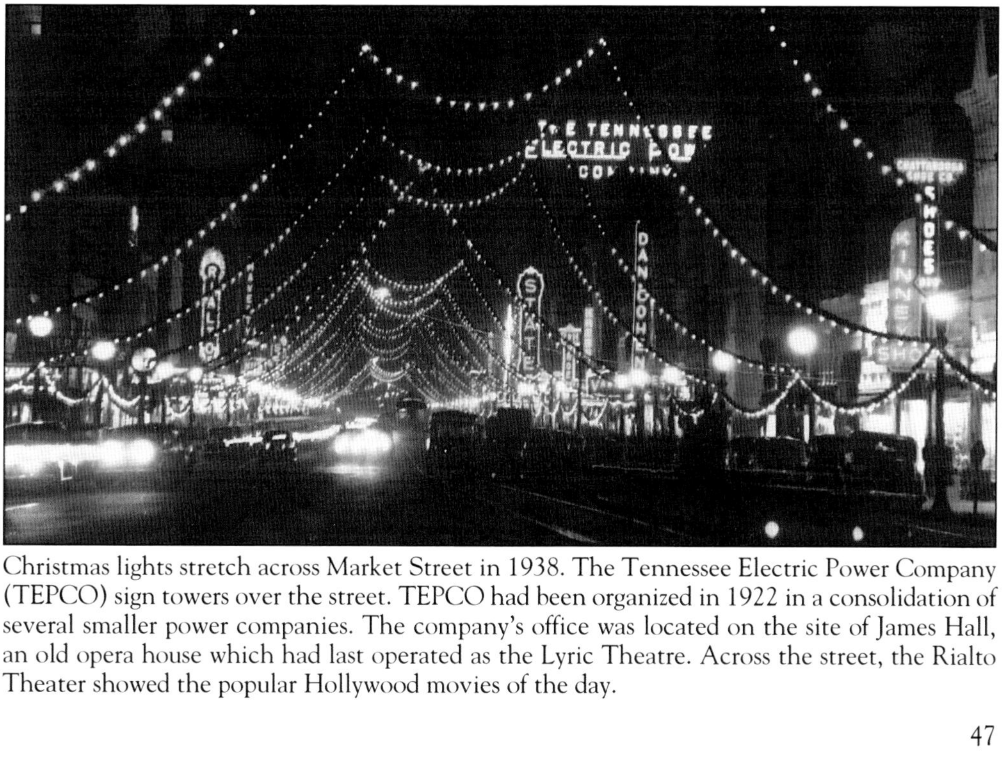

Christmas lights stretch across Market Street in 1938. The Tennessee Electric Power Company (TEPCO) sign towers over the street. TEPCO had been organized in 1922 in a consolidation of several smaller power companies. The company's office was located on the site of James Hall, an old opera house which had last operated as the Lyric Theatre. Across the street, the Rialto Theater showed the popular Hollywood movies of the day.

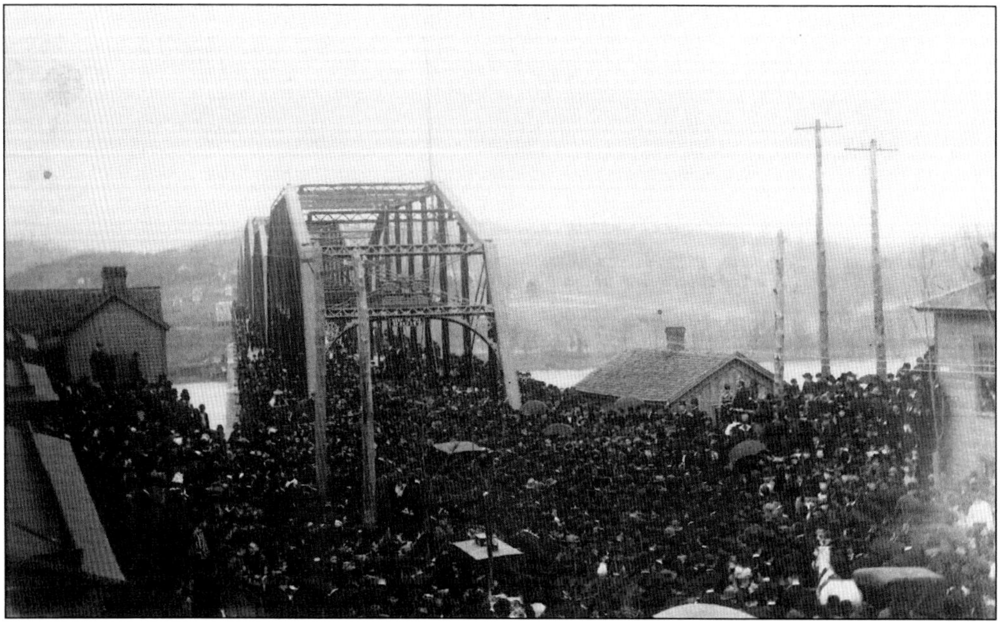

It was estimated that six thousand people attended the dedication ceremonies for the Walnut Street Bridge on February 18, 1891. The first bridge across the Tennessee River at Chattanooga since the ill-fated Meigs Military Bridge had been swept away by the 1867 flood, the Walnut Street Bridge eliminated the need for residents to take the ferry to settlements across the river. Several children of men connected with the bridge construction project drove in the last nails of the structure during the ceremony.

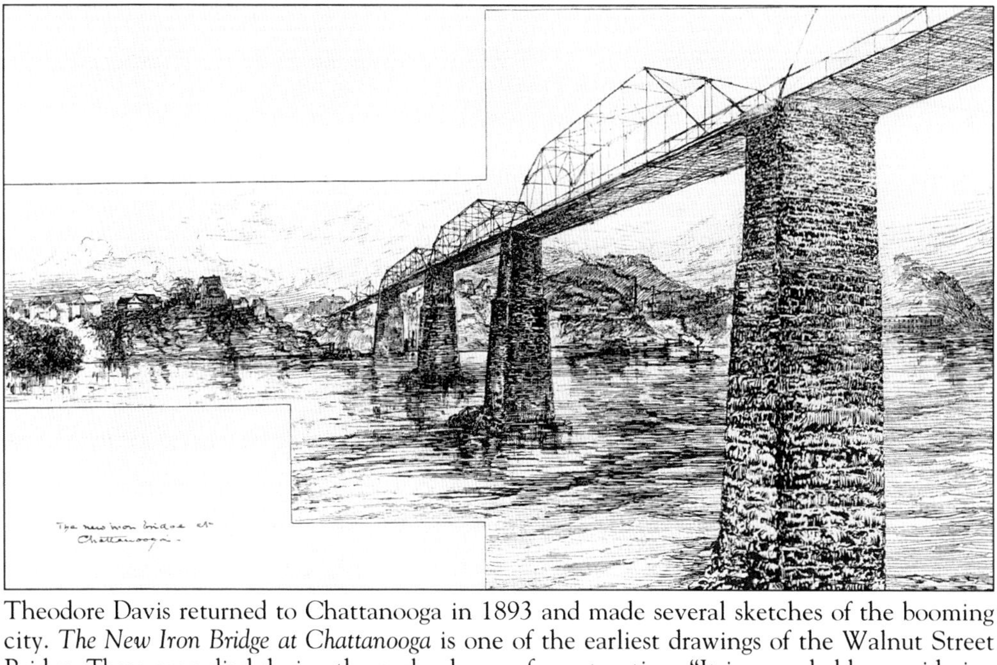

Theodore Davis returned to Chattanooga in 1893 and made several sketches of the booming city. *The New Iron Bridge at Chattanooga* is one of the earliest drawings of the Walnut Street Bridge. Three men died during the early phases of construction. "It is remarkable considering the carelessness with which the workmen went back and forth on the narrow beams at such height, that there are not more casualties to be chronicled," reported the *Chattanooga News*.

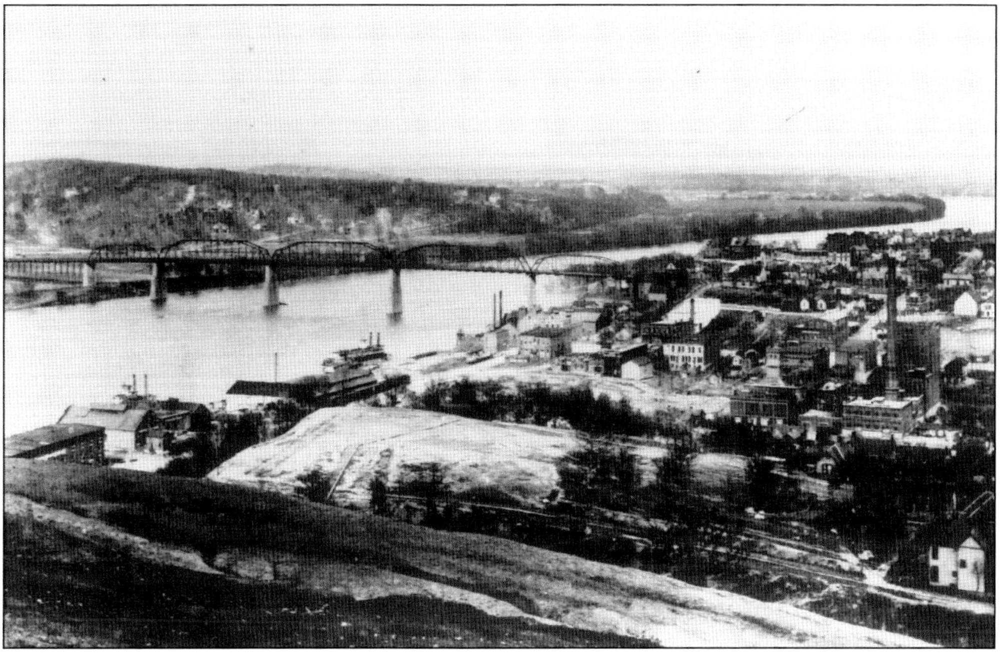

The impressive scale of the Walnut Street Bridge is evident in this photograph taken from Cameron Hill. To the right, the smokestacks of the various riverside industries are plainly visible. The bridge was eventually considered unsafe for traffic and closed in 1978. Today it is used as a popular pedestrian walkway.

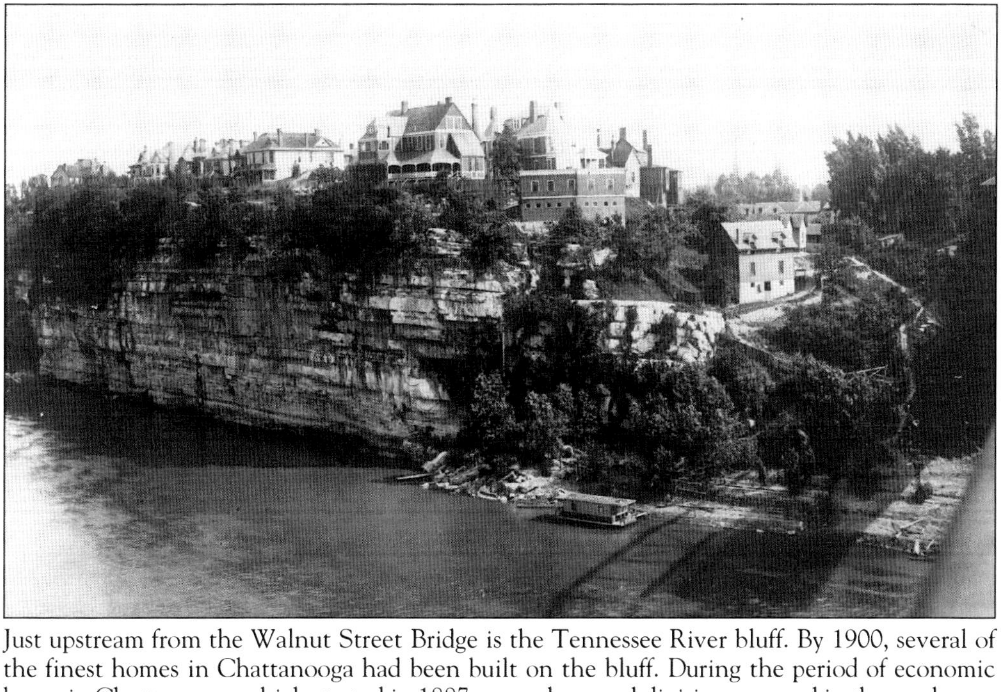

Just upstream from the Walnut Street Bridge is the Tennessee River bluff. By 1900, several of the finest homes in Chattanooga had been built on the bluff. During the period of economic boom in Chattanooga, which started in 1887, several new subdivisions opened in the rural areas outside of city limits, including St. Elmo, East Lake, Alton Park, and Hill City. Prices for local real estate skyrocketed and real estate offices began to crowd Market Street.

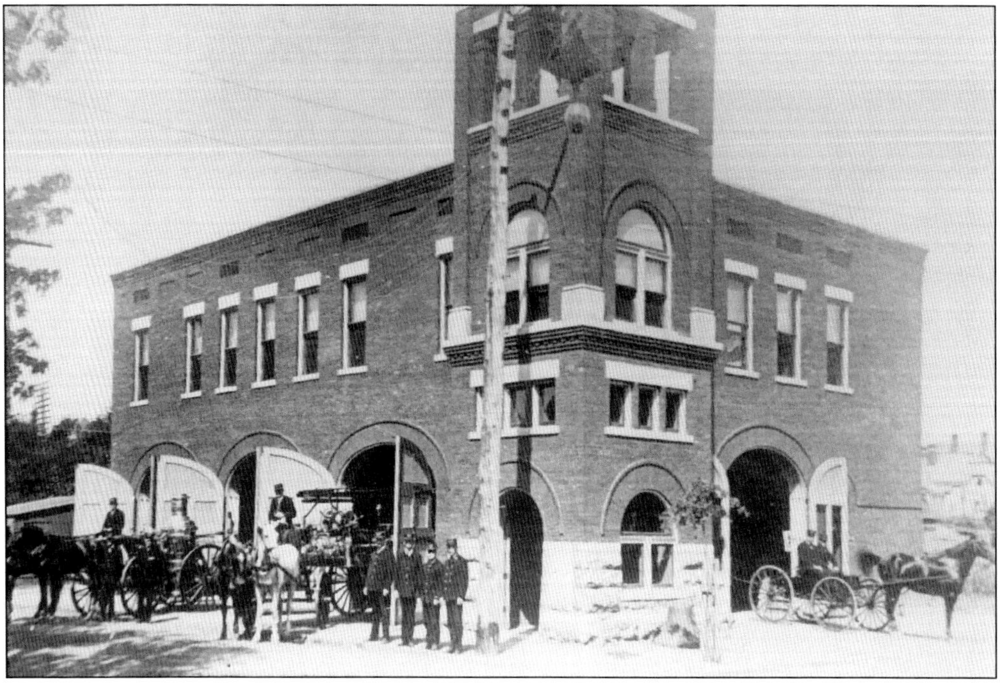

The rapid construction of so many new buildings in the city made a permanent fire station a necessity. Before this fire station was built on Eighth Street, the "Lookouts" of the Lookout Volunteer Fire Company had attempted to run a fire service, but they were constantly short of equipment. Indeed, during the fire of 1871, the city's only fire engine was in Rome, GA, due to problems with city bonds used to pay for it.

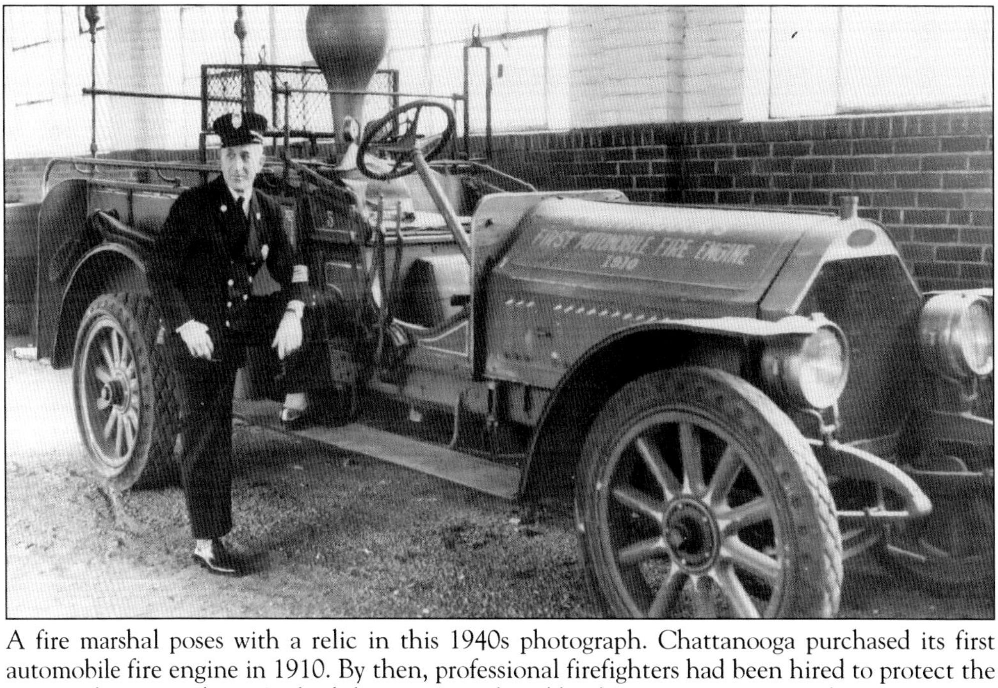

A fire marshal poses with a relic in this 1940s photograph. Chattanooga purchased its first automobile fire engine in 1910. By then, professional firefighters had been hired to protect the city. Today, more than 430 firefighters are employed by the city to serve at 21 fire stations.

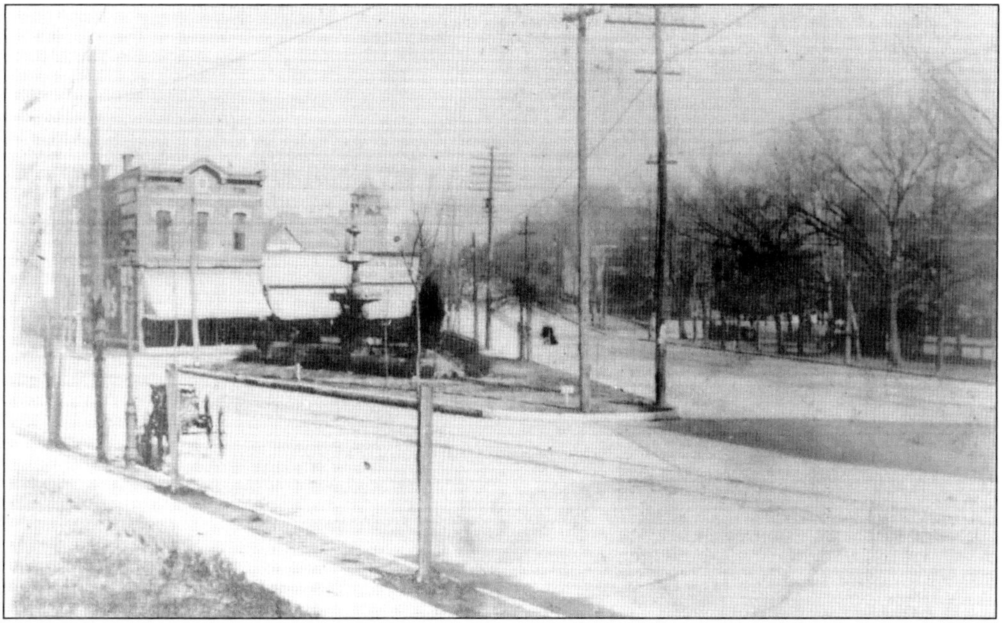

In June 1887, the Bee Hive Store fire broke out on Fourth Street. Two firemen, Matthew Peak and Henry Iler, were killed in an explosion caused by the fire. A memorial to the fallen heroes was dedicated on a small plot of ground near the county courthouse. The area around "Fireman's Fountain" soon became known as Fountain Square.

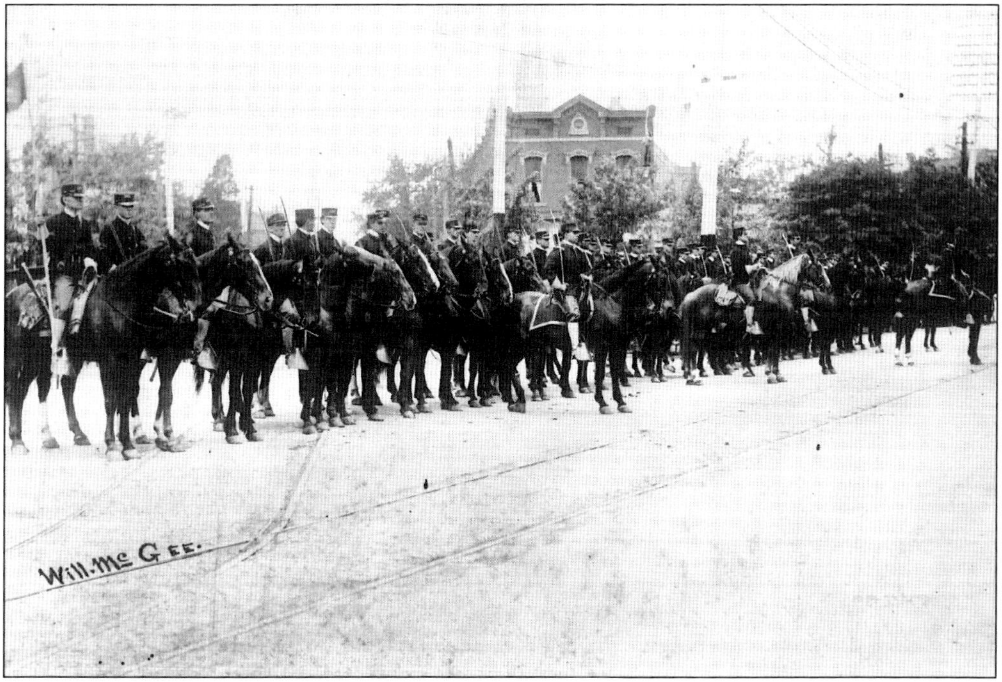

Firemen on horseback bring swords to salute during memorial ceremonies at Fountain Square. Perhaps the most disastrous fire in Chattanooga's history took place in August 1888. Several buildings along the Sixth and Seventh Street blocks were completely destroyed, including the Bradt Printing Company and the popular Tschopik's Garden, a center of social life in the city.

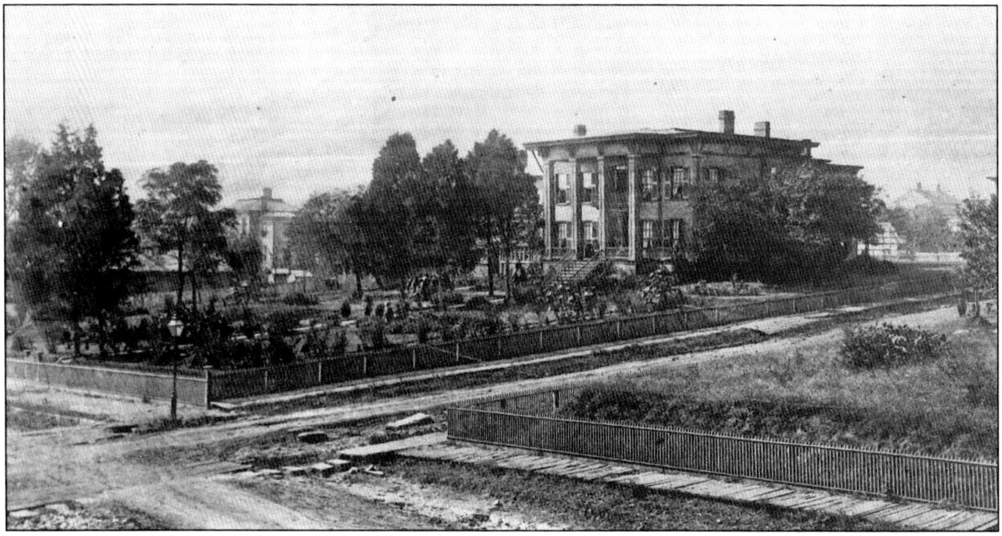

Efforts to save or preserve historic buildings in Chattanooga have occasionally been unsuccessful. The Grant headquarters and the Union depot were casualties of economic pressures. The Nottingham house (shown here), built in 1857 at Pine and Sixth Streets, also fell to the bulldozer in 1959, a victim of the Golden Gateway development plan. The house had been used as headquarters by both armies during the Civil War.

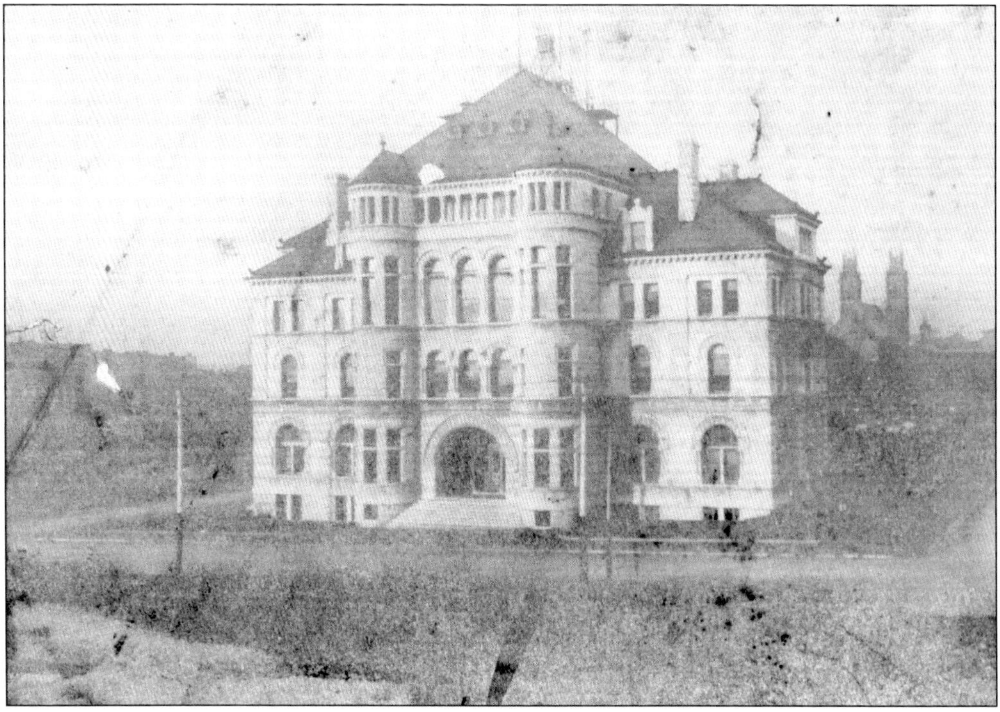

The Old Post Office-Custom House on Eleventh Street, is, however, a restoration success story. Built in 1893 on an old battery called the "Stone Fort," a large rock outcropping used as a defensive position by Union forces during the siege of Chattanooga, the post office is the South's most prominent example of Richardsonian Romanesque architecture. The building was given a complete facelift before the one hundredth anniversary celebrations in 1993.

The Lookout Mountain Inn was, perhaps, the most impressive hotel ever built in Hamilton County. The large hotel commanded a grand view at the end of the Broad Gauge Railroad line. Opened in 1890, the Lookout Mountain Inn had a large staff: the kitchen alone employed twelve cooks, twelve helpers, and sixty-two waiters. Amongst the hotel's leisure facilities were a bowling alley and a billiards room. Even the fire that burned it to the ground in 1908 was impressive, as it was visible for miles around.

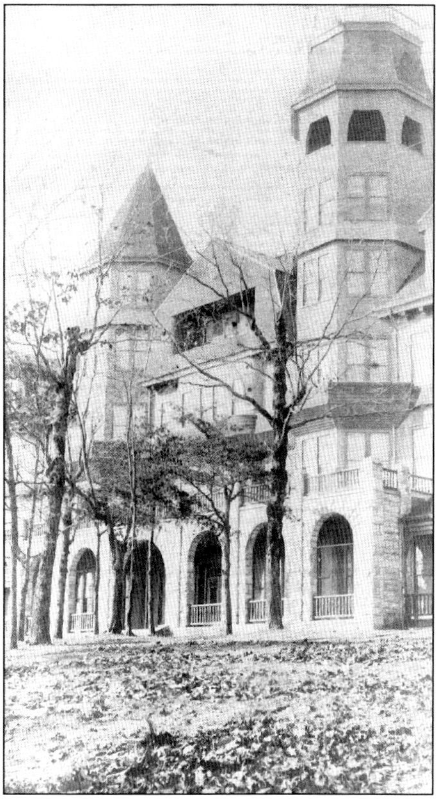

A number of other hotels on Lookout Mountain were very popular in the period before World War I. The Natural Bridge Hotel, comprising 45 rooms in a building set in 14 acres, opened just after the Civil War. Natural attractions, such as iron-rich springs, clean mountain air, and a rock bridge drew tourists seeking a healthful environment to the area. Spiritualist meetings were held on the site during the 1880s.

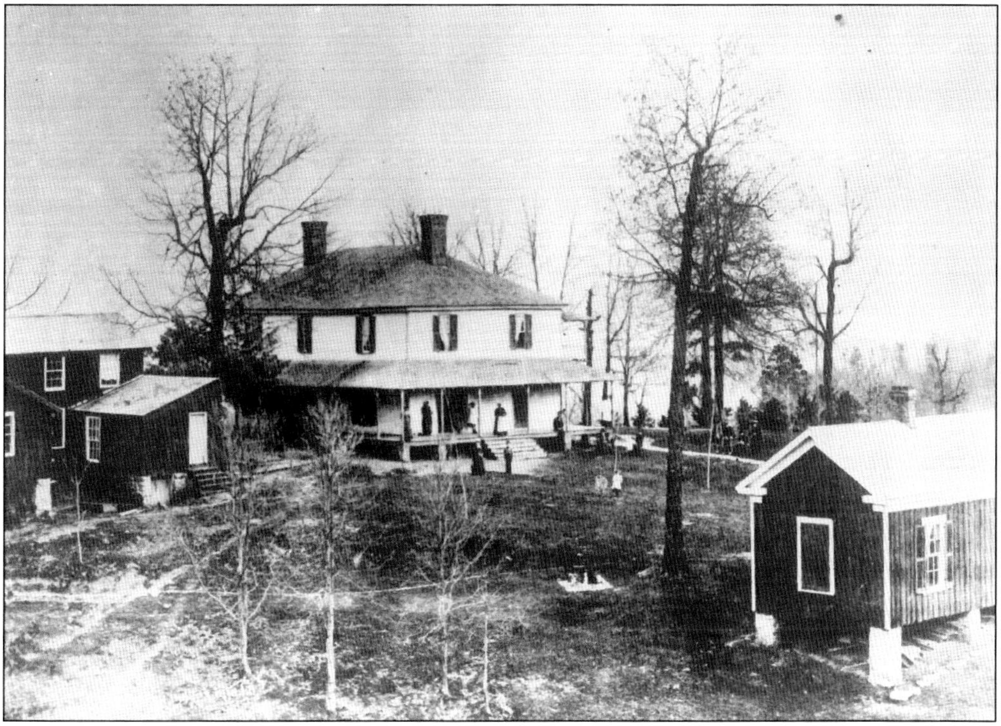

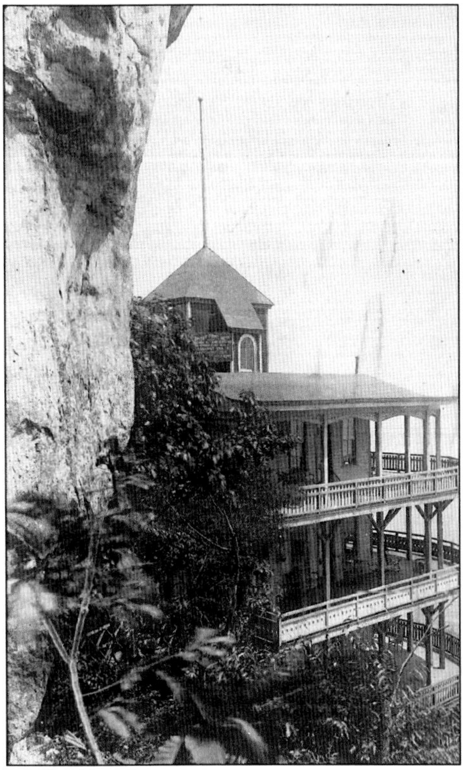

Photographs of Point Hotel are always interesting. Built by the McDaniel and Mighton Company of Chattanooga and located just below the Point of Lookout Mountain, the hotel was completed in 1888. The impressive structure featured four levels of balconies which wrapped around the building, giving patrons a commanding view of the valley below. Each guest room in the building had its own bath. Room charges ranged from $2.50 to $4.00 per day.

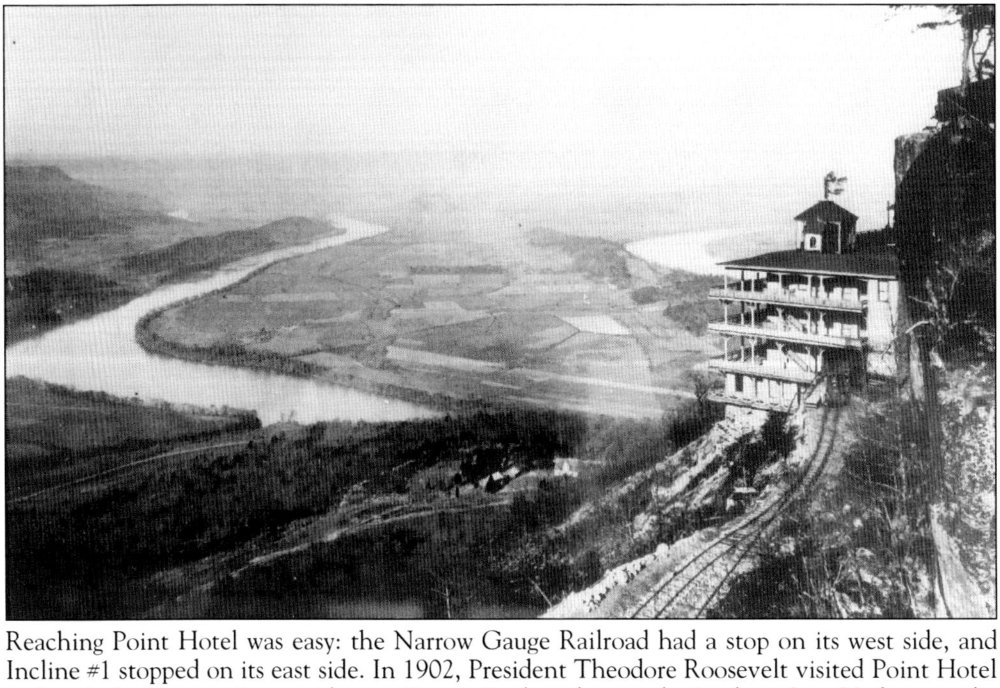

Reaching Point Hotel was easy: the Narrow Gauge Railroad had a stop on its west side, and Incline #1 stopped on its east side. In 1902, President Theodore Roosevelt visited Point Hotel and took the Narrow Gauge ride past Sunset Rock and up to the Lookout Inn. Unfortunately, Point Hotel never experienced great success due to competition from other hotels. It was finally demolished in the 1920s.

A streetcar rolls past the Cravens House on the old Broad Gauge Railroad line in the late 1910s. The Iowa Civil War monument is in the foreground. A horse-drawn streetcar system made its debut in Chattanooga in 1875, operating over a fifteen-block route in the downtown area. In 1887, an electric streetcar started service between Seventh Street and Missionary Ridge and by 1925 over 100 miles of trolley lines reached every part of the city. Fares were 7¢.

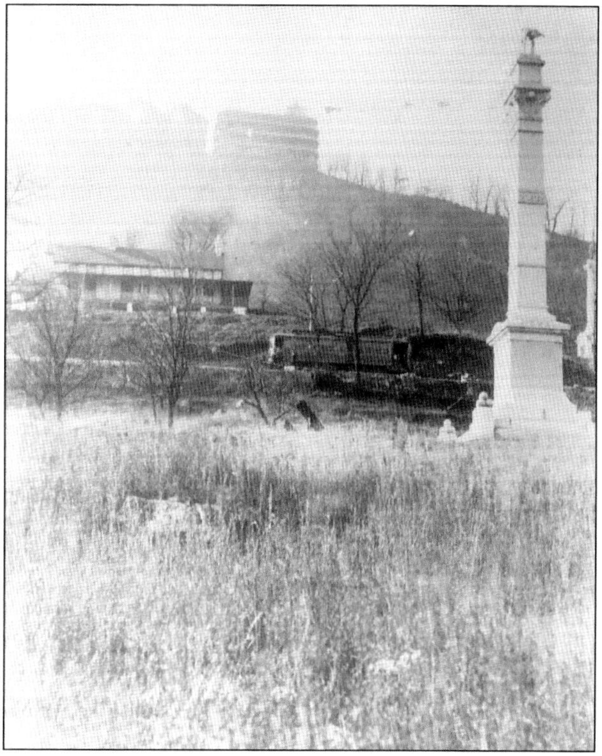

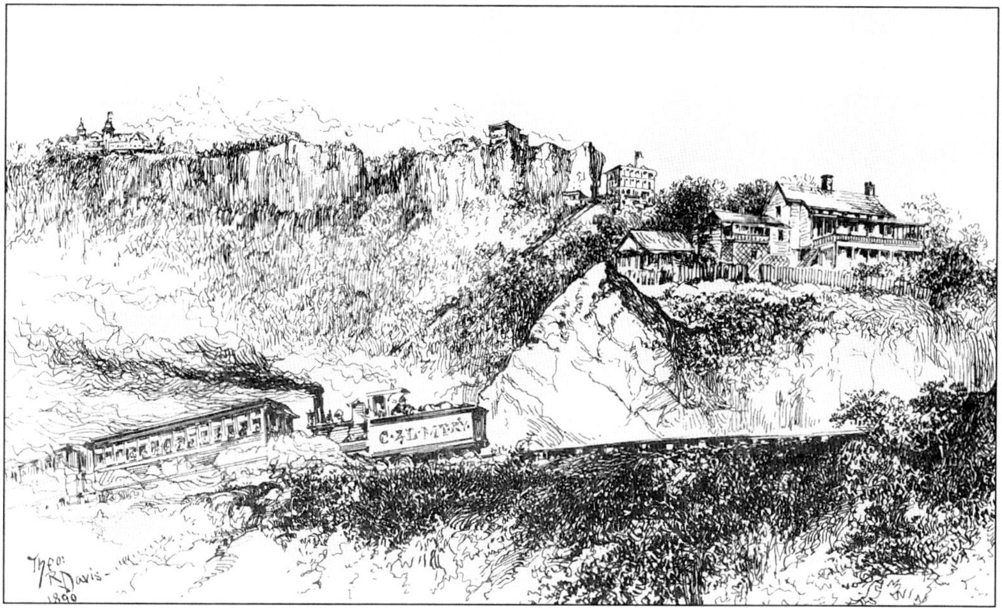

Theodore Davis tried to include all of the local landmarks in this fun depiction of a trip up Lookout Mountain. The Lookout Inn, Point Hotel, the Linn Photographic Studio, and the Cravens House can all be seen in this drawing. Following the Civil War, Davis continued his career in journalism. He traveled west drawing Colorado mining camps and United States Cavalry battles with the Cheyenne and Sioux. He also found time to work on several important works of art, including the *Atlanta Cyclorama*. He died in 1894.

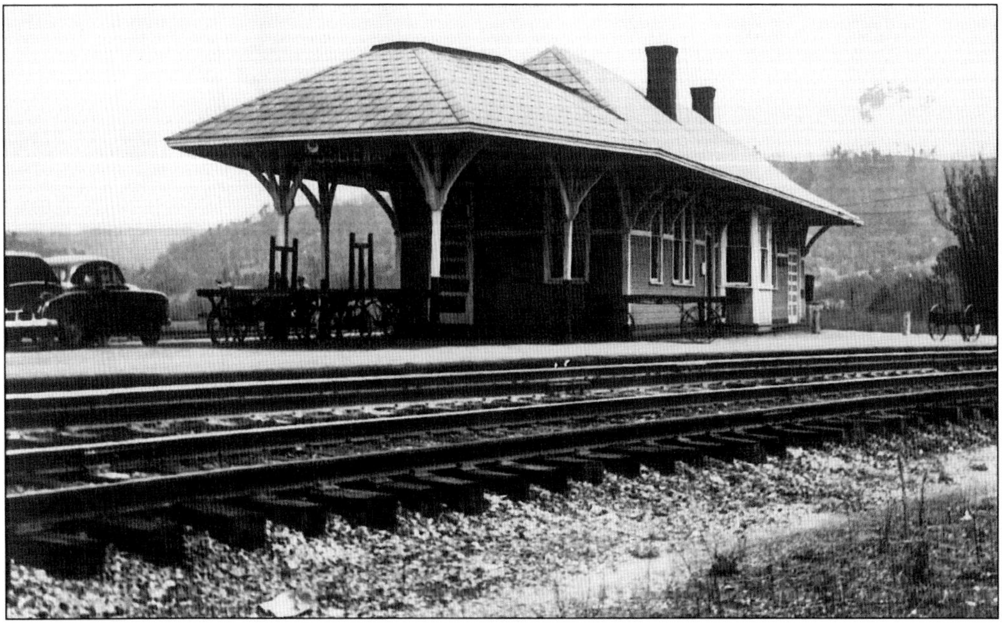

As Chattanooga grew, so did the once rural communities on its outskirts. Outlying communities in Hamilton County began to develop as soon as trains and streetcars made it possible for the average citizen to commute to the city from homes in the country on a daily basis. This photograph shows the Ooltewah depot.

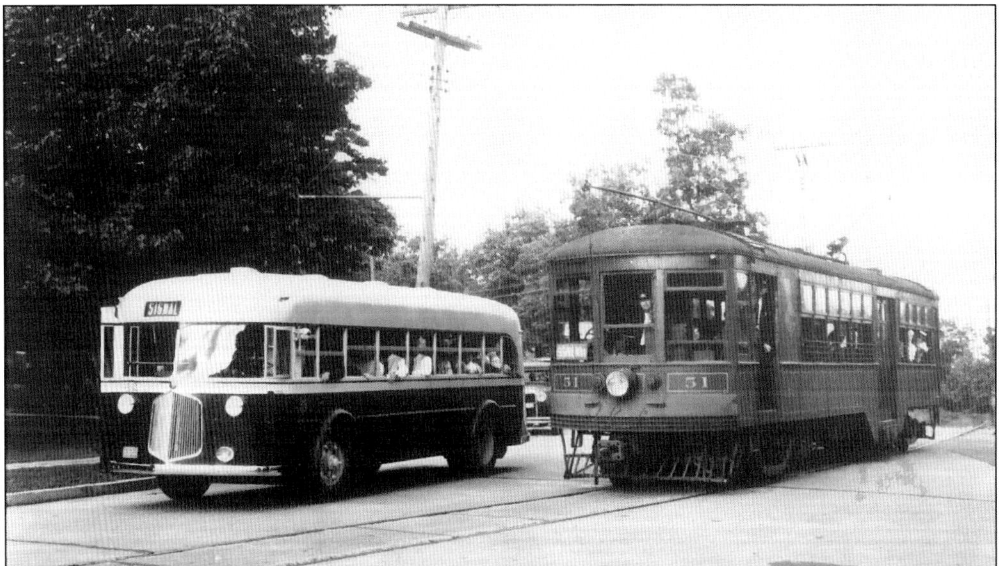

Streetcars eventually even reached the top of Signal Mountain, brought there by the enterprise of one man, Charles E. James. In 1911, James, a tireless promoter, began erecting a resort hotel on the mountain. At the same time, he built a 13-mile streetcar line to the summit, which he chartered as the Chattanooga Traction Company. A casino and golf course were soon added, along with cottages and permanent residences, and so the community of Signal Mountain was born. James became the first mayor of Signal Mountain and served in that capacity until his death in 1925.

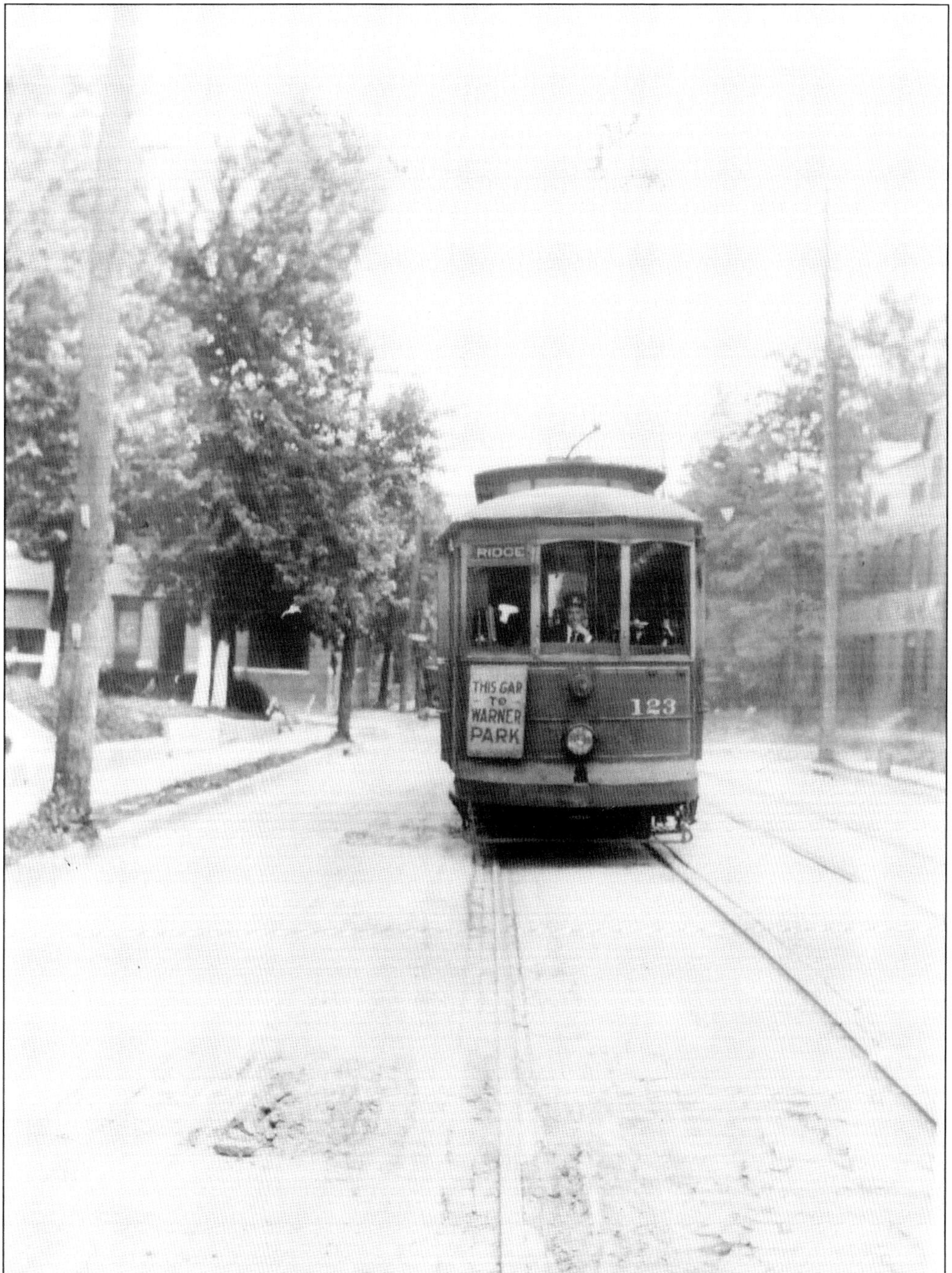

In order for the streetcars to remain successful, patrons had to have a place to go, so enterprising operators began building parks and lakes that could be reached by their streetcar lines. In 1890, the Electric Railway Company sponsored the building of Olympia Park. The park featured horse racing, a zoo, baseball diamonds, a bandstand, and other attractions. In 1912, the City of Chattanooga bought the property and renamed it Warner Park in honor of the city commissioner who helped develop it as a public park.

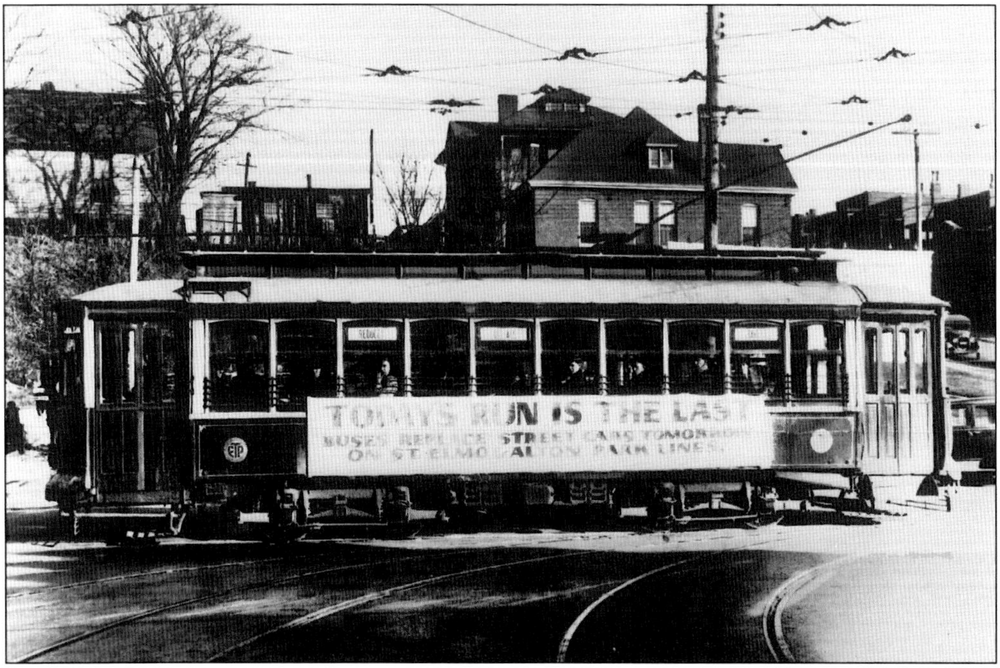

Eventually, the automobile rendered the streetcar obsolete. The completion of the Dixie Highway in the 1920s prompted improvements to other local roads. By the time this photograph was taken in 1932, most of the main roads in Hamilton County had been paved. According to the 1925 City Directory, by that date Chattanooga alone had over 155 miles of paved streets.

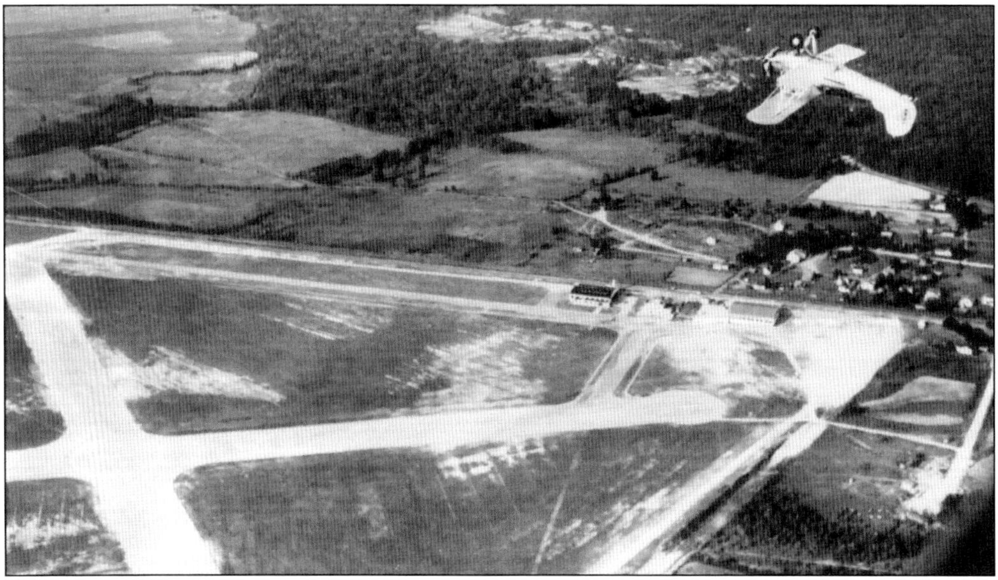

Marr Field, near Missionary Ridge, opened in East Chattanooga in 1919. Over three thousand spectators showed up to watch a few planes do circus tricks. However, a larger and safer airport to serve the Chattanooga region was needed. Named after a local aviation promoter, Lovell Field opened in 1930 on 130 acres of land near Chickamauga. In 1934, Eastern Airlines made its first stop at Chattanooga's new airport.

Four

The Business of Chattanooga Is Business

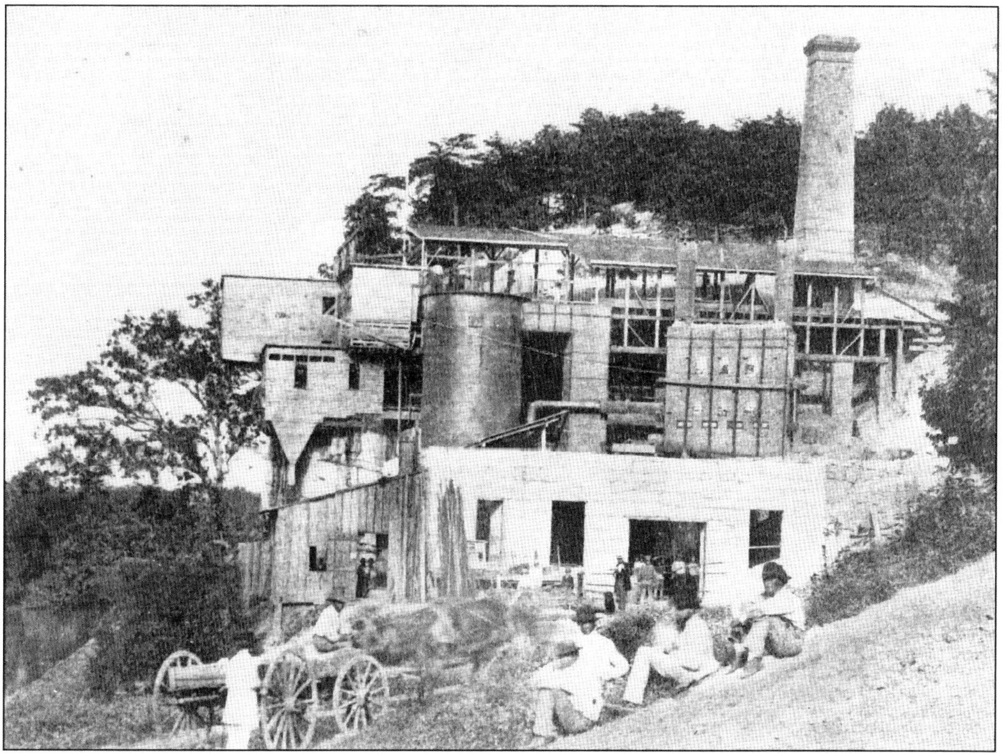

When railroads began developing lines into Chattanooga in the 1850s, the rural character of the city began to change, with industries taking advantage of the new, efficient transportation systems. The Bluff Furnace was constructed in 1854 by Robert Cravens and James Whiteside, using charcoal as a fuel. In 1859, it became the first blast furnace in the Southern Appalachian region to use coke as a fuel. The Civil War interrupted operations and the Bluff Furnace was destroyed by Union troops in 1864. In the late 1970s, archaeological explorations of the site were conducted. The Bluff Furnace site has now been turned into a historic park along the Riverfront Walkway. The only known photograph of the blast furnace (shown above) is in the collection of the Chattanooga Regional History Museum.

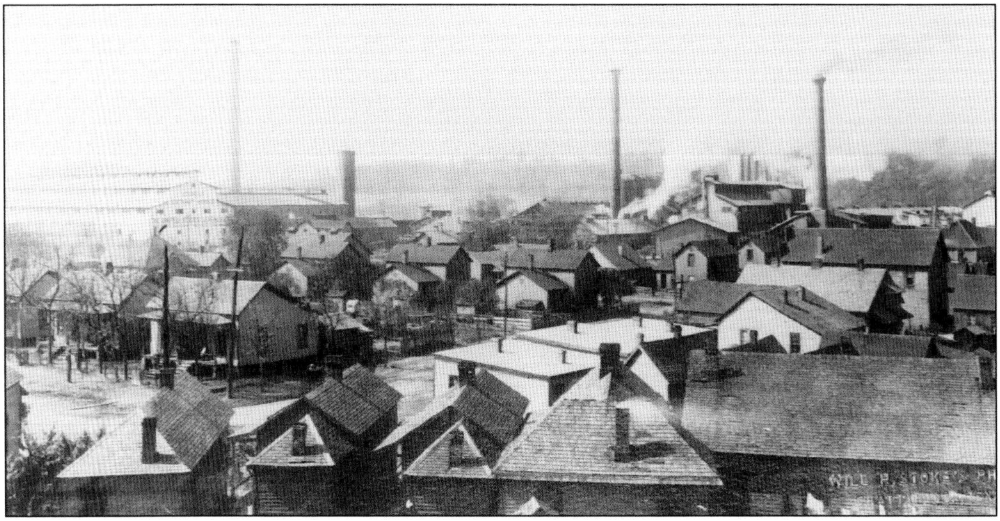

The trend towards industrialization, interrupted by the Civil War, continued in the 1870s. The area known as "Tannery Flats," between the west side of Cameron Hill and the Tennessee River, saw substantial growth in this period. This photograph shows Lookout Extract Works (also known at various times as the Hoyt Company, Fayerweather and Ladew Tannery, and Union Tannery) on the left, off Fourteenth and Elm Streets. In the center of the photograph is the Chattanooga Iron Furnace Company, an operation started by Dr. J.N. McLane, an Indiana native who arrived in Chattanooga in 1873.

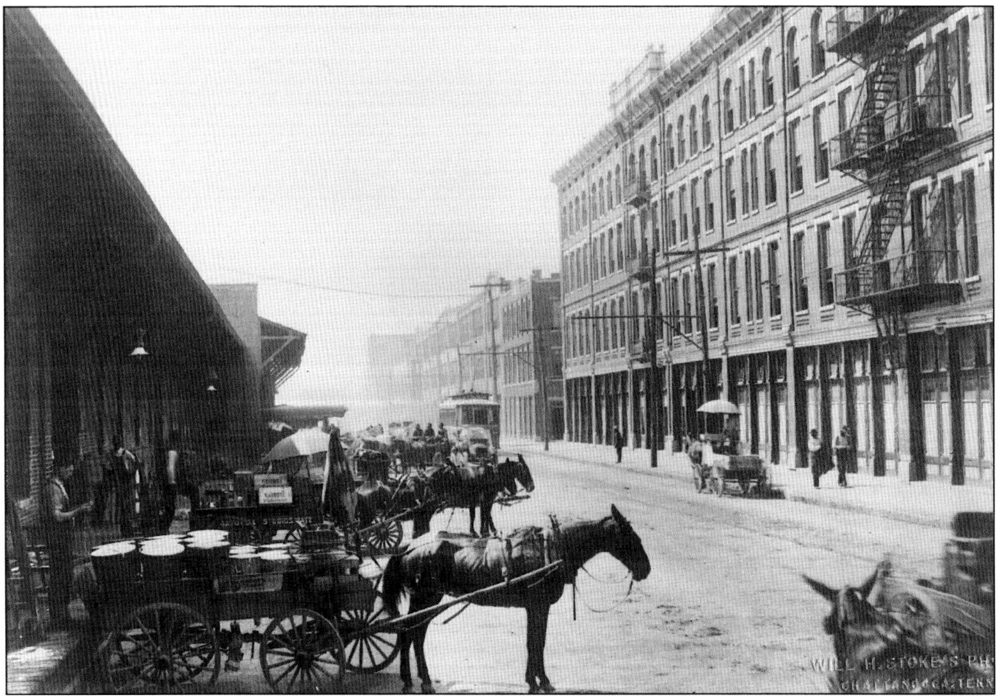

A streetcar rides past horse-drawn wagons loaded with goods awaiting delivery at the W & A Union depot freight dock on Chestnut Street in the 1880s. Across the street is the Southern Hotel, a triangular shaped building that was originally called the Palace Hotel. The hotel was built in 1887 and had 140 guest rooms and 8 rooms which served as offices on the first floor.

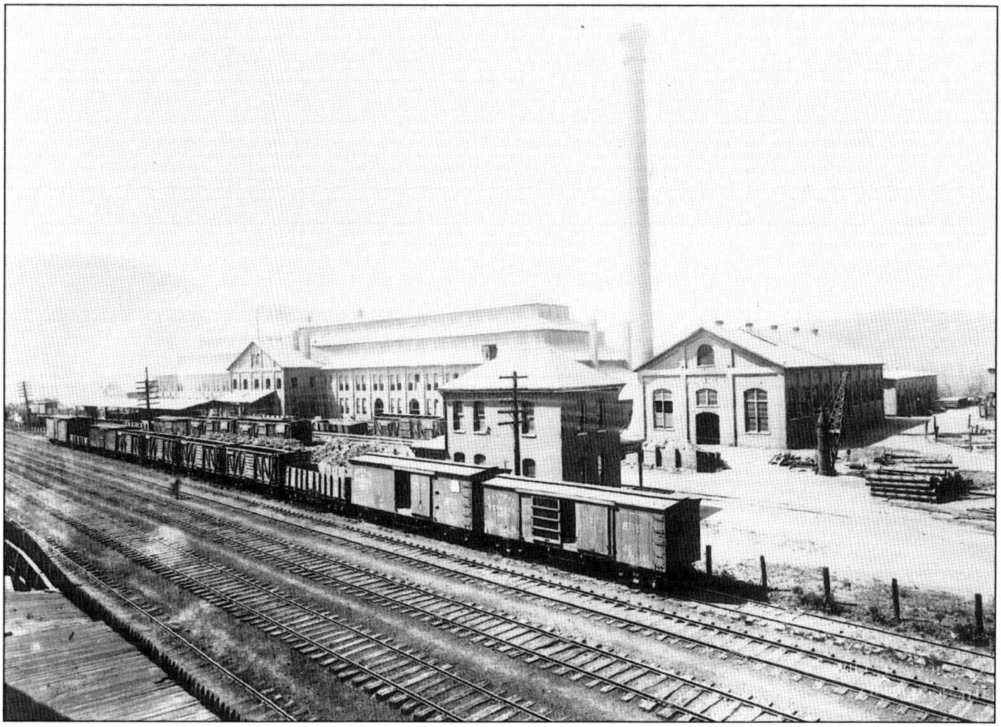

The United States Pipe and Foundry Company is shown in this 1930s photograph. The tracks of the Nashville, Chattanooga, and St. Louis Railroad, as well as those of the Central of Georgia Railroad, can be seen in the foreground. The United States Pipe and Foundry Company opened in Nashville in 1867. In 1877, David Giles, the founder, opened another plant in Chattanooga, manufacturing pit-cast pipe. Giles remained as president of the company through several reorganizations until his death in 1910.

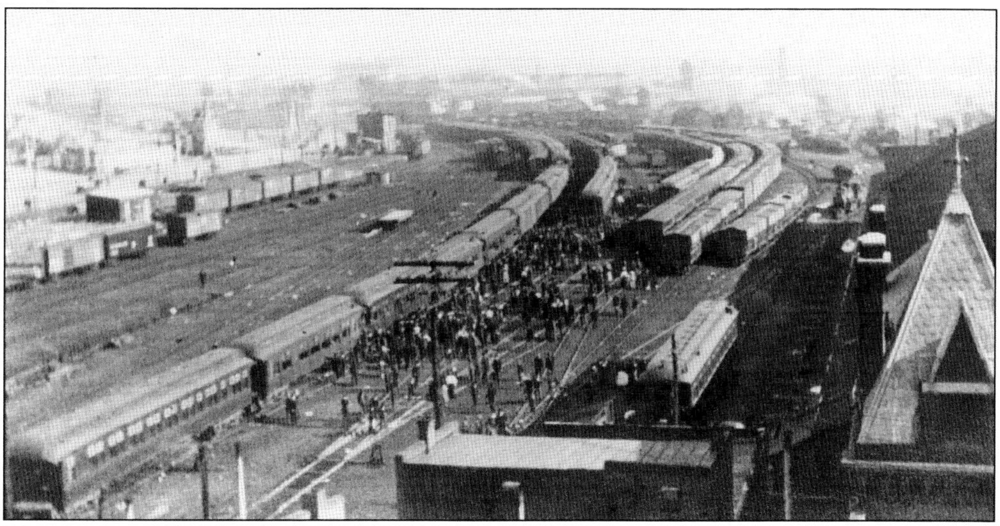

This picture of the view looking south over the rail yards was taken from a window in the Read House. The men in the picture are in transit to Fort Oglethorpe to serve in the 1898 Spanish-American War. Visible in the background are the old ice plant and the Stanton House Hotel. The Stanton House was torn down in 1906; the Terminal Station was built on the site in 1909.

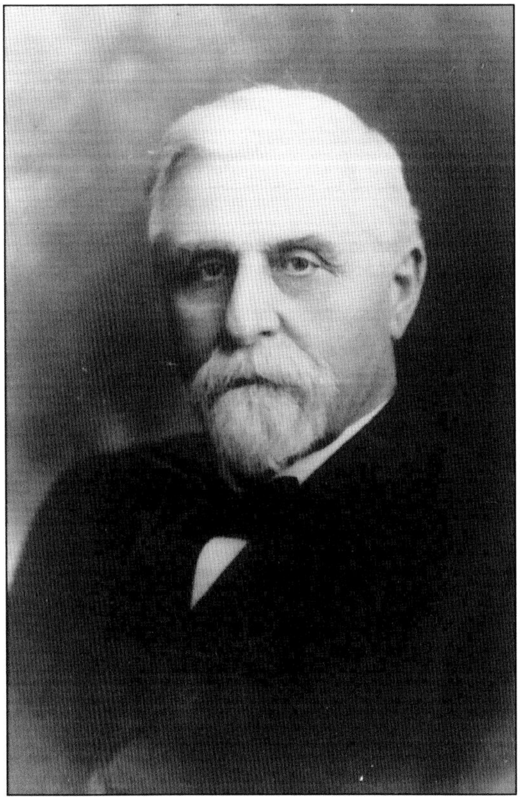

George Washington Wheland was another of those Civil War veterans who saw opportunity in Chattanooga. A native of Pennsylvania, Wheland had come to Tennessee to study the machinist trade with his uncle in Athens. Unfortunately, Wheland's uncle was killed in an accident just three months after his arrival, so in 1873 Wheland moved to Chattanooga and established a foundry near the Scholze Tannery just south of Chattanooga Creek.

The Wheland Foundry and workers in a photograph dating from 1875. The foundry also included a machine shop, a blacksmith shop, and a pattern shop. Specializing in the construction of grist mills, saw mills, cane mills, and water wheels, the Wheland Foundry experienced a period of great success in the 1870s and 1880s. Even the great flood of 1886 did little to slow the company's progress. George Wheland took an active role in the company until his death in 1929.

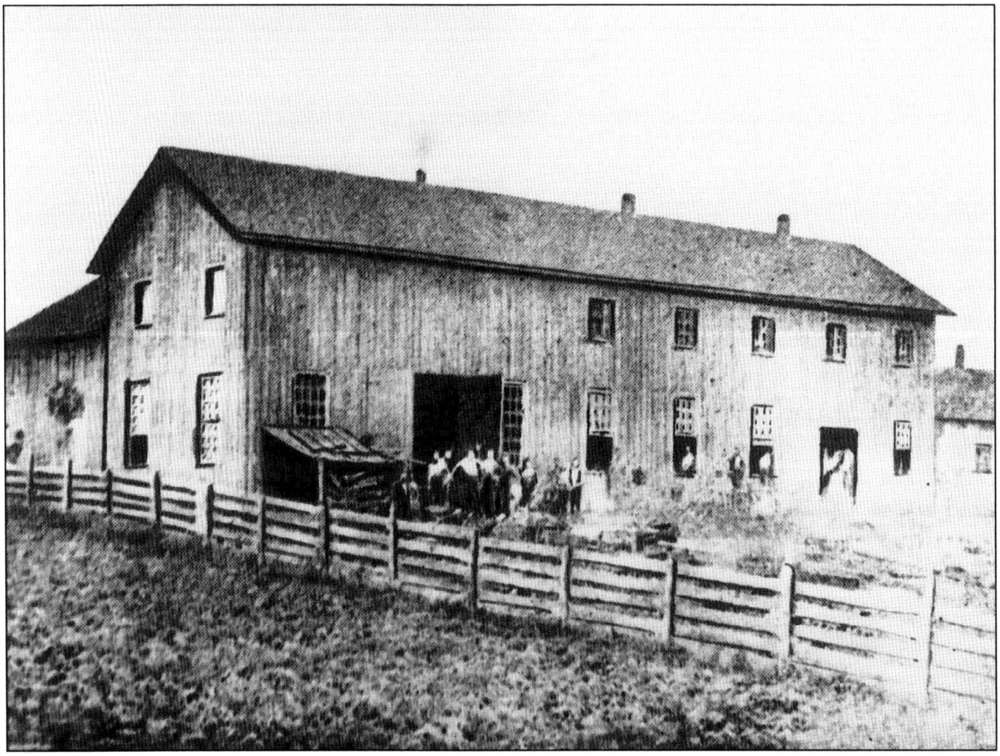

Over the years the Wheland Foundry continually adjusted its products to meet the demands of its customers, manufacturing at various times cookware, drilling equipment, steam engines, and anchor windlasses. Today, the foundry continues to be a major industrial presence in Chattanooga. A subsidiary of North American Royalties, Inc., the company is the largest independent producer of cast iron automotive brake components in the United States. In an average week in 1991, 15 rail cars and 130 trailer loads of castings were shipped to Wheland's customers.

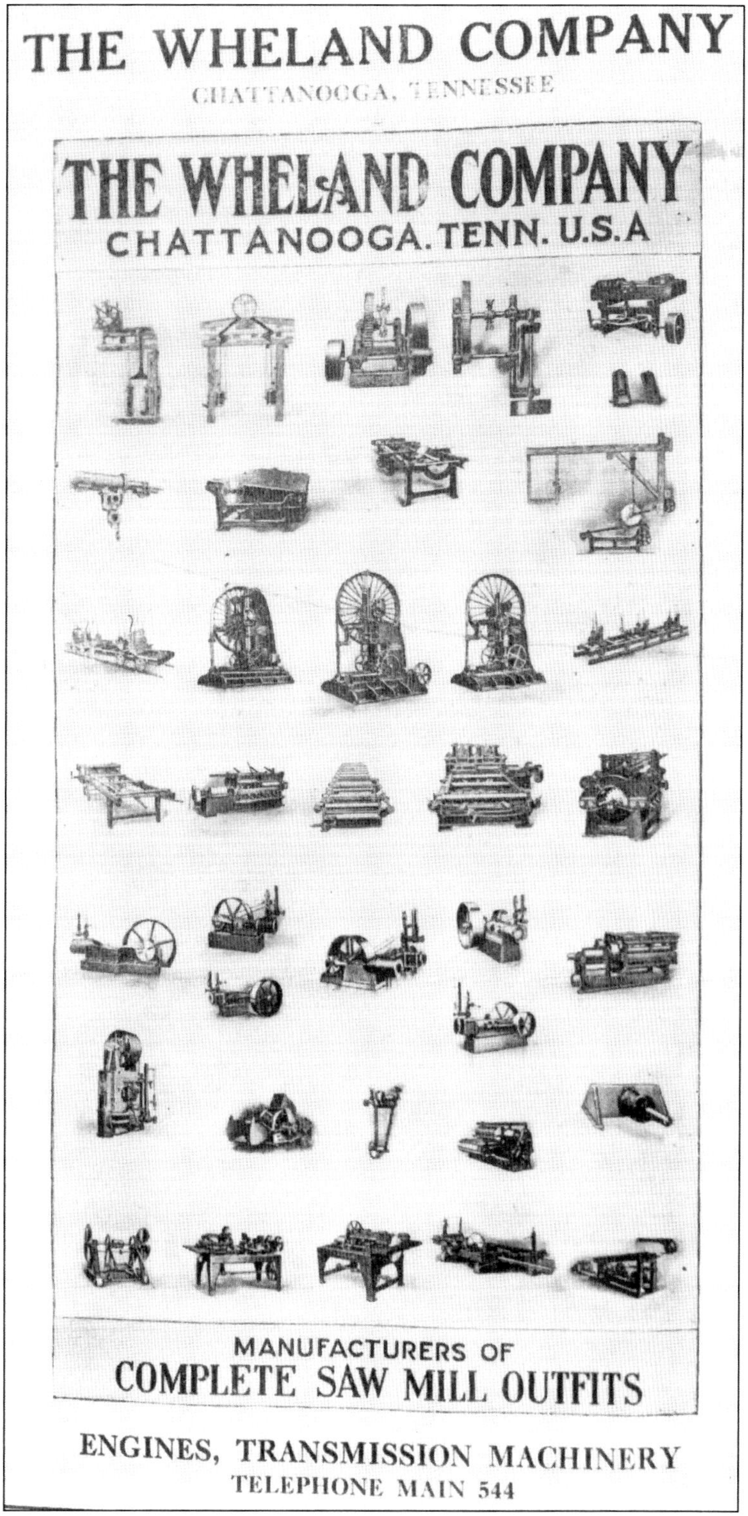

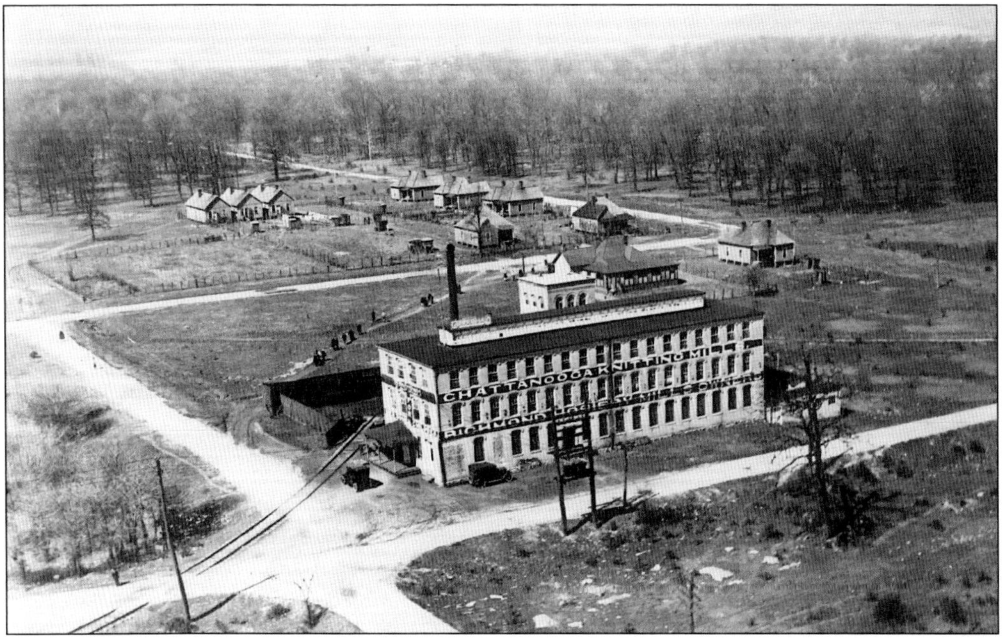

After several abortive attempts to establish a textile industry in Chattanooga in the 1870s and 1880s, Garnett Andrews organized the Chattanooga Knitting Mills in 1896. The mills specialized in cotton hosiery and employed thirty people. With Edward G. Richmond, the firm was reorganized as Richmond Hosiery Mills in 1898. The Chattanooga Knitting Mill was one of the first businesses in the city to use electrical power.

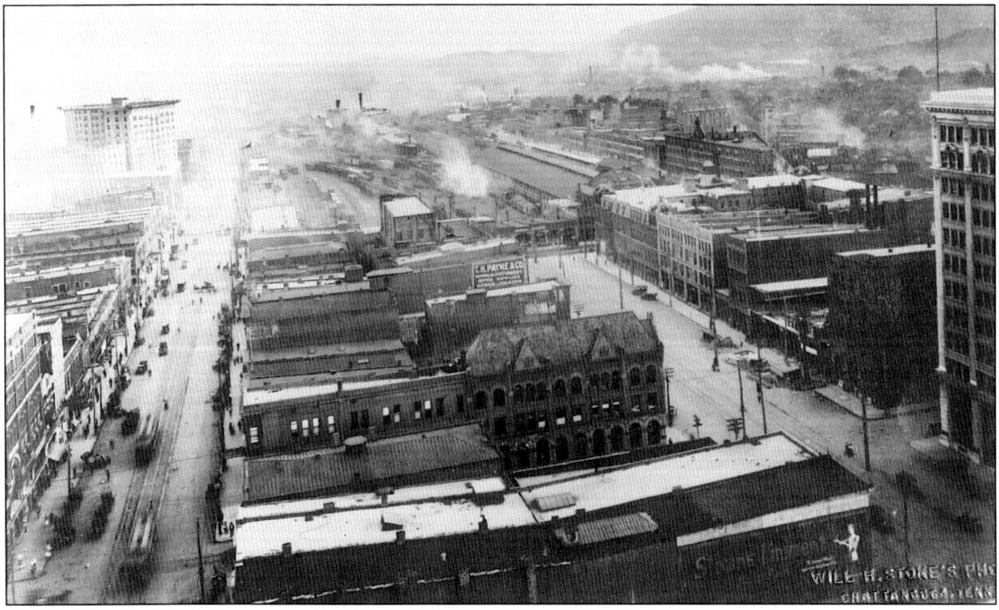

Local photographer Will H. Stokes took this photograph of the view looking south down Market (left) and Broad (right) Streets. The tall structure on the right is the James Building. Smoke and other pollutants from the rail yards and factories cloud the horizon, but Lookout Mountain can be seen in the background. By the 1960s, Chattanooga had the worst air quality of any city in the country.

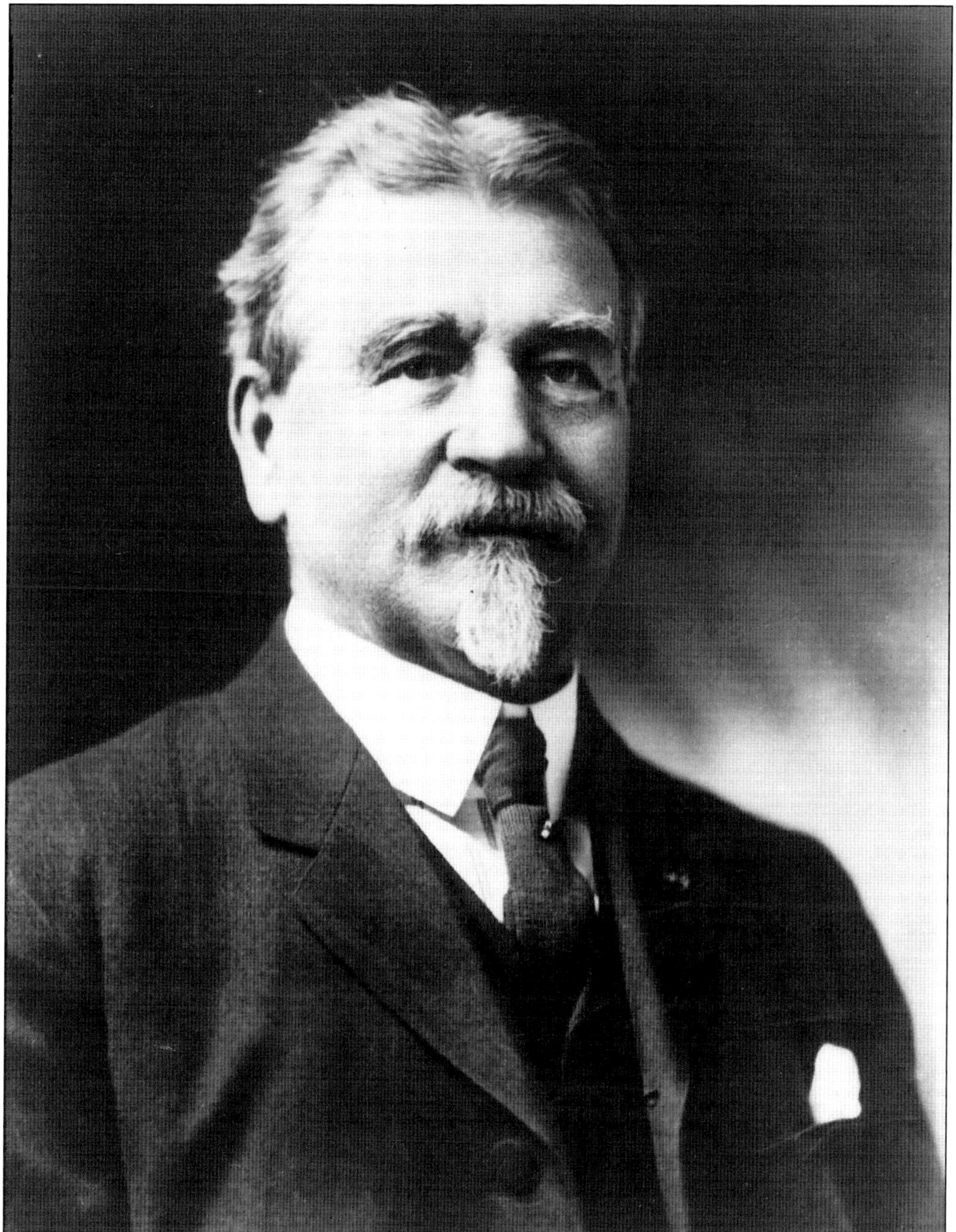

Hiram Sanborn Chamberlain had served in an Ohio cavalry unit during the Civil War. In 1871, he moved to Chattanooga to become general manager of the Roane Iron Company. He eventually served as president of the Citico Furnace Company, in operation in 1884 near the Citico Creek. Chamberlain became quite involved in the civic affairs of Chattanooga. In the 1890s, he was listed by the *New York Tribune* as one of seven millionaires in the city. The Citico furnace was dismantled in 1913.

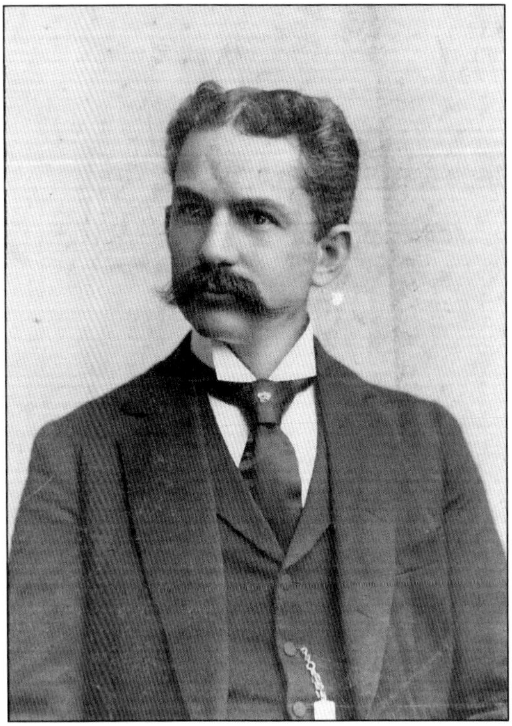

In 1899, two Chattanoogans, Ben F. Thomas and Joseph B. Whitehead, convinced the owner of a popular soda fountain drink in Atlanta to let them bottle the product throughout the United States (with a few territorial exceptions). Because they needed capital, John Thomas Lupton (left), the lawyer and treasurer of the Chattanooga Medicine Company, was brought into the venture. After the country was divided into territories, the world's first franchised Coca-Cola bottling company was established in Chattanooga.

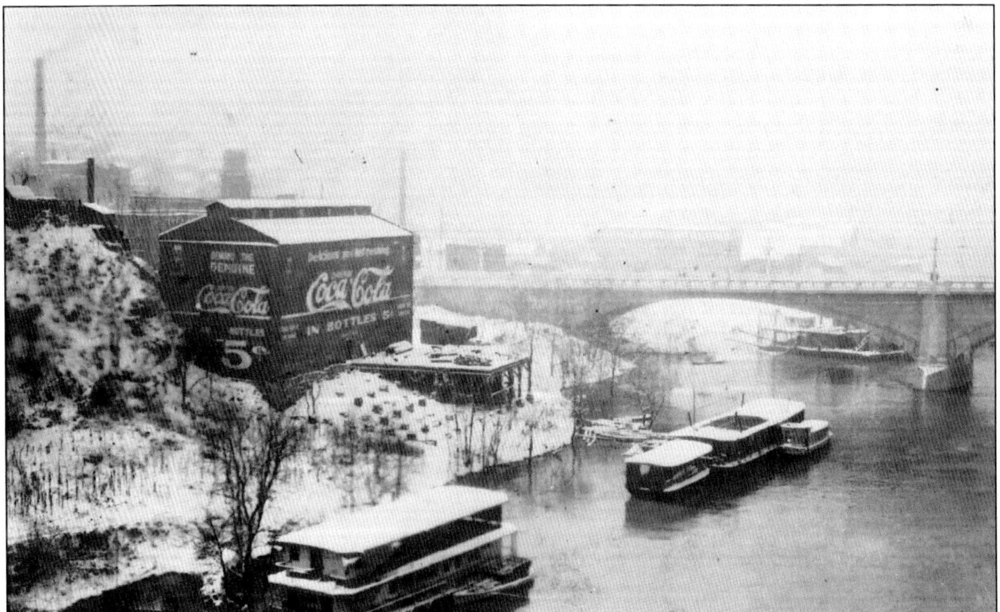

Snow blankets barges on the Tennessee River near the Market Street Bridge and an early Coca-Cola advertisement adorns a warehouse near the river. John T. Lupton became one of the richest men in the country; "Lyndhurst," his home overlooking the Tennessee River, was considered one of the finest in the South. The Lyndhurst Foundation, established in 1977, has funded many projects in Chattanooga and the Southeast, including the permanent exhibit at the Chattanooga Regional History Museum.

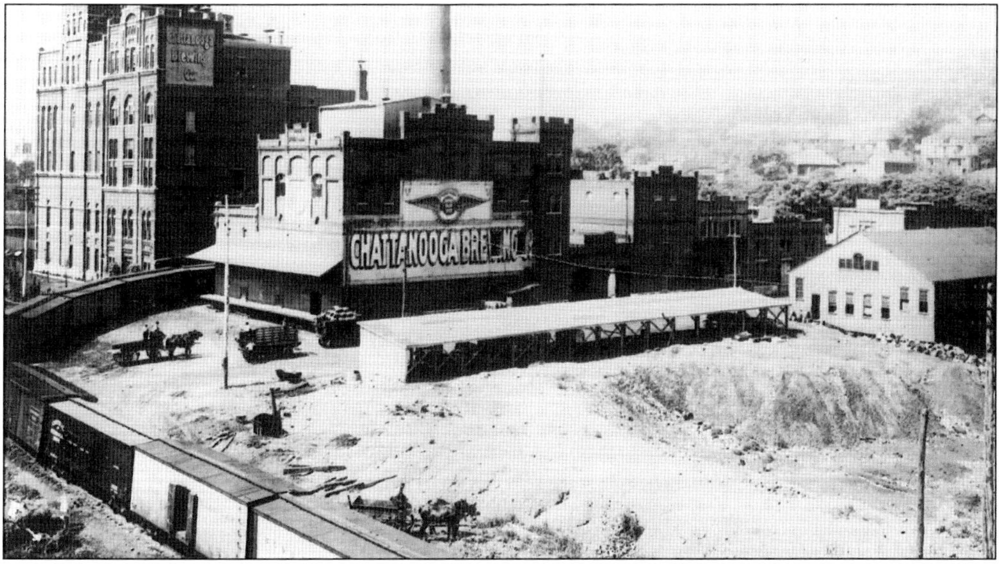

Several brewers began operations in Chattanooga after the Civil War. The first was Conrad Geise and Company on Broad and Third Streets. A six-story brick building, the brewery also included an ice factory and wagon house. After the company changed ownership, it was renamed the Chattanooga Brewing Company. The passage of the prohibition amendment in 1919 effectively ruined the company and the building was demolished in the late 1920s to make way for a new Chattanooga Coca-Cola Bottling Company plant.

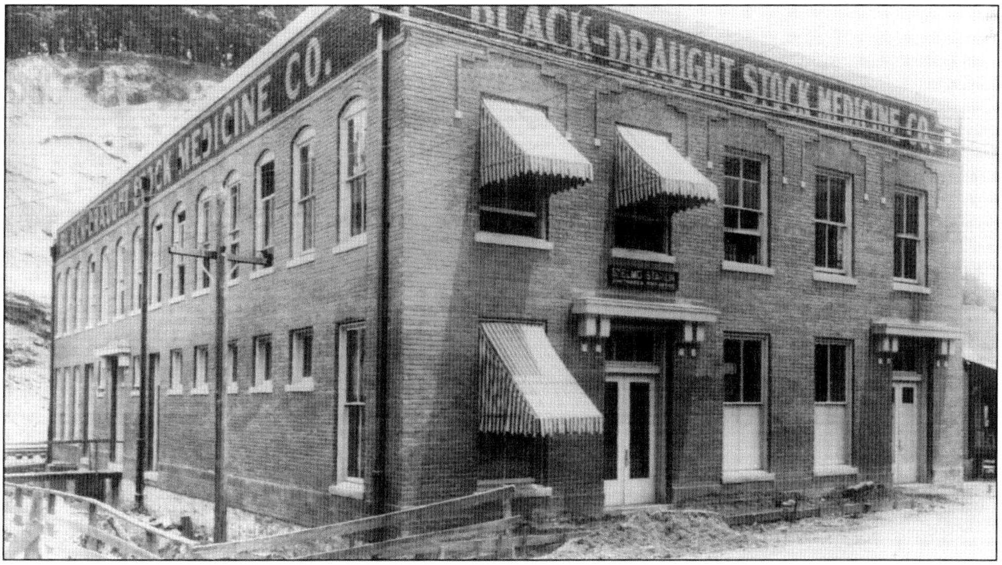

The Chattanooga Medicine Company (now Chattem) was organized in 1879 with Frederick Wiehl as president and Z.C. Patten as secretary-treasurer. The company obtained the rights to two popular medicines, "Black Draught," a liver regulator, and "Wine of Cardui," a preparation for women. In a bold marketing move, the company sent out 7,000 bottles of the latter product "on condition that they are to be paid for only if benefit is derived." The product was a success as 6,500 women voluntarily paid for the medicine. The correspondence between the company and its customers was so great that the company was assigned its own government-paid post office (shown above) at its headquarters in St. Elmo.

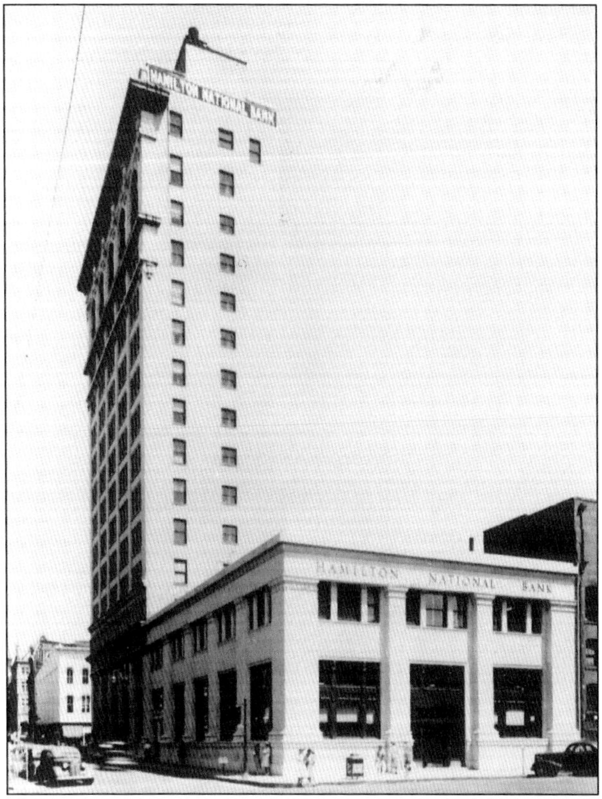

Making sense of the banking business at the turn of the century is difficult. Bankruptcies and mergers were commonplace. One of the most stable of the Chattanooga banks was the Hamilton National Bank. The bank was founded in 1905 and located at Seventh and Market Streets. After merging with the Hamilton Trust and Savings Bank in 1920 it became the largest bank in eastern Tennessee.

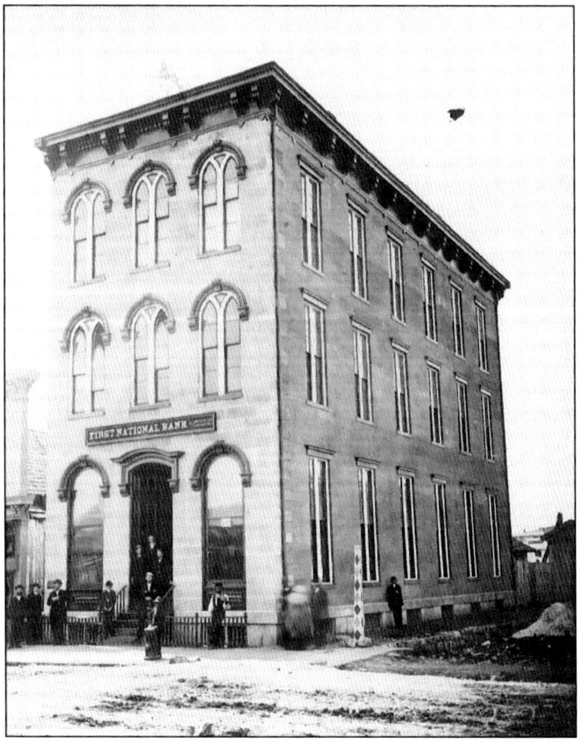

Bank patrons, a street sweeper, and a musician pose in front of the First National Bank. The bank was founded in 1865 by William P. Rathburn and Theodore G. Montague. Setting up a bank in a war-torn city was risky but the venture proved successful. Soon, the bank was able to move to new offices at Sixth and Market Streets, shown above. A great deal of the post-war recovery of the area was made possible by the progressive loan policies of this bank.

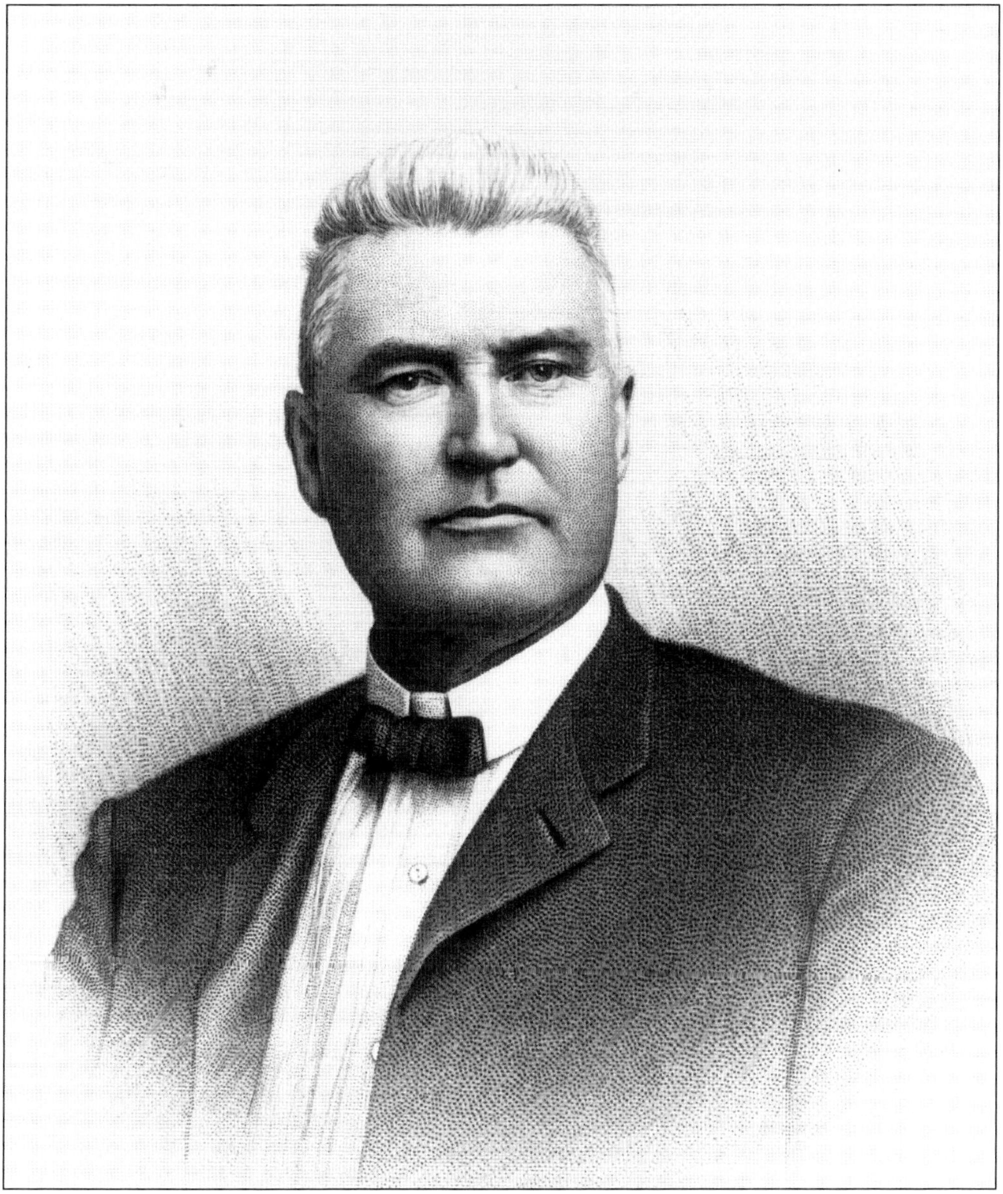

When the Civil War was over Zeboim Cartter Patten, a young Union veteran, decided that Chattanooga offered his best chance for success: he certainly made the most of it. As a founder of the Chattanooga Medicine Company, the Stone Fort Land Company, and the Volunteer State Life Insurance Company (among other enterprises), Patten was heavily involved in the civic affairs of the community. His wife, Sarah Key Patten, was a leading force in the preservation of historic homes in the region.

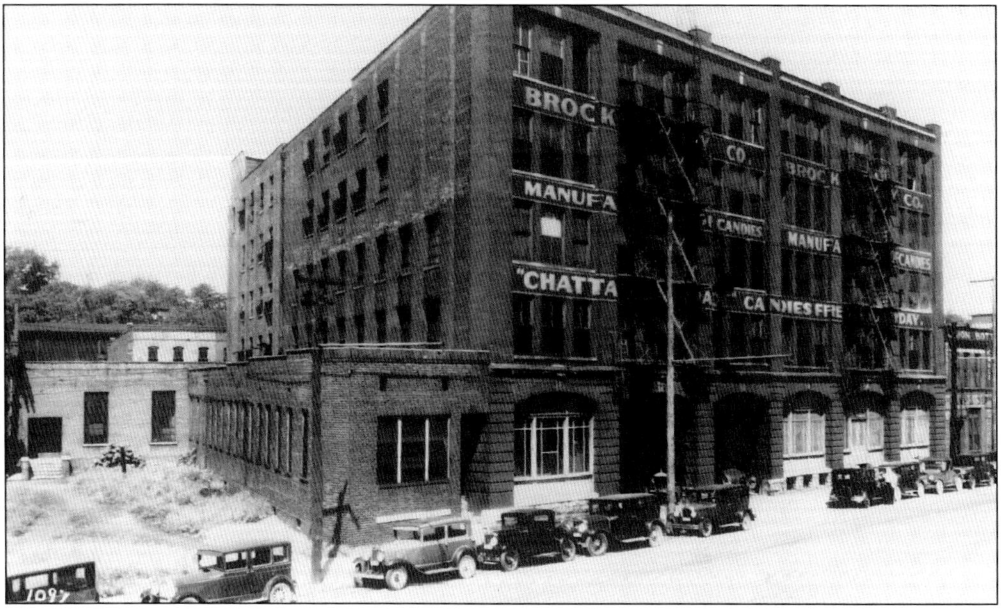

In 1909 William Emerson Brock purchased a small venture known as the Trigg Candy Company using borrowed funds. The Brock Candy Company, located on Chestnut Street, became such a success that Brock was elected president of the National Confectioners Association. In 1929, he was appointed to the United States Senate to fill an unexpired term. He became a leader in the fight to bring the TVA to Hamilton County.

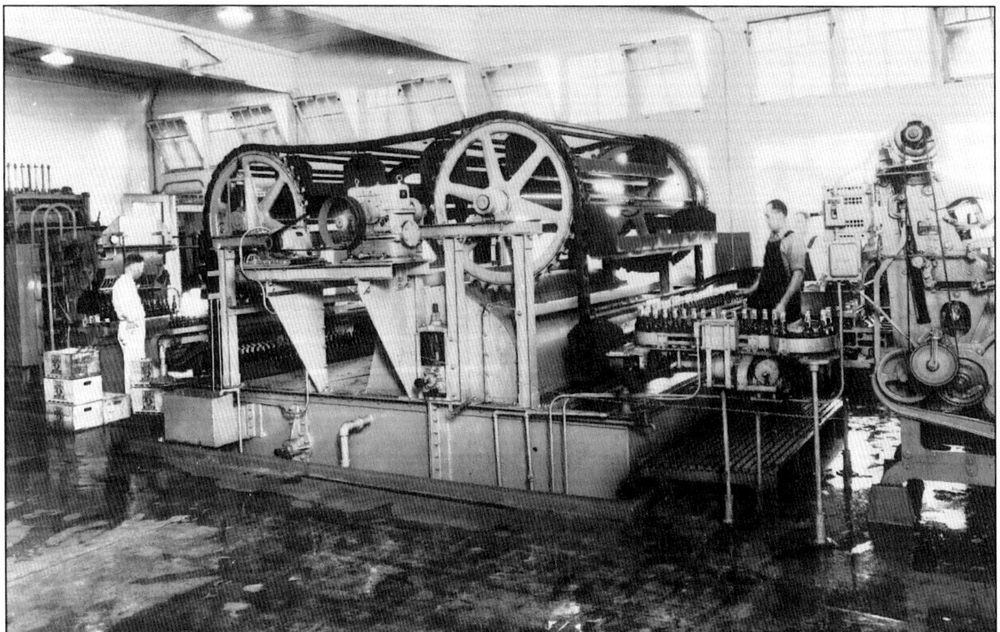

Three men attend machinery at the Southeastern Brewing Company in this October 1934 photograph. Following the repeal of Prohibition, a short-lived attempt was made to revive the brewing industry in Chattanooga. Most operations were unable to compete with national breweries; by 1950, there were no breweries listed in the city directory.

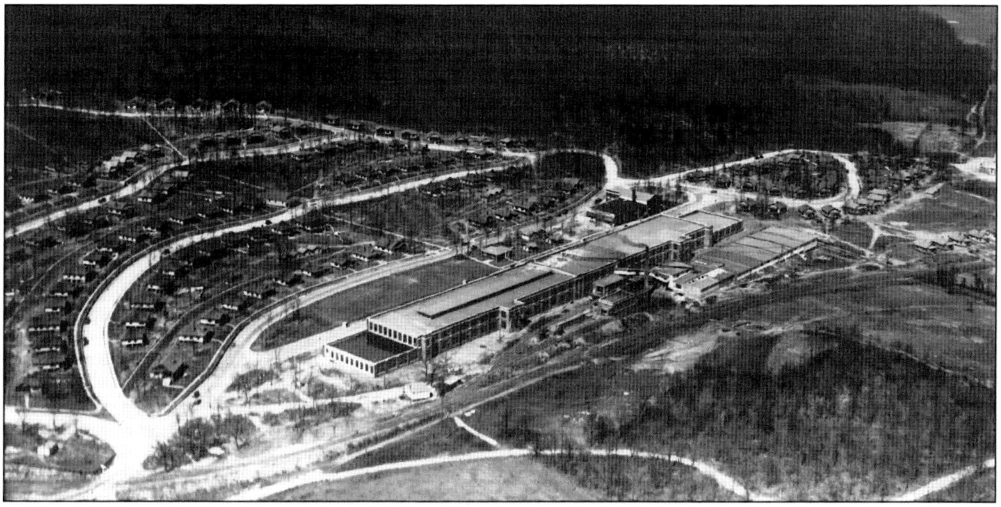

Dixie Mercerizing was established by a group of local textile businessmen backed by John T. Lupton, and the company's spinning plant was built on property owned by Lupton near Hixson. Workers lived in a community near the plant which became known as "Lupton City." In 1964, the name of the company was changed to Dixie Yarns. At one time, the company owned eighteen plants and employed four thousand people.

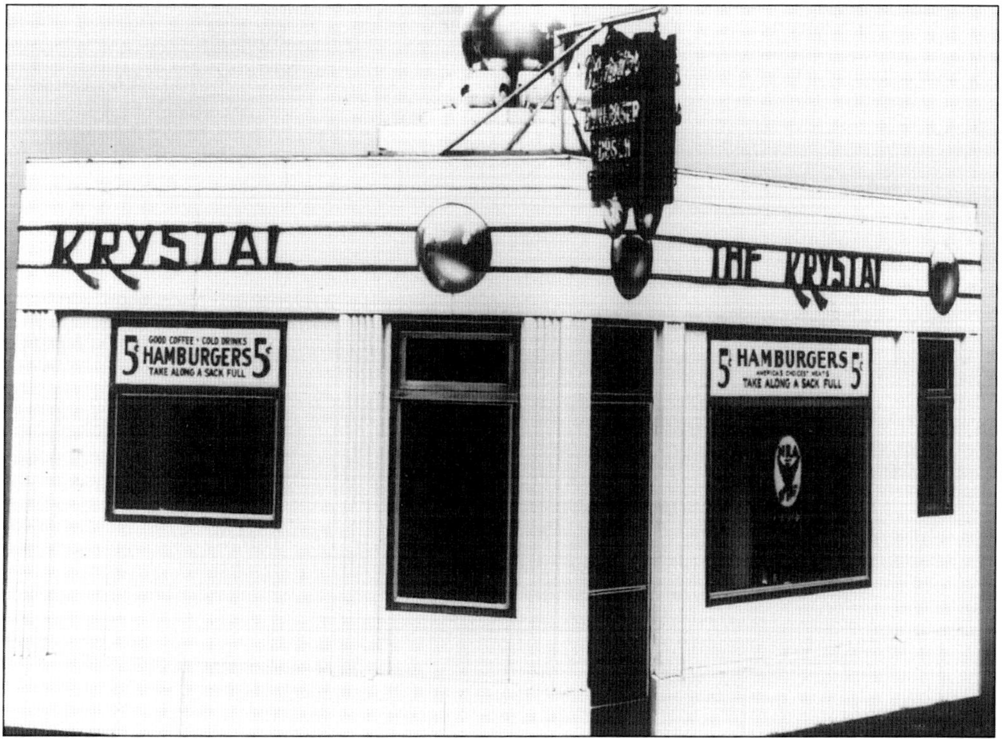

The first Krystal restaurant opened in 1932 at the corner of Cherry and Seventh Streets. The restaurant, established by Rody Davenport, Jr., and J. Glenn Sherrill, at first specialized in low-price hamburgers and good coffee. The bright image suggested by the name was reflected in the use of porcelain enamel for the outside of the buildings. The Krystal restaurant business went on to become a major chain with restaurants located throughout the South.

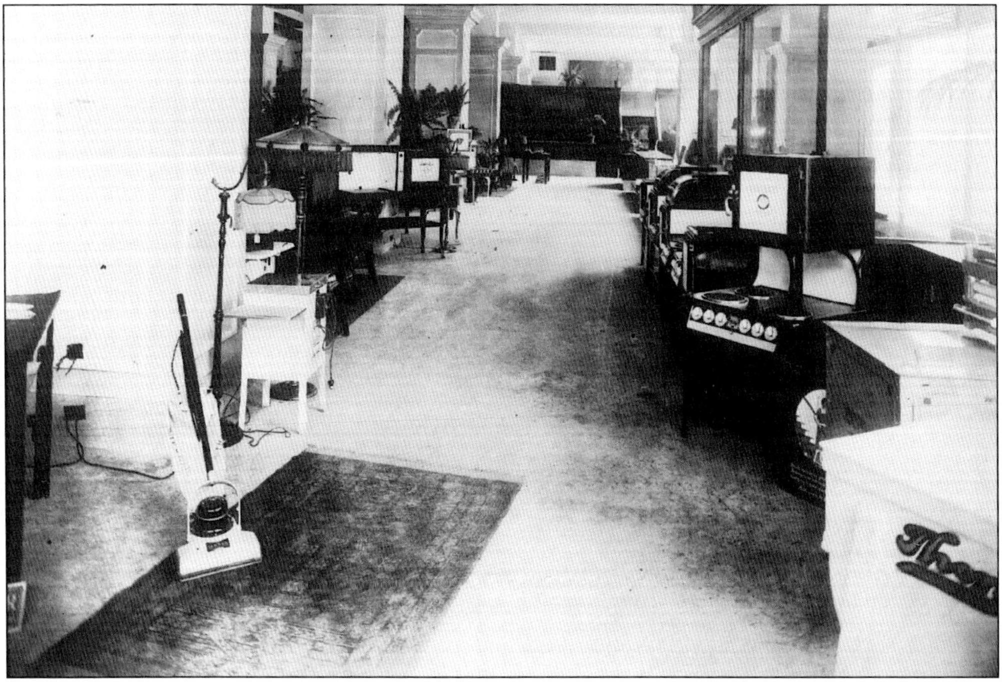

The latest electric appliances (washing machines, stoves, vacuum cleaners, sewing machines, etc.) are displayed in this 1930s photograph of the interior of the Electric Power Board. The coming of the TVA had an immediate effect on the number of appliance stores found in the Chattanooga region.

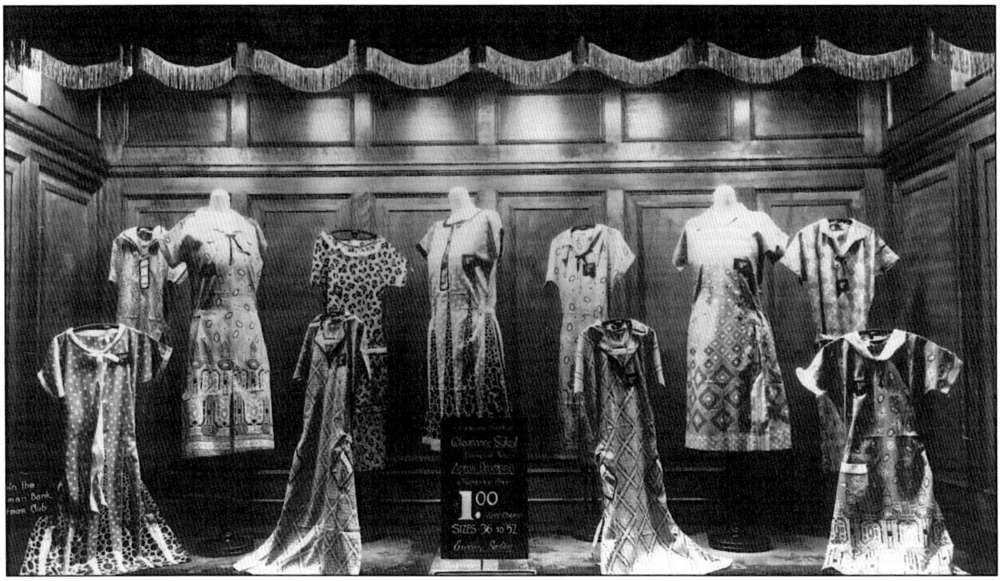

The dresses displayed in the window of the D.B. Loveman Department Store were selling for $1.00 during the Depression. D.B. Loveman bought the popular New Orleans Store in 1875. The store moved to a new 38,000-square-foot building in 1886, and had separate general sales, dress-making, and carpet departments. When that building was destroyed by a fire in 1891, a new four-story store was built featuring electric elevators. A fifth story was added in 1906.

Five

People

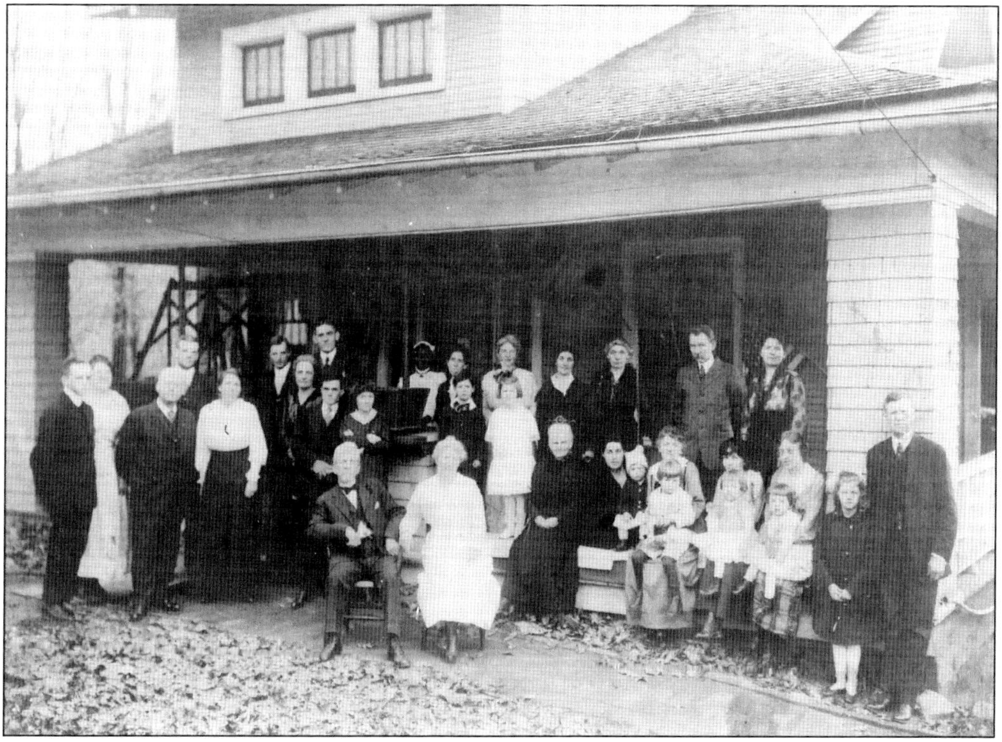

The people of Chattanooga, like the people of the United States as a whole, come from a wide variety of ethnic and cultural backgrounds. Basically, three large groups still dominate the mix. Hearty Scotch-Irish settlers first filtered down the Tennessee Valley in the eighteenth century. The removal of the Cherokee in 1838 created a vacuum into which these settlers rapidly moved. The African-American segment of the population, a group originally introduced as slaves, has always been substantial, peaking at 33% of those living in Hamilton County in 1890. German settlers arrived in small numbers prior to the Civil War and during the war many Union soldiers of German origin fought in the Battles for Chattanooga. A great number of Germans returned to the area with their families after the war. Immigrants of numerous other ethnic groups also came to the Chattanooga area seeking work before the country's borders were tightened in the 1920s.

A comfortable existence is shown in this photograph of the Stoops family of Lookout Mountain. George Washington Stoops, seated in front, celebrated his seventy-fifth birthday on February 22, 1918, with his family. Stoops had other presidential connections beyond his name: he claimed to have shaken the hand of Abraham Lincoln. The Stoops clan was famous for its various restaurants and other enterprises, such as the largest roller skating rink in the South, a billboard business, a couple of hotels, and Chattanooga's first roller coaster.

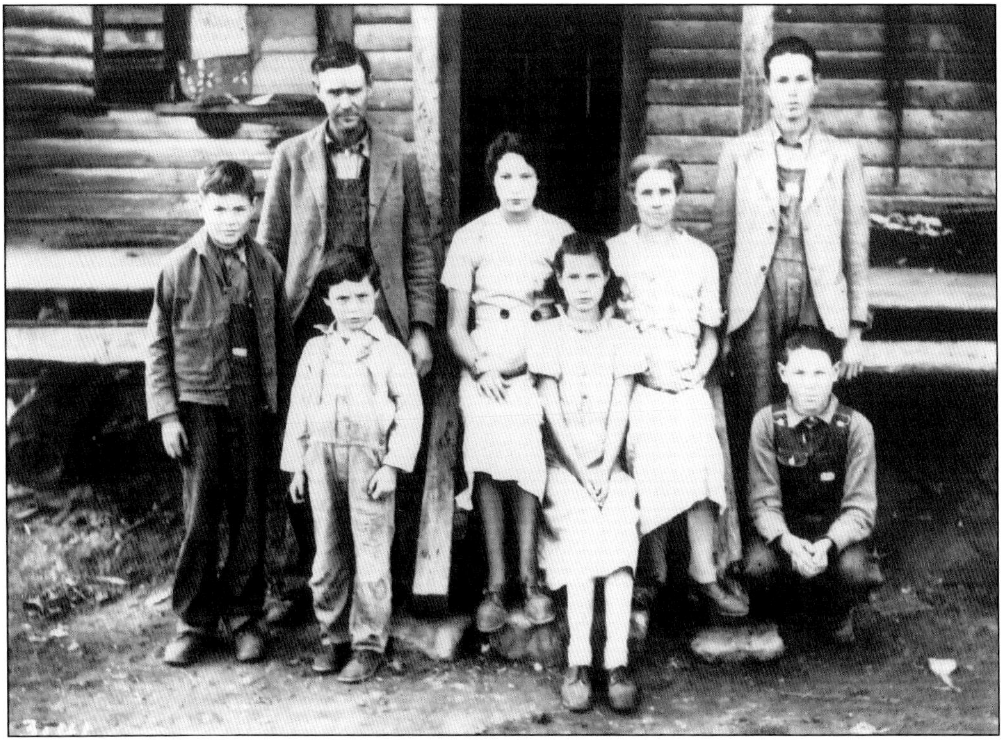

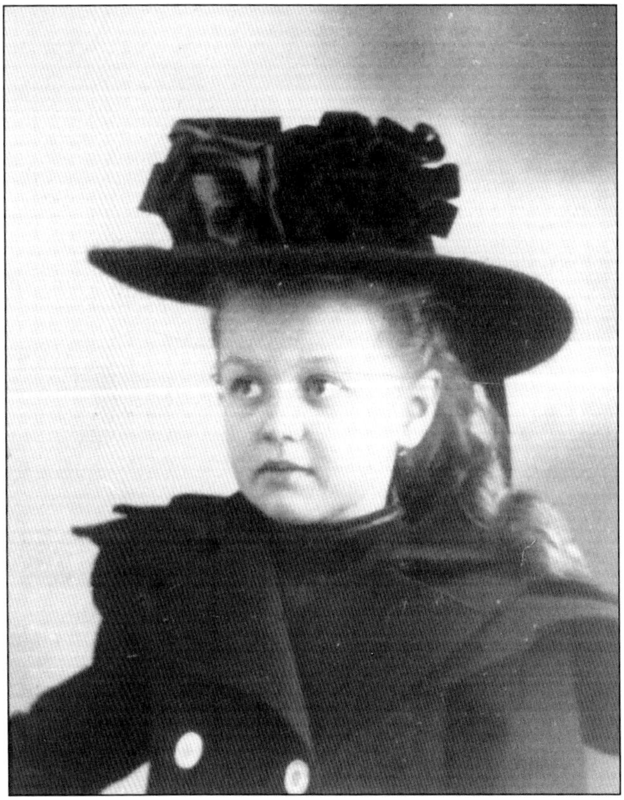

This unknown Waldens Ridge family had their picture taken during the 1930s. During the Depression, and indeed prior to that period, the Southern Appalachian area experienced some of the worst poverty in the nation. Stereotypical notions of "hillbilly" life are still widespread today: mountain folk are supposedly unconcerned about their lot in life but make up for their laziness with a love of music, folksy wit, and common sense.

Unfortunately we cannot identify the young girl in this photograph. Marked only "Leona," the picture was taken around 1900 at Pickard's Penny Photographs at 820 Market Street. An advertisement on the back reads, "Get 12 nice Photos for 25 cents."

Chattanooga had its share of the newly rich. Fortunes were made and lost in railroads, soft drink bottling, lumber, real estate, banking, candy, streetcars, medicine, and any other endeavor in which a buck could be made. This beautiful lady, obviously of the elite, poses in a fine gown at the Schmedling Gallery in the 1880s.

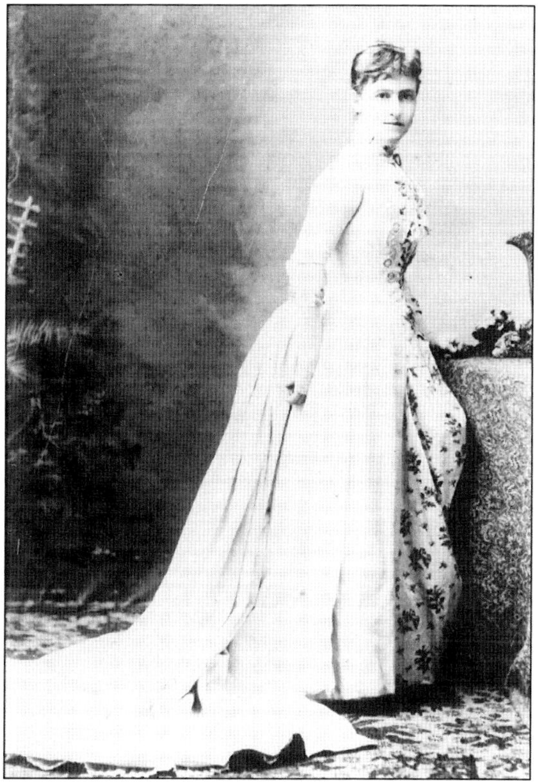

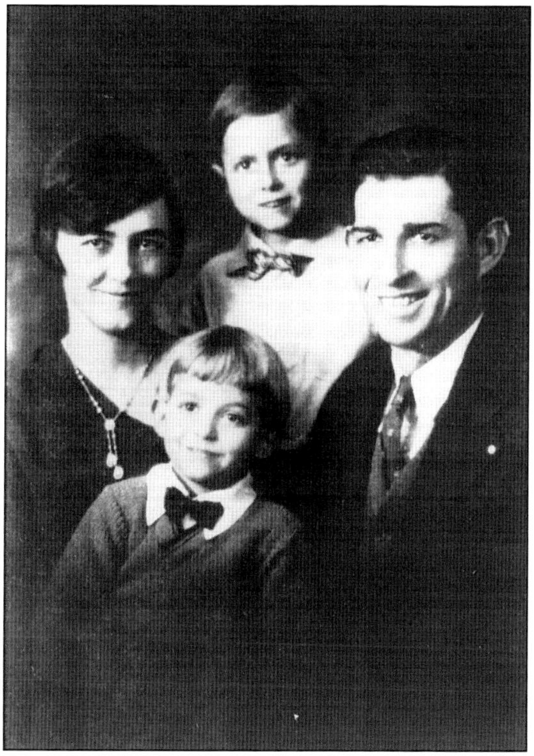

A portrait of a typical God-fearing and law-abiding Chattanooga family. James and Ida Taliaferro and their sons, James, Jr., (top) and Edward (bottom), lived in a modest home near Missionary Ridge. Both sons attended McCallie School in the late 1930s and early 1940s. James, Jr., was captured by the Germans at the Battle of the Bulge in World War II and spent several months in a prisoner ofwar camp. Unknown to him, his brother had been killed in France a week prior to his capture.

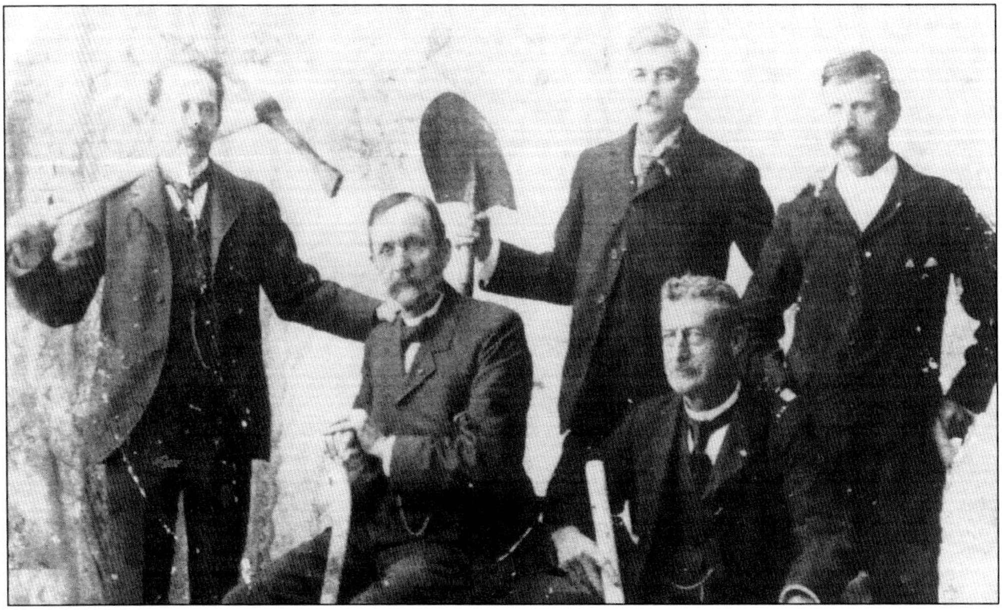

It was customary for prominent Victorian Chattanoogans to make social calls at the homes of friends and neighbors at New Year. Several downtown businessmen had calling cards printed up to leave after each visit. In this card, D.B. Loveman, Frederick Wiehl, John B. Nicklin, L.T. Dickinson, and T.H. Payne carry groundbreaking tools.

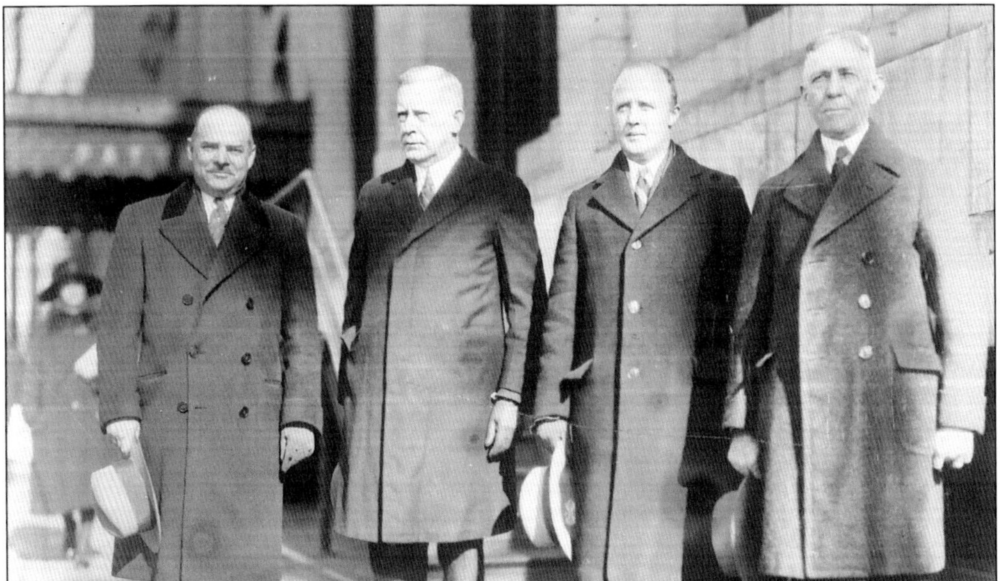

Two individuals greatly affected the landscape of Chattanooga in the twentieth century: architect Rueben Harrison Hunt and Judge William Cummings. Rueben Harrison Hunt (second from the left) moved from Elbert County, GA, to Chattanooga in 1882, at the age of twenty. He soon became the city's most prolific and imaginative architect. A few examples of his designs are the present-day Hamilton County Courthouse, the Federal Building, the James Building, the Central Baptist Church, the Lookout Mountain Hotel (now Covenant College), and Memorial Auditorium.

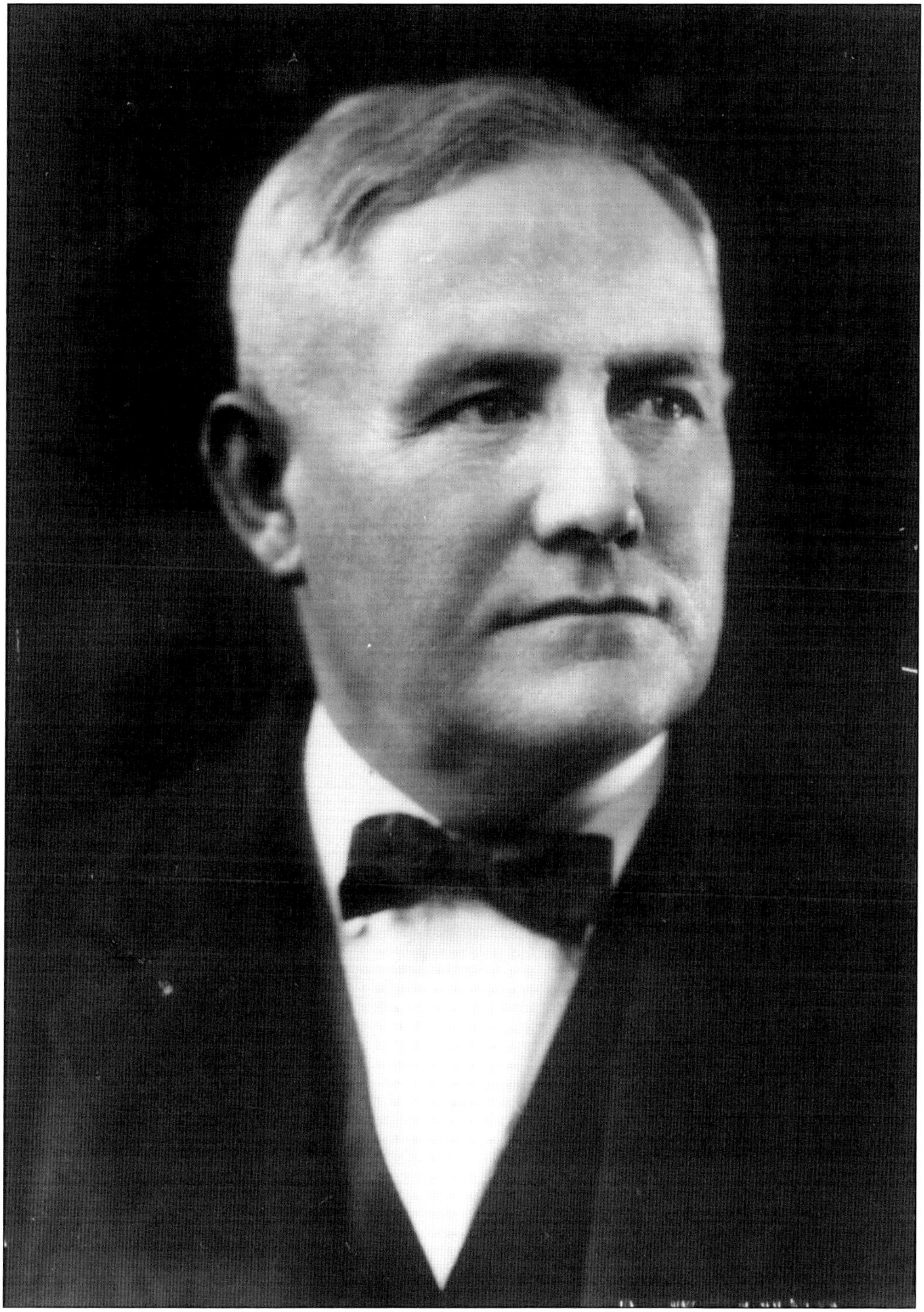

Will Cummings was born on his family farm at Wauhatchie in 1872. At the age of twenty-two, he entered politics, serving as a judge for many years. He is known for his energetic promotion of the Market Street Bridge project, highways, and the Tennessee Valley Authority. The Will Cummings Highway runs from Jasper to Chattanooga.

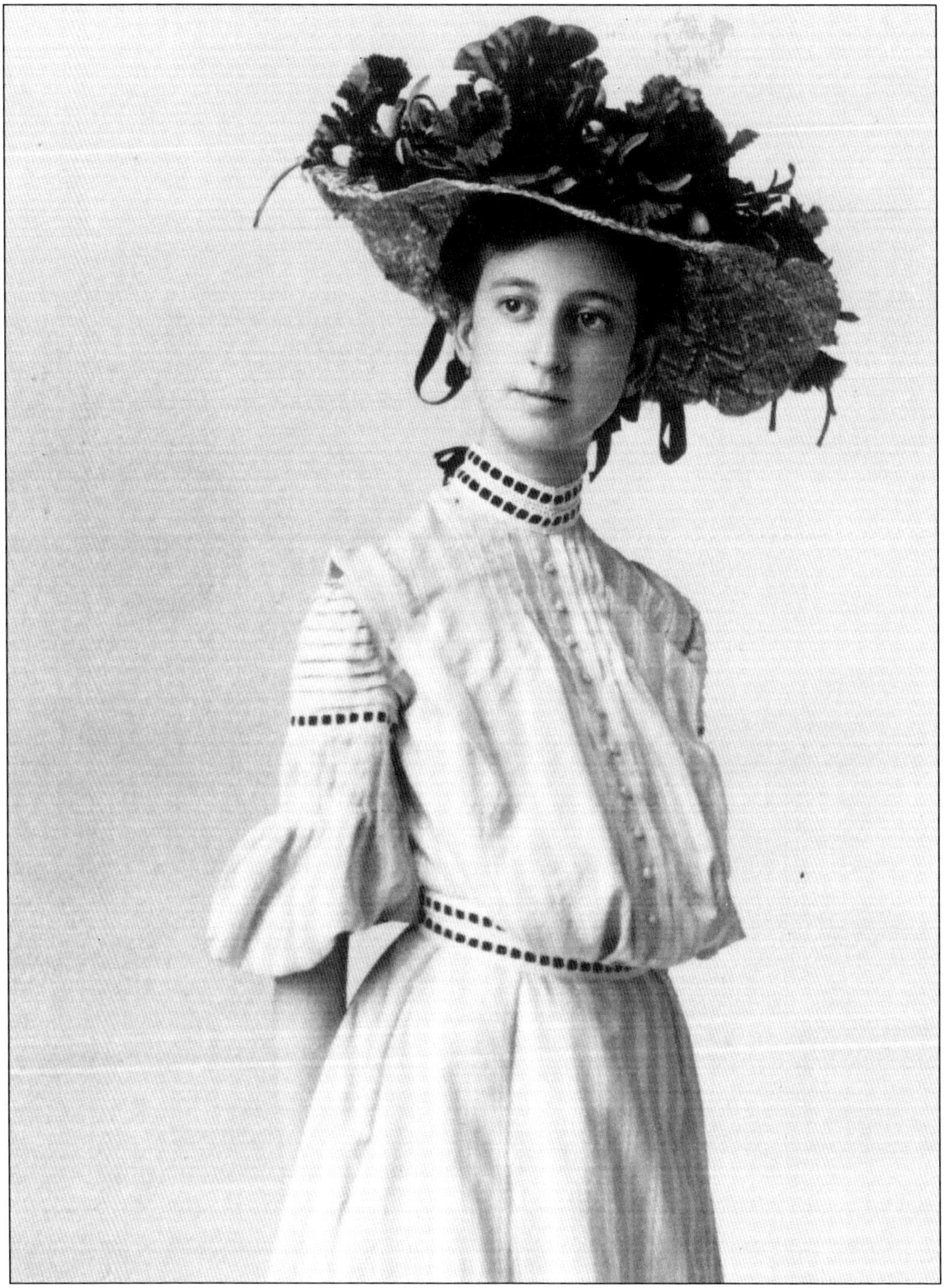

The very embodiment of the "Gibson girl," "Tot" Henderson wears the simple clothing of the early 1900s. As women began to take work in offices, shops, and factories, comfortable clothing became a necessity. The 1902 Sears, Roebuck catalog sold waists and skirts for $2.50. McCall and Butterick sold hundreds of thousands of dress patterns. As no woman would set foot outside without a well-adorned hat, early home shopping catalogs also sold feathers, lace, ribbons, and flowers.

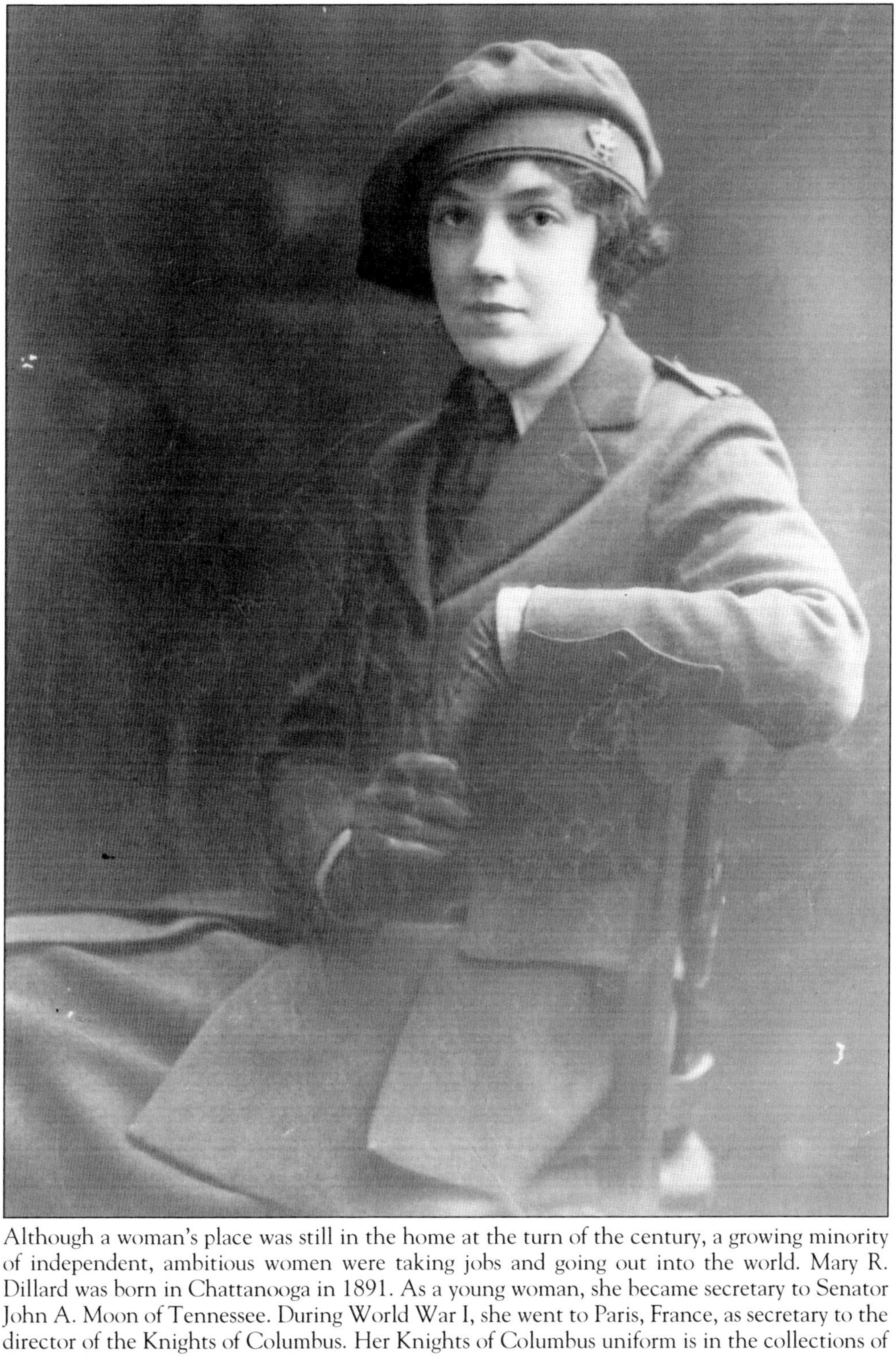

Although a woman's place was still in the home at the turn of the century, a growing minority of independent, ambitious women were taking jobs and going out into the world. Mary R. Dillard was born in Chattanooga in 1891. As a young woman, she became secretary to Senator John A. Moon of Tennessee. During World War I, she went to Paris, France, as secretary to the director of the Knights of Columbus. Her Knights of Columbus uniform is in the collections of the Smithsonian Institution.

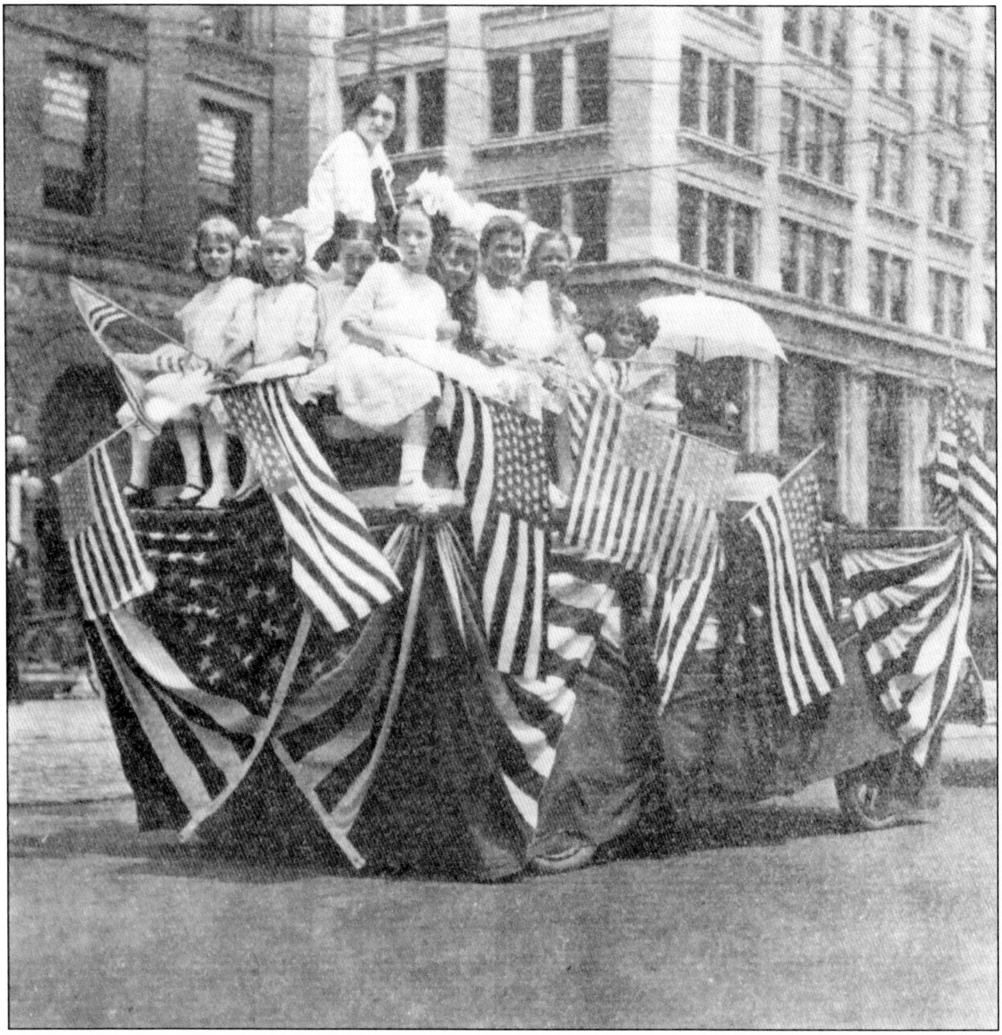

Young girls riding a float during one of Chattanooga's July 4th parades in the early 1900s. The lives of these girls would be very different from those of their mothers. Inexpensive, labor-saving kitchen and household devices made it possible for women to devote more time to public causes, political action, and, if they had them, careers. Father's comfort would now compete with the women's club.

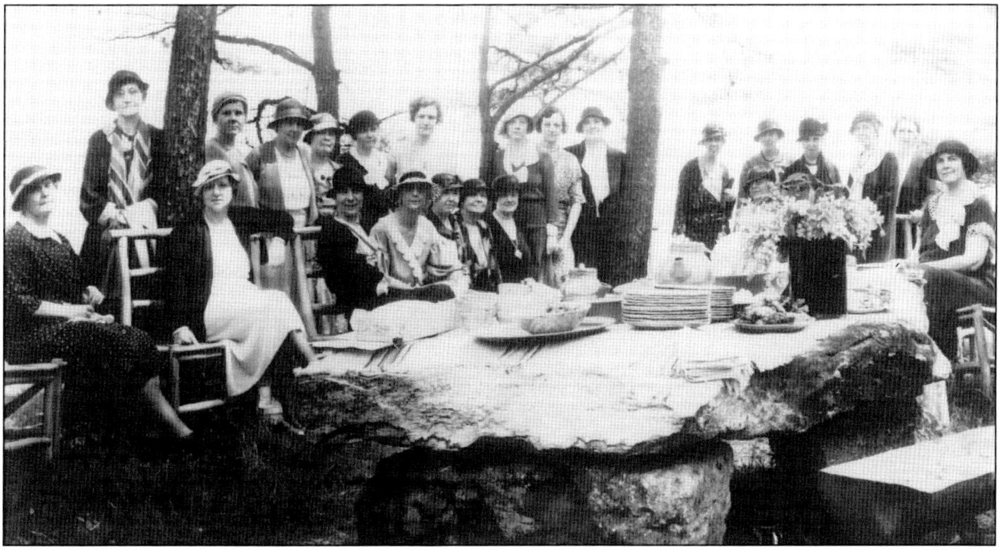

Members of a women's club pose before enjoying a picnic lunch on Lookout Mountain. Several prominent women's clubs were formed in the area, including the Kosmos Woman's Club, the Chattanooga Woman's Club, and branches of the Daughters of the American Revolution and the Daughters of the Confederacy. The leading social club for men was probably the Mountain City Club. First organized in 1889, the club now has its headquarters in a beautiful building on Chestnut Street. Other clubs included the Turner Club, the Elks, the Calumet Club, and the Masonic Lodge.

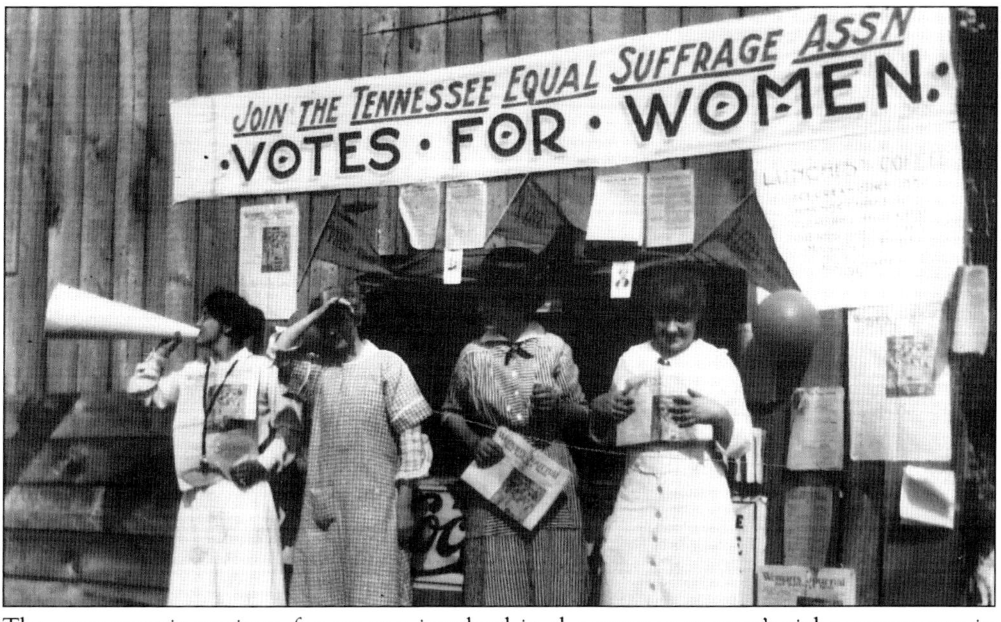

The most prominent issue for women involved in the nascent women's rights movement in the early twentieth century was that of voting rights. The Suffragettes were very active in Chattanooga: this photograph shows four ladies campaigning for equal rights in front of a street booth in 1912. One speaks into a megaphone while the others pass out pamphlets. When she cast her vote in 1918, Mrs. Newell Sanders of Lookout Mountain was the first woman in Tennessee to vote in a municipal election.

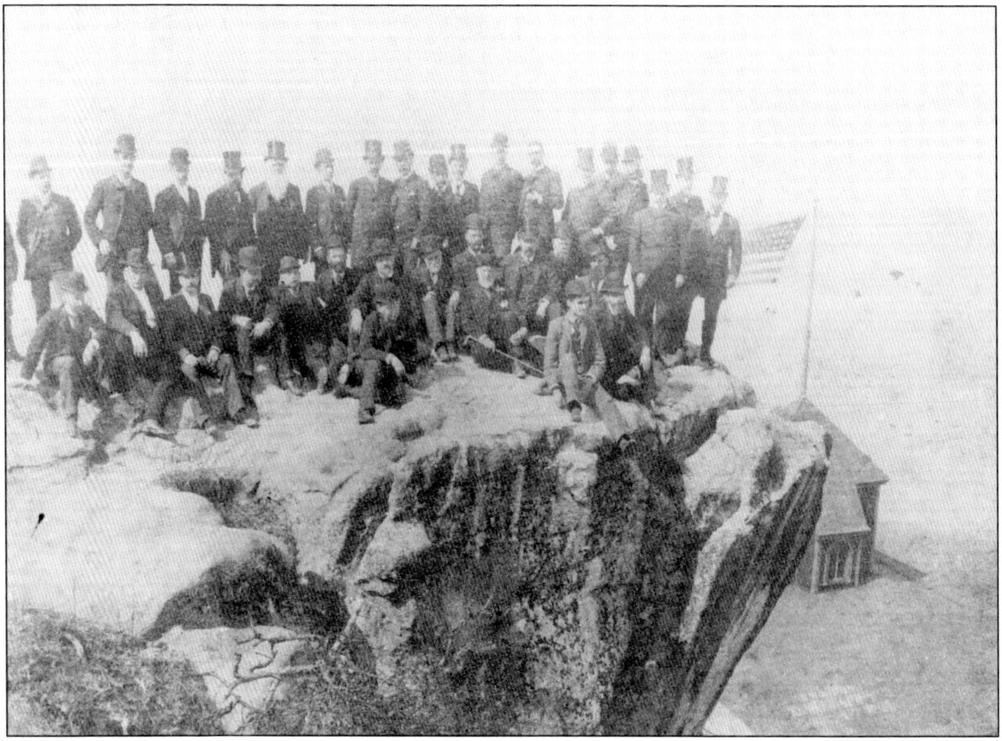

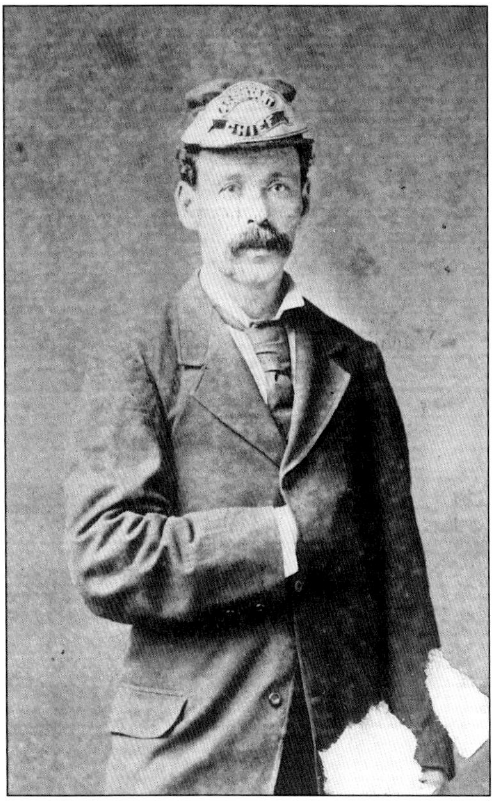

A group of prominent Chattanoogans posing at Lookout Point (just above the roof of Point Hotel) in 1895. William G. McAdoo, a former Chattanoogan who would eventually become secretary of the treasury under Woodrow Wilson, was in attendance, along with John Nicklin, Summerfield Key, Hiram Chamberlain, Adolph Ochs, H. Clay Evans, Hugh Whiteside, and Henry V. Boynton (a prime mover in the founding of the National Military Park).

This "carte de visite" (an early calling card with a photograph on one side) belonged to William Friedman, a member of the fire volunteers. He wears a hat which reads "Assistant Chief," a position prominent enough to warrant this Napoleonic pose. The portrait was made by Thomas Schleier in 1890.

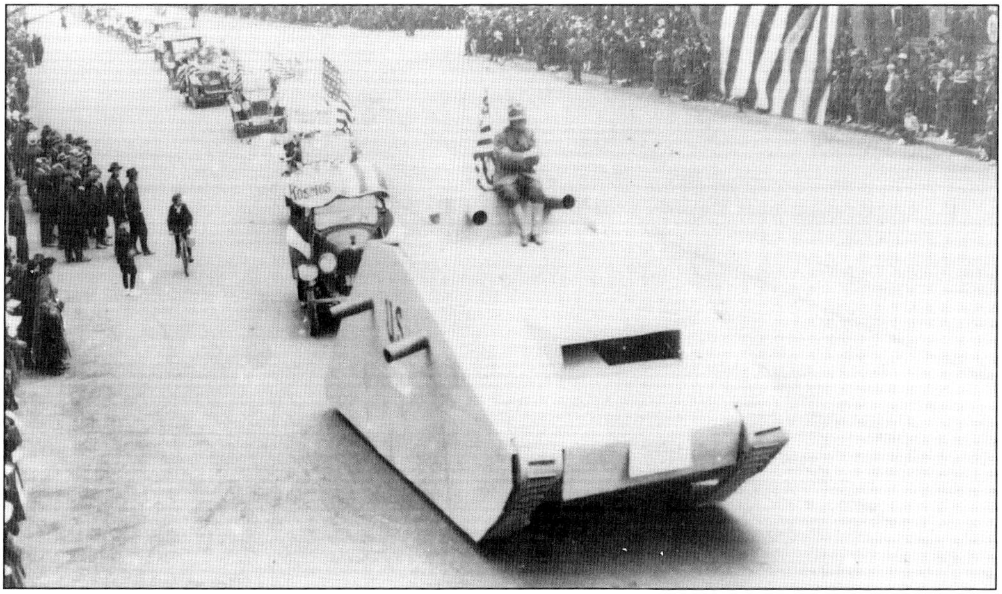

A float designed to resemble an early tank rumbles down Market Street in this 1917 War Bond parade. The training camps and barracks for officers, medical personnel, and forty-three thousand enlisted men that were built at Fort Oglethorpe, GA, at this time tested the service organizations of the city, as this large camp relied heavily on Chattanooga for certain essential services. Over ten thousand Hamilton County men served in the armed forces during World War I; two hundred lost their lives in service to their country.

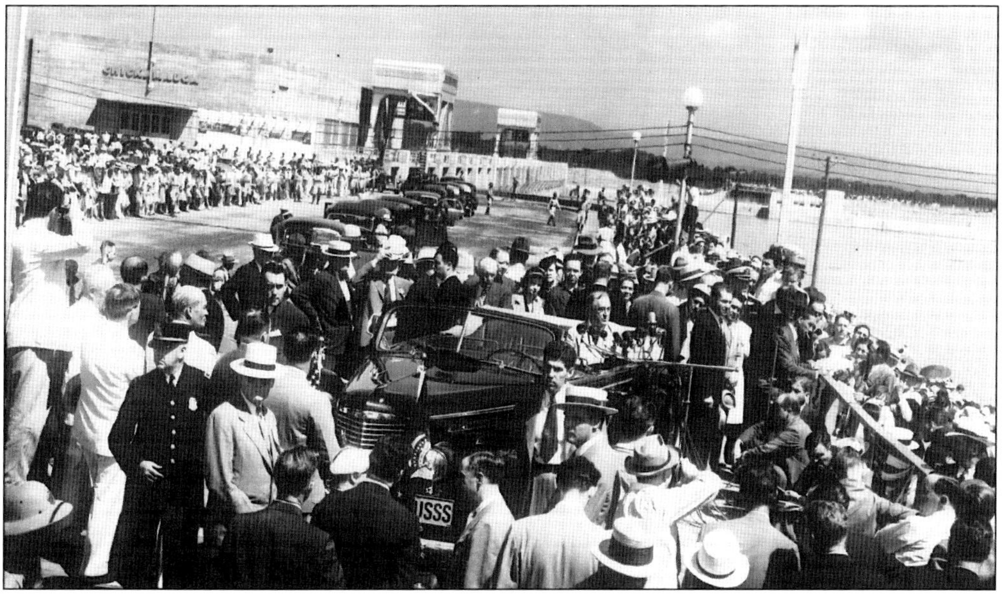

Thousands gathered in 1940 to hear President Franklin Roosevelt give the dedication address which formally opened the Chickamauga Dam. Following the creation of the Tennessee Valley Authority in 1933, local citizens, led by Judge Will Cummings, lobbied for the creation of the dam near the city. It changed Hamilton County forever, partially because it provided flood control and electrical power, but also because it meant new recreational areas near the 33,500-acre Chickamauga Lake.

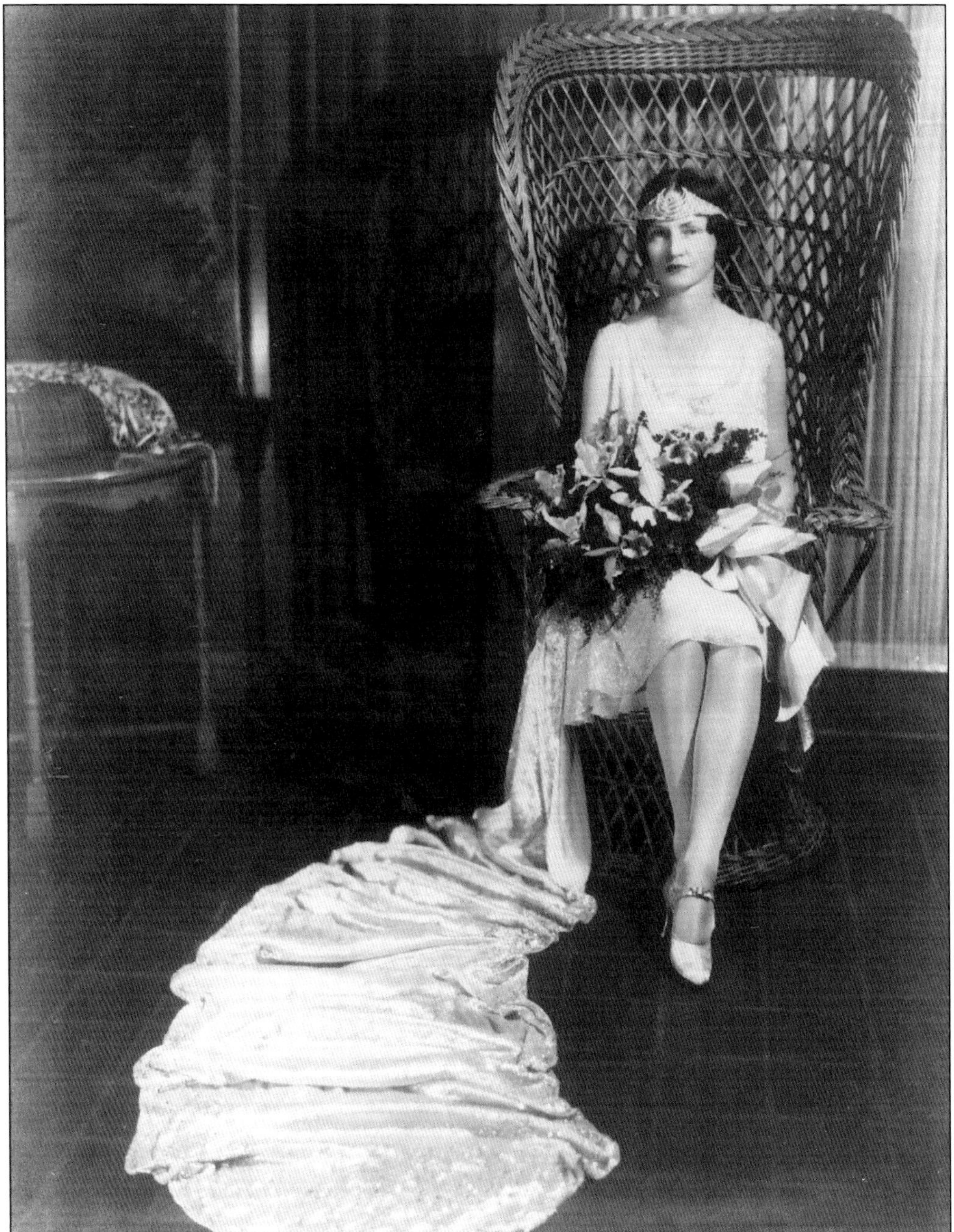

Mrs. Samuel C. Hutcheson, queen of the Junior League ball, is shown in all her regal splendor in this 1928 photograph. Her husband operated the Mountain City Mills for many years. In the 1970s, Mrs. Hutcheson became a major contributor to the eye care center at the Erlanger Hospital. The gown in this picture is in the collection at the Chattanooga Regional History Museum.

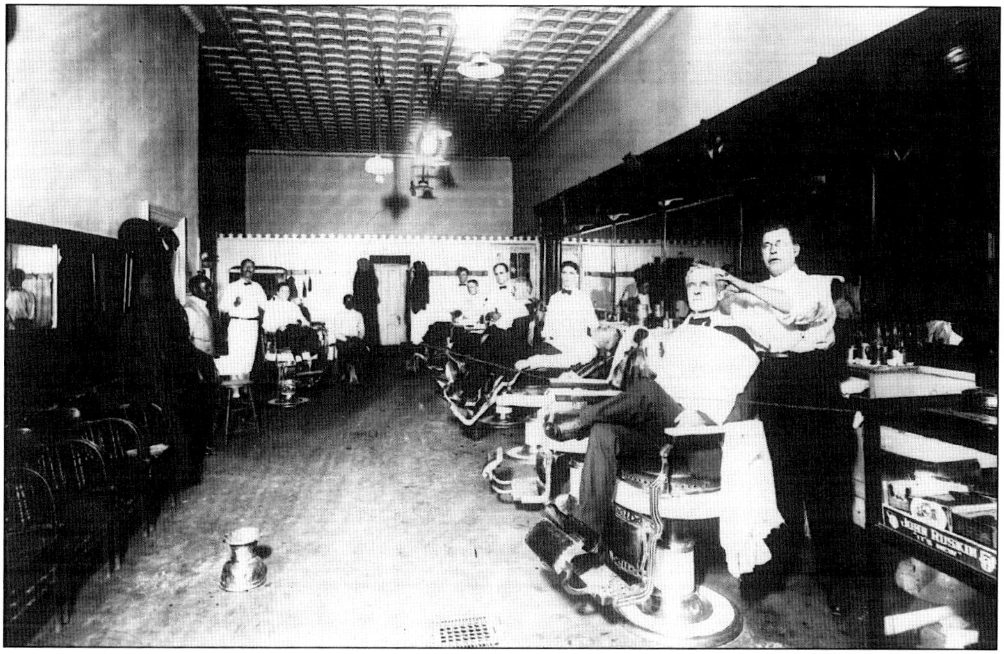

Proprietors J.B. and H.A. Horton are hard at work in this photograph of the interior of the Horton Barber Shop on Cherry Street. The Chattanooga City Directory of 1925 listed, amongst other businesses: 110 barber shops, 26 automobile dealers, 25 tailors, 58 dentists, 5 optometrists, 63 shoemakers, 533 grocers, 156 lawyers, and 1 wholesale banana company.

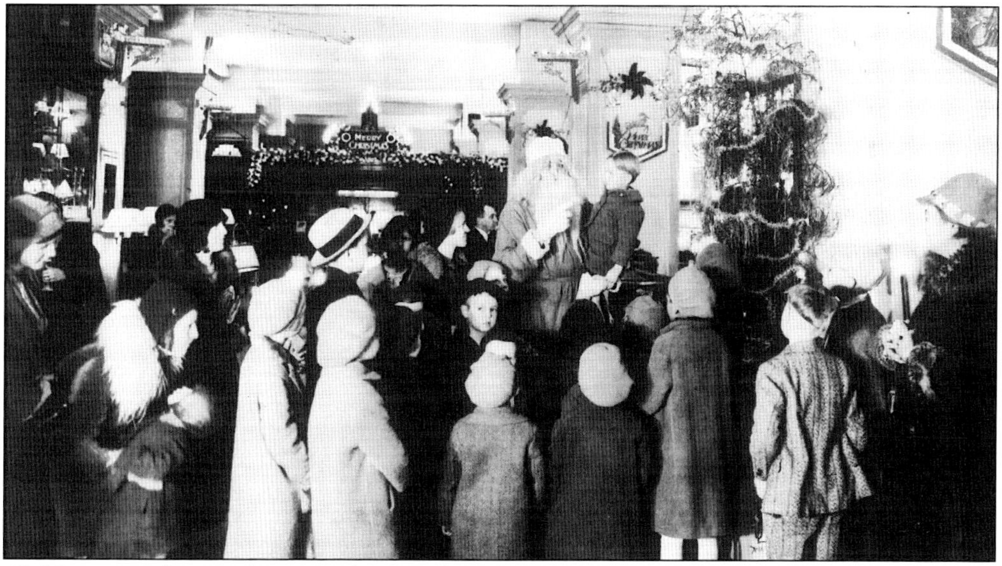

Children crowd around Santa Claus in the Electric Power Board office on Market Street in 1930. The early years of the Depression were difficult ones for the citizens of Hamilton County. By 1932 over four thousand people were being fed by the City of Chattanooga each day; eight thousand were registered as unemployed. The homeless lived in shanty towns with names like Hell's Half Acre, Onion Bottom, and Hayne's Flats. Tennessee Valley Authority construction projects in the mid-1930s provided some relief for the jobless, but the impact of the Depression was still severe in this part of Tennessee.

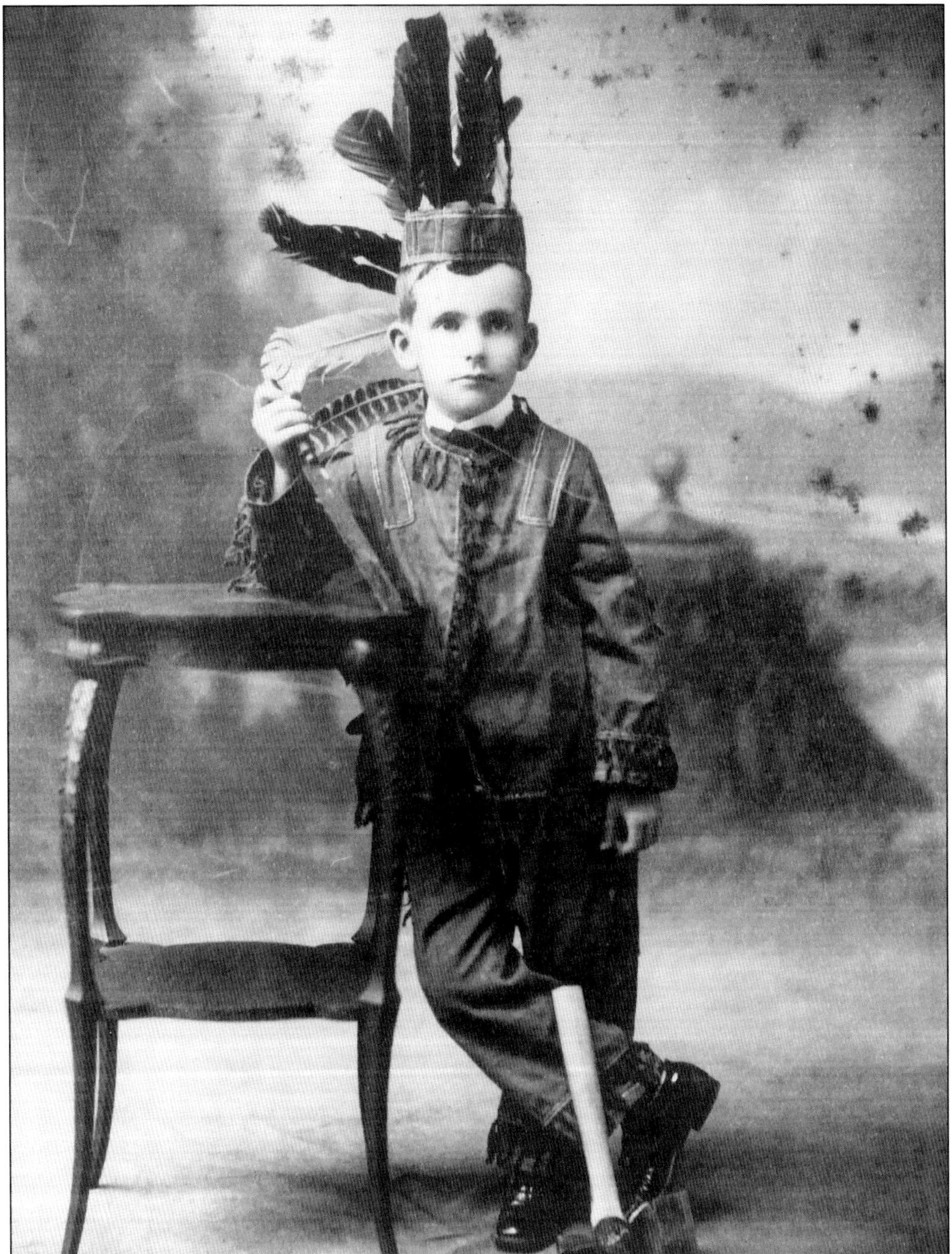

This young "Indian" poses tranquilly with his weapons before going on the warpath in a photograph taken in the 1890s at the Judd Photographic Studio on the east side of Market Street. Amos Wilson Judd was a Civil War veteran who set up his studio in Chattanooga in 1877. His son continued the business after his father's death in 1929. The studio finally closed in 1946.

Six

People at Work

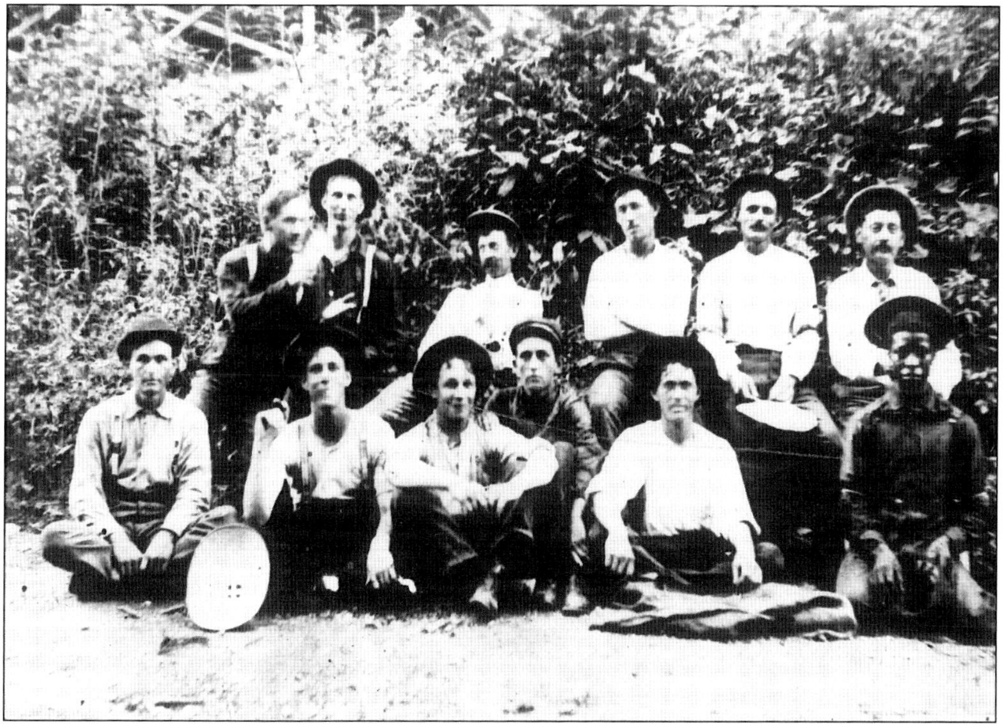

Workmen in a survey party working on the Muscle Shoals Canal project relax before going back to work on a hot summer's day in the 1880s. An earlier attempt at this project—to bypass a dangerous area of rapids on the Tennessee River—had failed in the 1830s. The second canal project was started in 1875 and took fifteen years to complete. The new canal, however, failed to reinvigorate the freight shipping trade on the Tennessee River. The railroad, with its monopoly on shipping rates, continued to dominate trade in the area.

Through financial panics, depressions, failed projects, and dashed expectations, the people of Chattanooga have remained hardworking and hopeful.

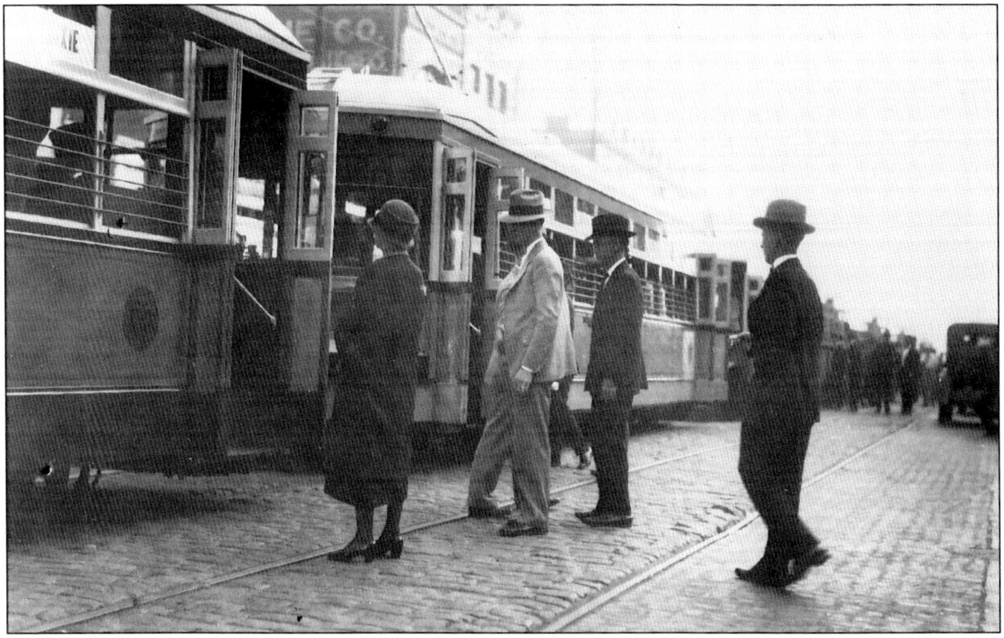

Quitting time! This 1930s photograph shows streetcars lined up on Broad Street waiting to carry passengers to their homes outside the city. Electric streetcars had operated in the city since 1889; electric shuttle buses continue to move passengers in the city today.

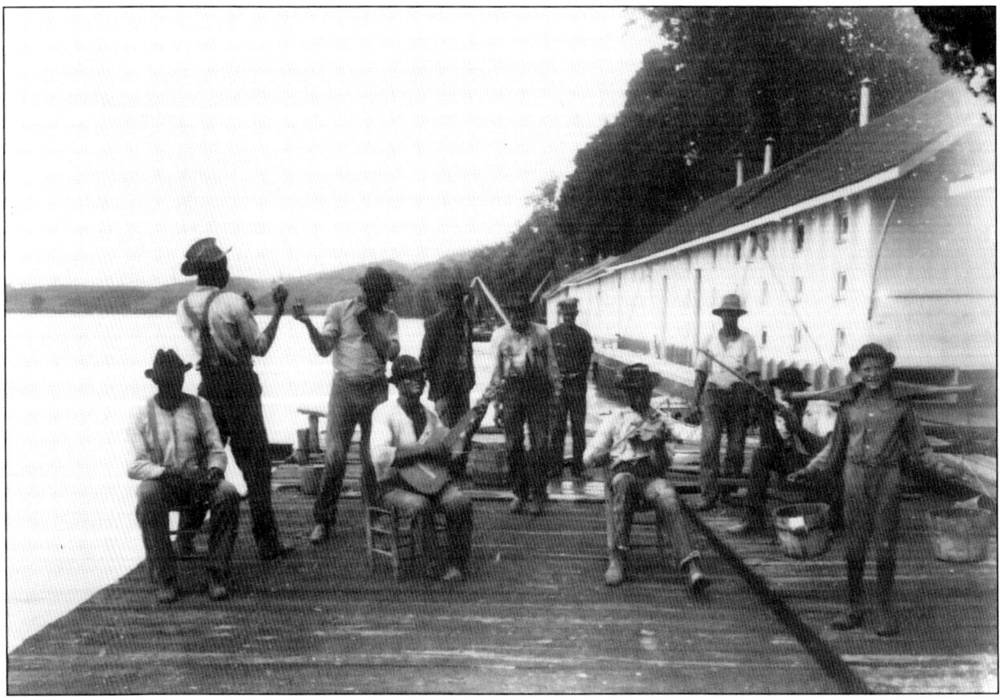

Workers along the Tennessee Riverfront "pan it up" for the camera during a rest break. River barges have long run the length of the Tennessee River: in 1933, 1 million tons of shipments traveled along the entire length of the Tennessee River; in 1980, 2.8 million tons were shipped by river from Chattanooga's docks alone.

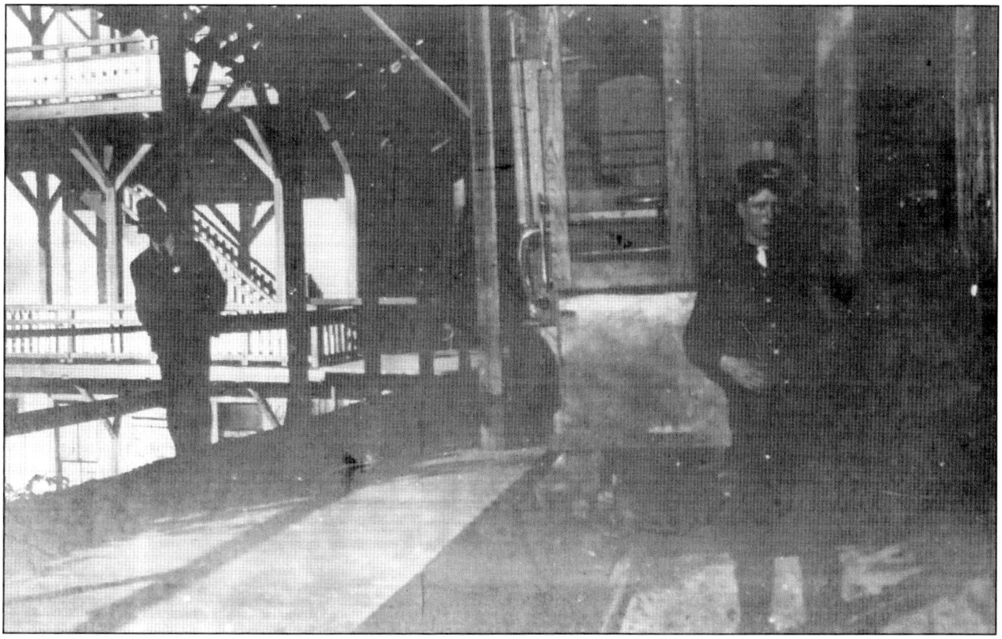

A young worker on the Narrow Gauge Railroad awaits passengers at Point Hotel on Lookout Mountain in the late 1890s. Wages for the average railroad worker were 16¢ an hour, or about $425 a year, in 1900. The work week varied from 45 to 60 hours.

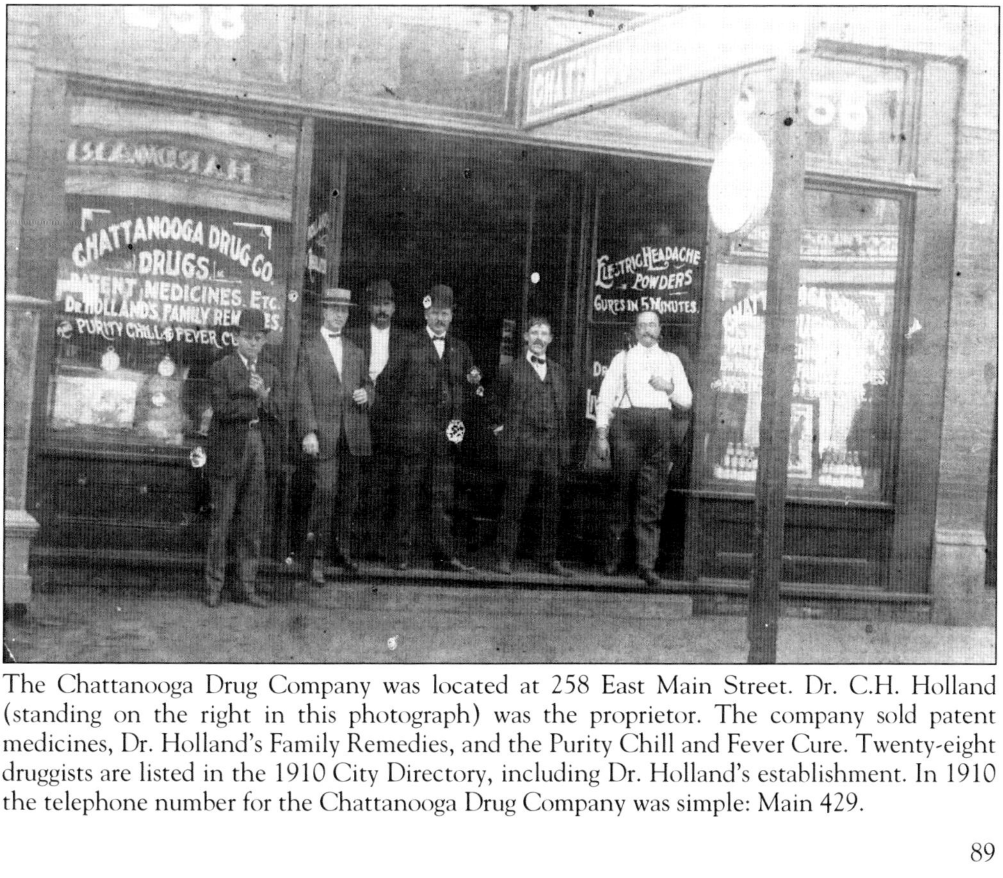

The Chattanooga Drug Company was located at 258 East Main Street. Dr. C.H. Holland (standing on the right in this photograph) was the proprietor. The company sold patent medicines, Dr. Holland's Family Remedies, and the Purity Chill and Fever Cure. Twenty-eight druggists are listed in the 1910 City Directory, including Dr. Holland's establishment. In 1910 the telephone number for the Chattanooga Drug Company was simple: Main 429.

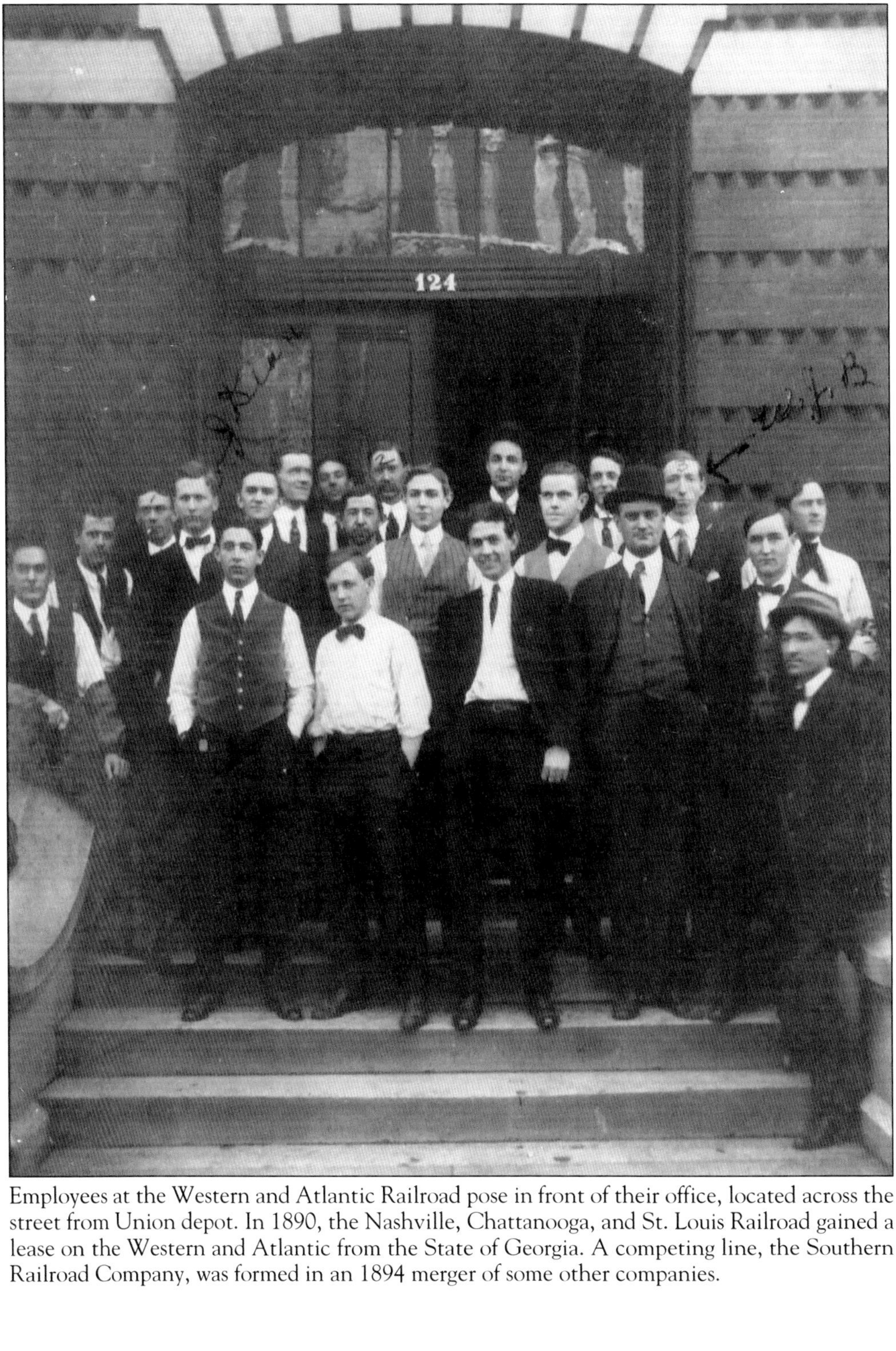

Employees at the Western and Atlantic Railroad pose in front of their office, located across the street from Union depot. In 1890, the Nashville, Chattanooga, and St. Louis Railroad gained a lease on the Western and Atlantic from the State of Georgia. A competing line, the Southern Railroad Company, was formed in an 1894 merger of some other companies.

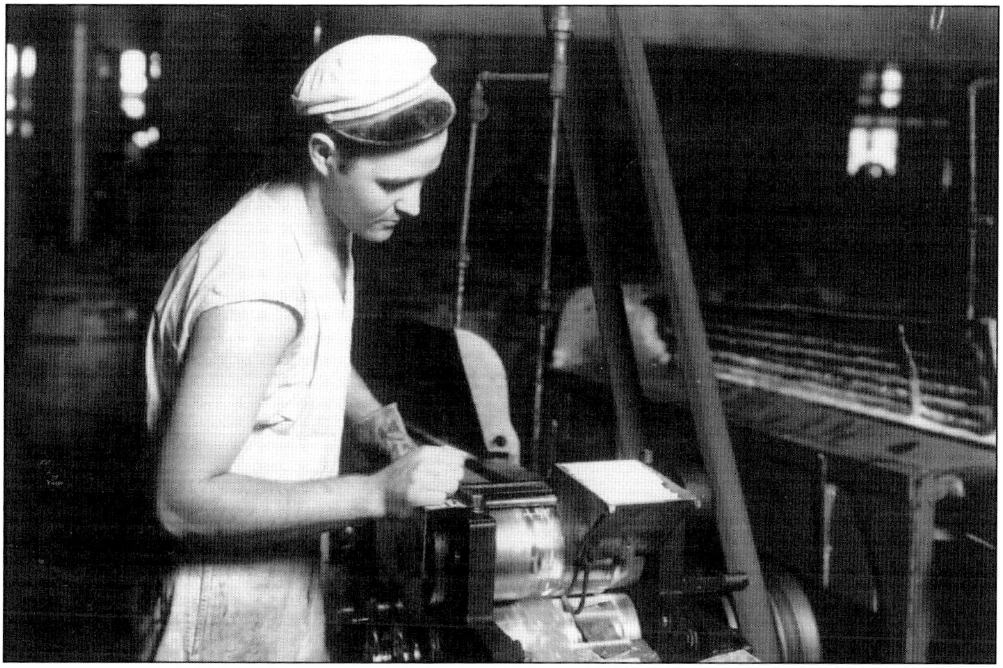

This 1930 photograph shows an employee of the Brock Candy Company attending a machine. The 1920s and 1930s were difficult times for the company and its employees. A rise in sugar prices after World War I and poor accounting practices resulted in a downsizing of the company. Sugar rationing in World War II also had an adverse effect on sales.

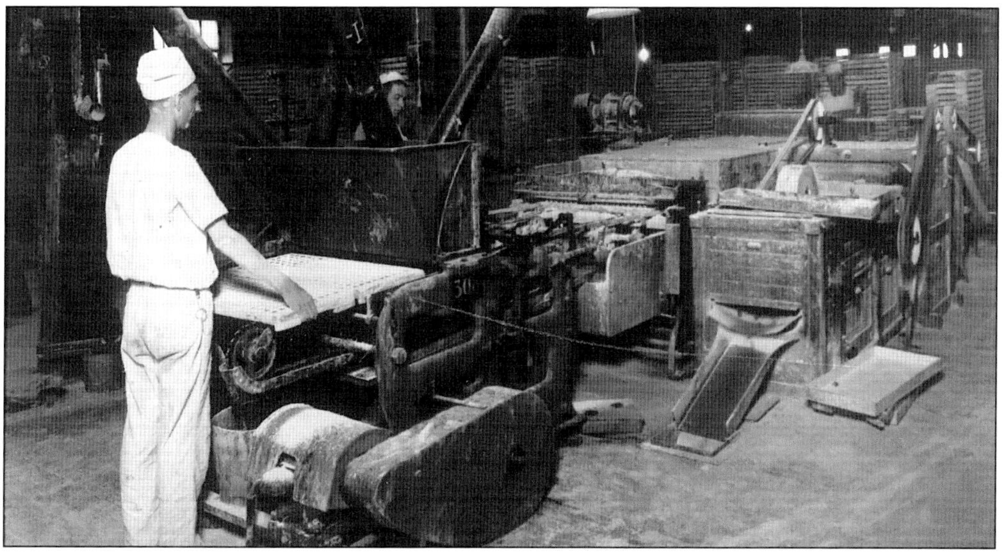

Three employees dressed in white prepare trays of candy with powdered sugar. William Emerson Brock built the company's reputation upon quality. The story of how the company achieved success in the Coconut Bon Bon business is illustrative of this point. Brock priced his Bon Bons 3¢ higher per pound than those made by the competition. When his salesmen complained, Brock replied that it was the only way to prove to the customer that the Brock Candy Company's Bon Bon was better than the others. It worked, and Brock's Coconut Bon Bon was soon outselling its New York competition.

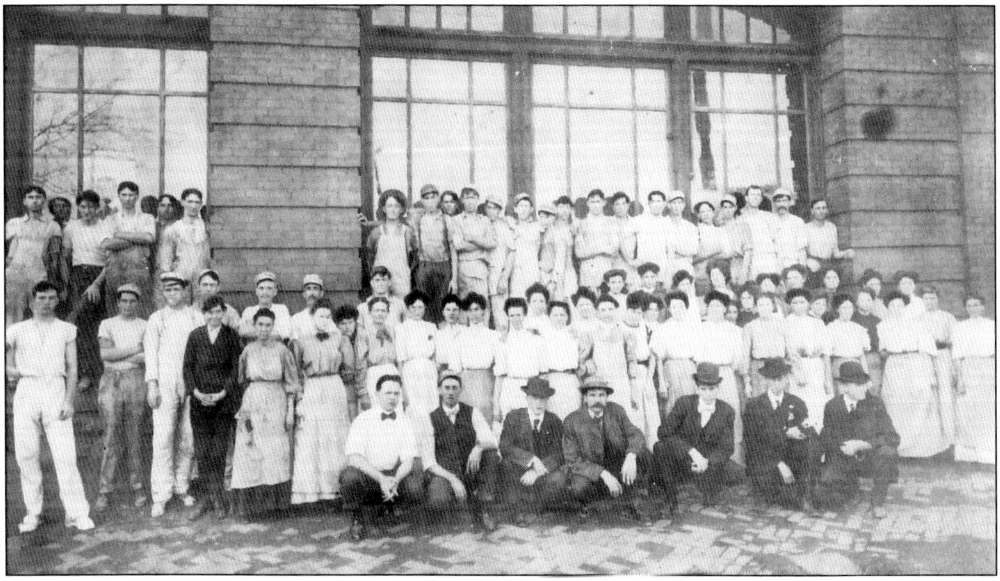

Brock Candy employees stand outside the factory on Chestnut Street. William Emerson Brock, the owner, kneels in front, second from the right. In the 1960s and 1970s, the company moved from its downtown location to a 30-acre tract of land near the airport on Jersey Pike. In the early 1970s the company was shipping nearly 40 million pounds of candy each year.

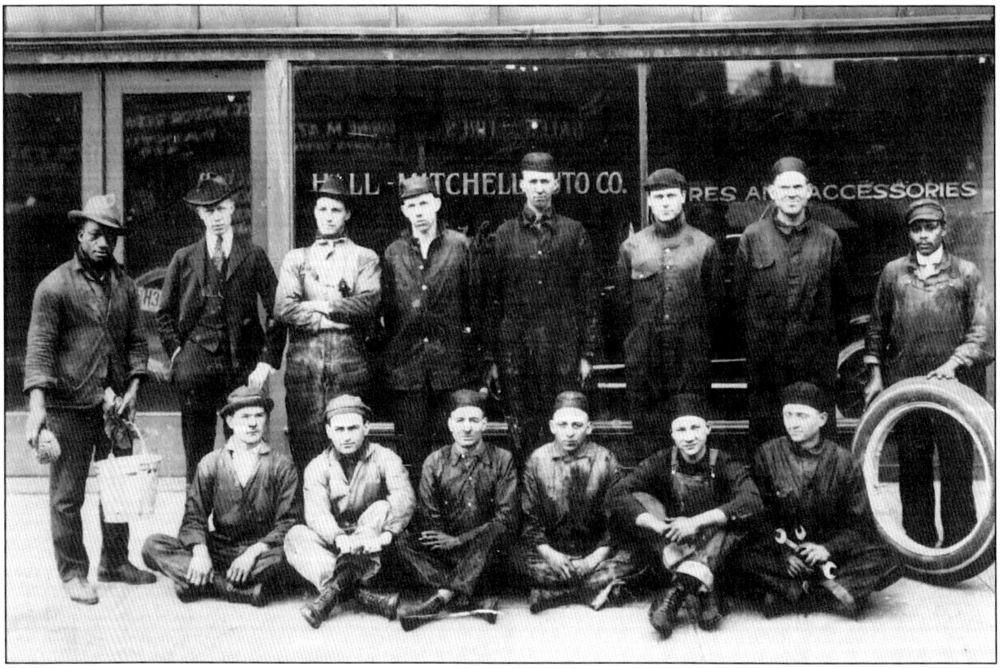

The proliferation of automobiles in the early twentieth century and the highway construction that followed completely changed the landscape of Chattanooga. As citizens moved into the countryside, the city began annexing the surrounding communities, increasing the city's acreage to equal one-fourth of Hamilton County. These men are posing outside of the Hall-Mitchell Auto Company at the 400 block of Market Street. The Hall-Mitchell Auto Company specialized in selling and servicing Studebaker automobiles.

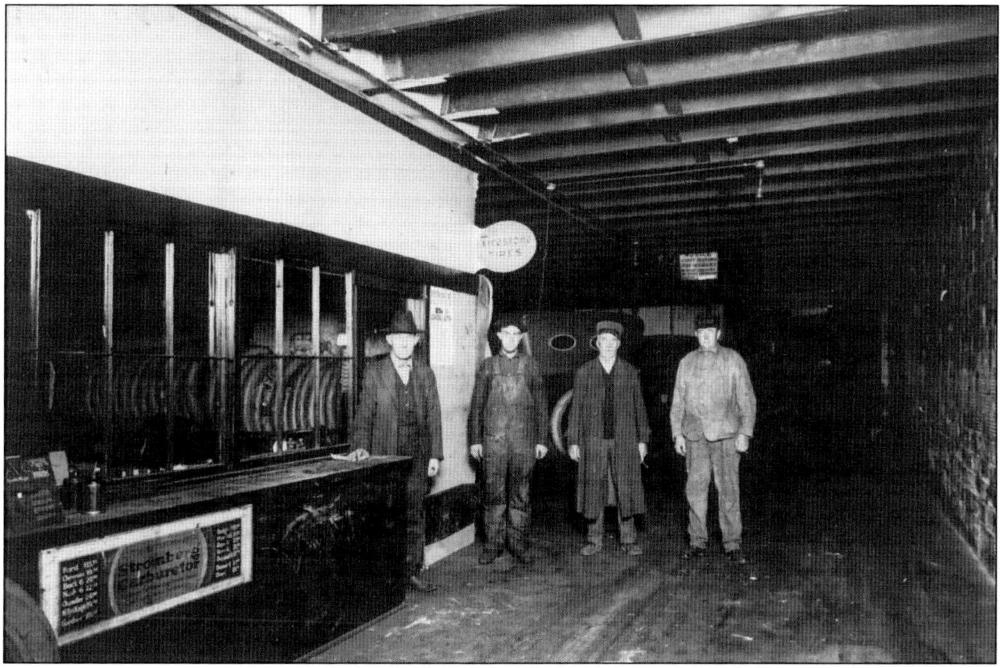

Four employees of an automobile repair shop pose next to the parts department. A sign lists prices for various Stromberg Carburetors. The 1905 City Directory lists two automobile repair shops, the Chattanooga Automobile Company and the Wallace Buggy Company. By 1925, that number had increased to fifty-seven.

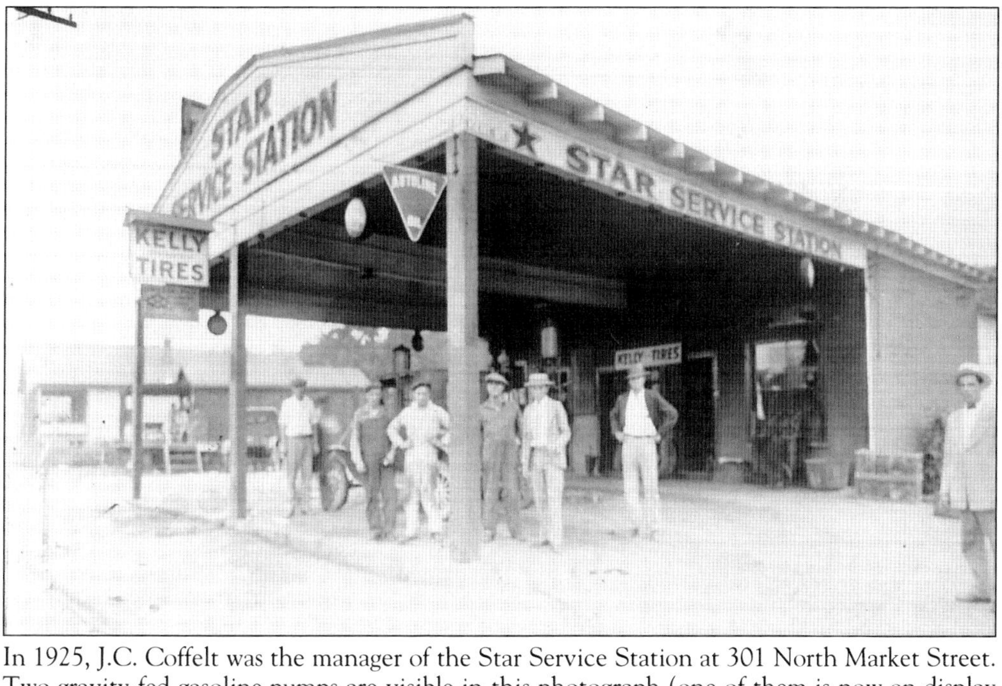

In 1925, J.C. Coffelt was the manager of the Star Service Station at 301 North Market Street. Two gravity-fed gasoline pumps are visible in this photograph (one of them is now on display at the Chattanooga Regional History Museum). After a rise in demand following World War I, gasoline prices stabilized at about 18¢ a gallon during the 1920s.

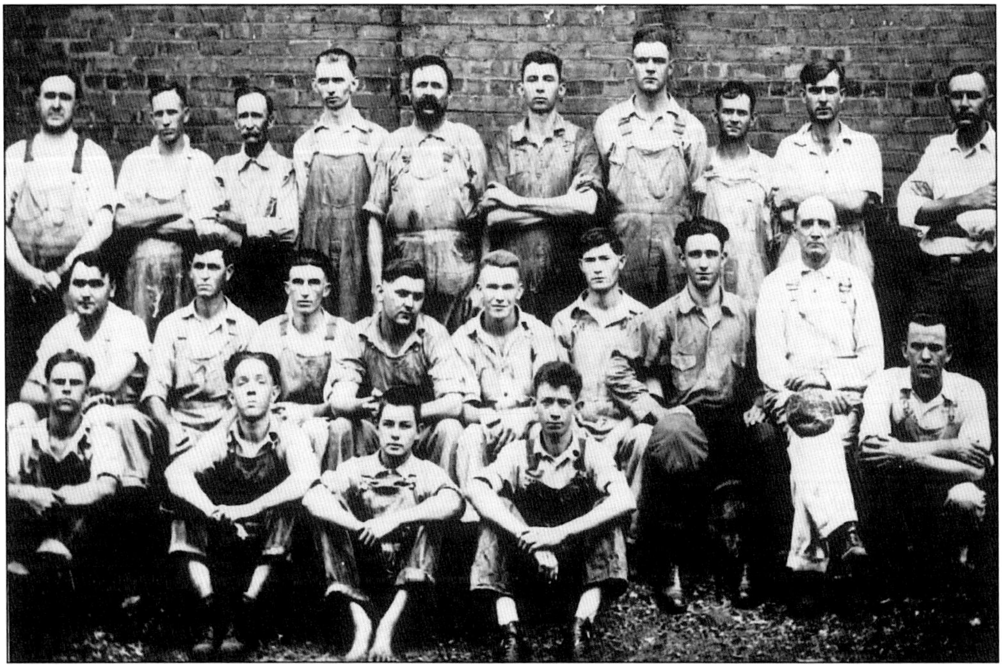

Employees of the Dixie Mercerizing Company pose outside their workplace. Notice the young men sitting in front, one without shoes. A mercerizing plant treats cotton thread with an alkali solution to strengthen it and give it a gloss. The thread is then shipped to textile factories.

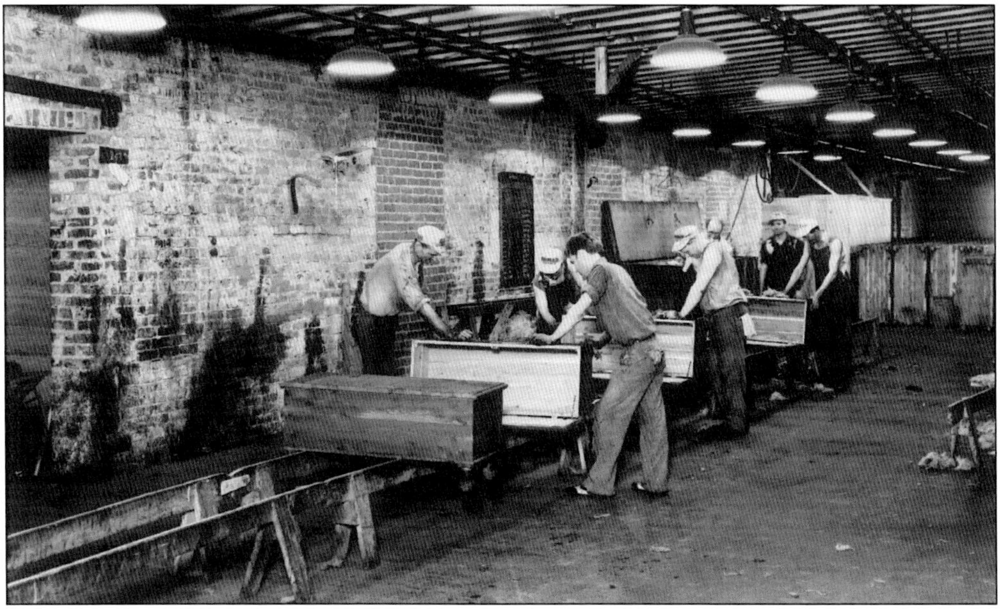

A cedar chest assembly line is shown in this photograph of the interior of the Tennessee Furniture Corporation. Located near the Tennessee River on Pine Street, the corporation was actually a conglomeration of various Chattanooga industries put together by Gaston Raoul after his arrival in the city in 1905. Included in the corporation was the old Loomis and Hart plant, the Keyser Manufacturing Company (makers of the "odorless refrigerator"), and the Acme Kitchen Furniture Company.

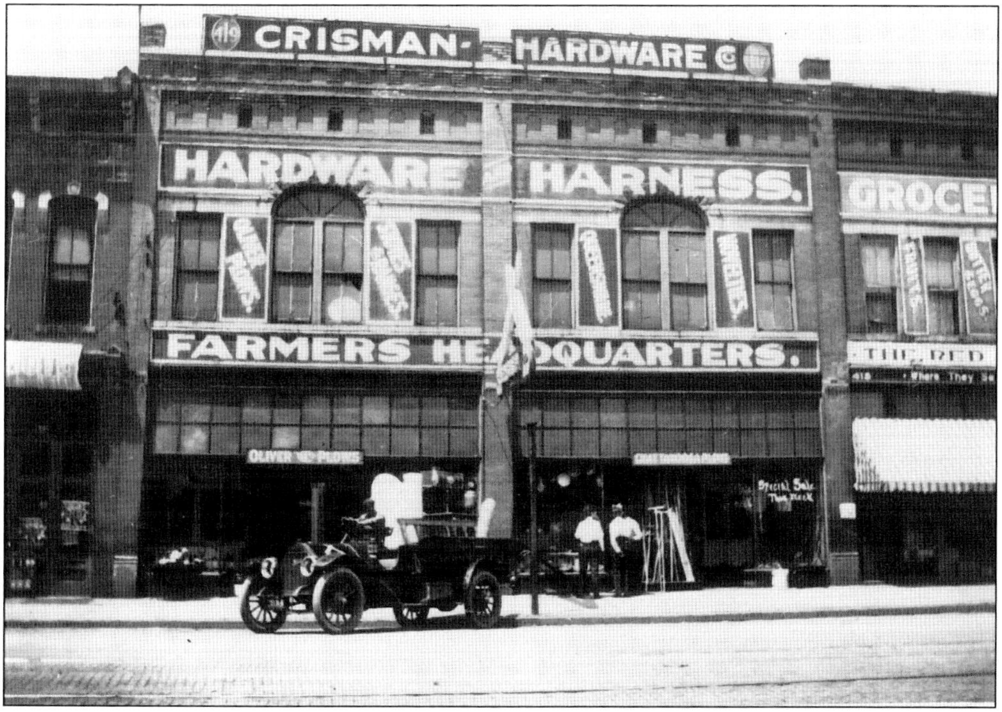

The Crisman Hardware Store had entrances on the 500 block of Market and Broad Streets. O.A. and B.A. Crisman were the proprietors. The store specialized in hardware, harnesses, stoves, ranges, guns, stoneware, plumbing supplies, and novelties.

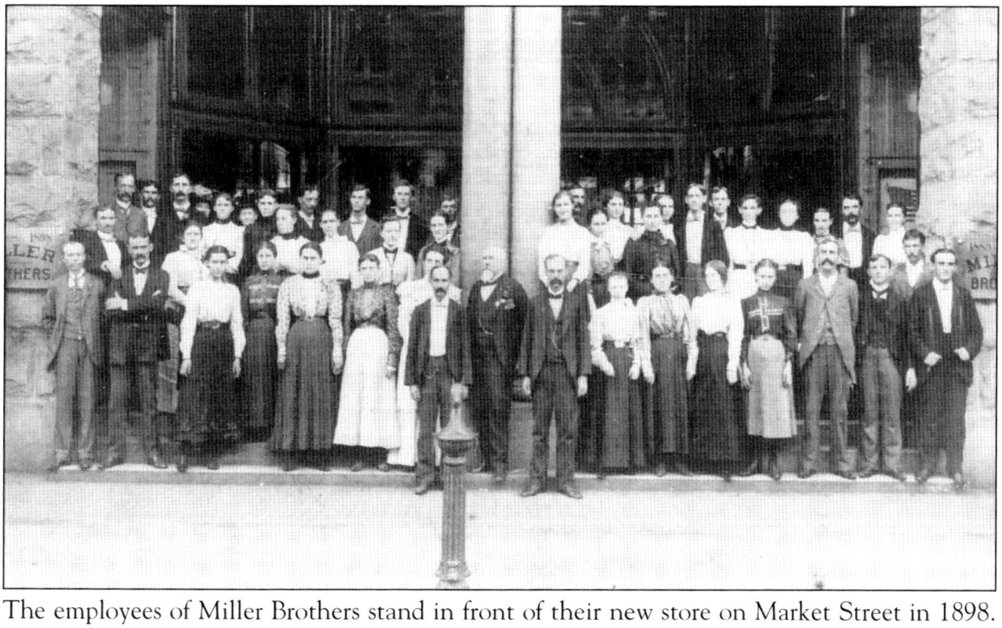

The employees of Miller Brothers stand in front of their new store on Market Street in 1898. Gustavus and Franklin Miller (flanking Mayor Watkins in the center) were born in Waco, TX. They moved east to enter the retail business, opening a small store in Chattanooga. When the Richardson building at Seventh and Market Streets burned in 1897, the Millers purchased the property and had a 100,000-square-foot-store, designed by R.H. Hunt, built.

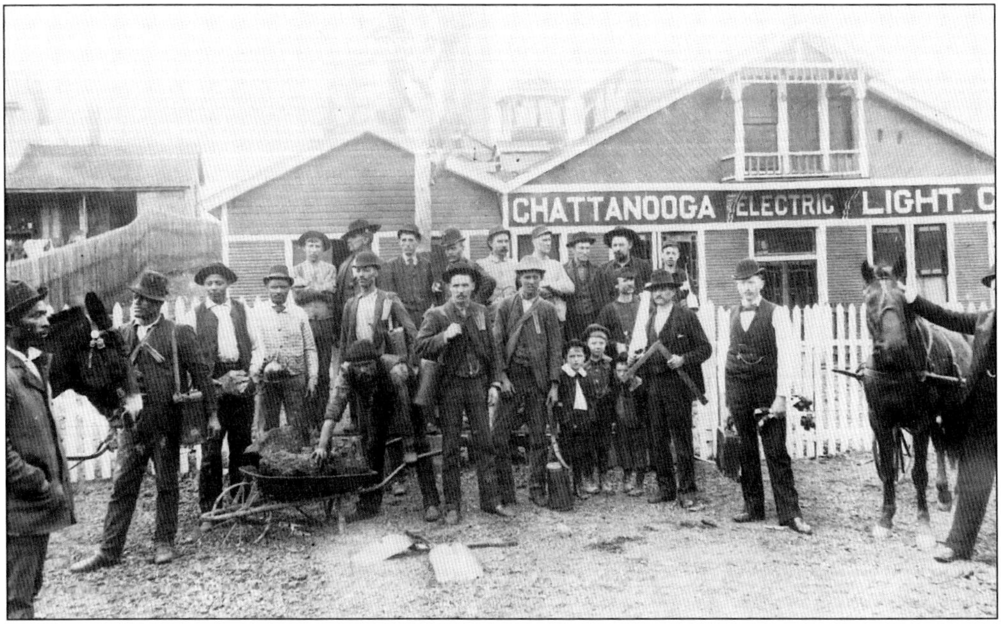

The Brush Electric Light Company first brought electrical power to Chattanooga on May 6, 1882. Miss Nellie Evans, the six-year-old daughter of H. Clay Evans, treasurer of the company, pressed the switch to turn on the twenty-five lamps that had been installed for the ceremony. In 1887, the Hauss Electric Lighting and Power Company was formed and in 1888 it merged with the Brush Electric Light Company to form the Chattanooga Electric Light Company. Employees of the company pose in front of and above the main office in this photograph from the 1890s.

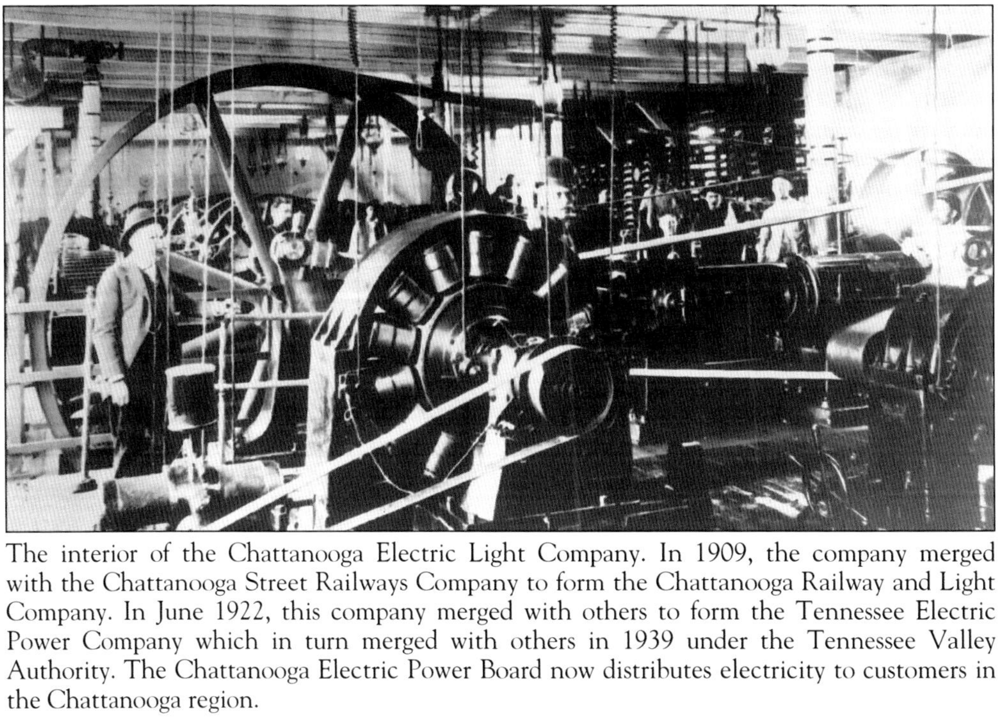

The interior of the Chattanooga Electric Light Company. In 1909, the company merged with the Chattanooga Street Railways Company to form the Chattanooga Railway and Light Company. In June 1922, this company merged with others to form the Tennessee Electric Power Company which in turn merged with others in 1939 under the Tennessee Valley Authority. The Chattanooga Electric Power Board now distributes electricity to customers in the Chattanooga region.

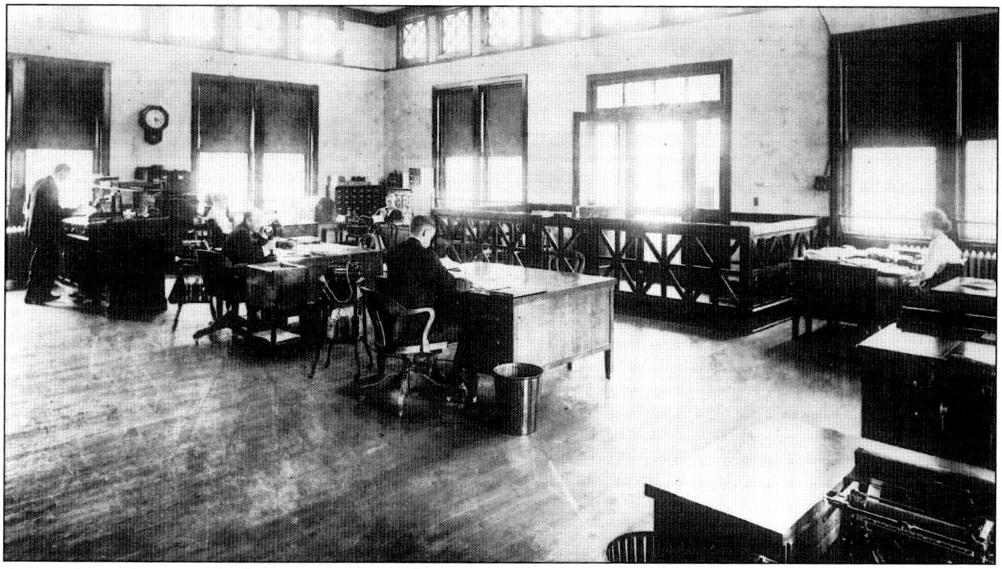

Several employees of Chattanooga Implement and Manufacturing Company are at work in the company's office in this photograph. The company was formed by Frances Powell Sholar with start-up capital of $650. At first specializing in steel plows, the company soon expanded into other farm products, such as disc plows, hullers, and hay presses.

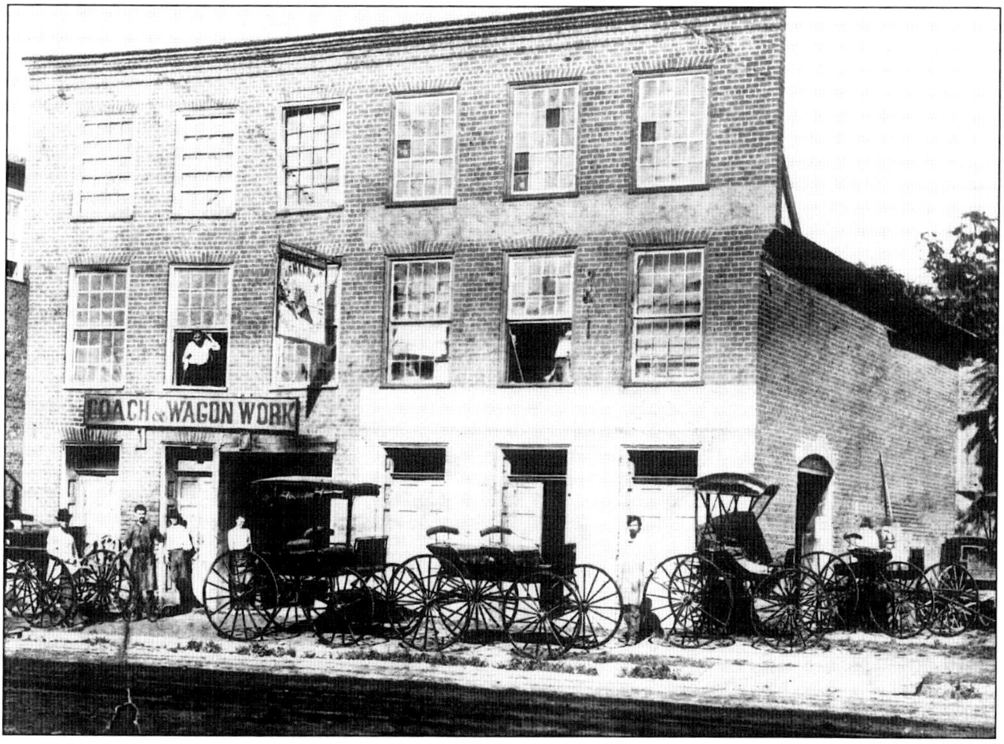

Employees of the A. Fassnacht Coach and Wagon Works on Carter Street posed for the camera some time in the 1880s. The owner of this business, Andrew Fassnacht, had come to America from Germany in 1855. The family was successful in converting to the manufacturing and distribution of truck equipment after wagons and carriages went out of style.

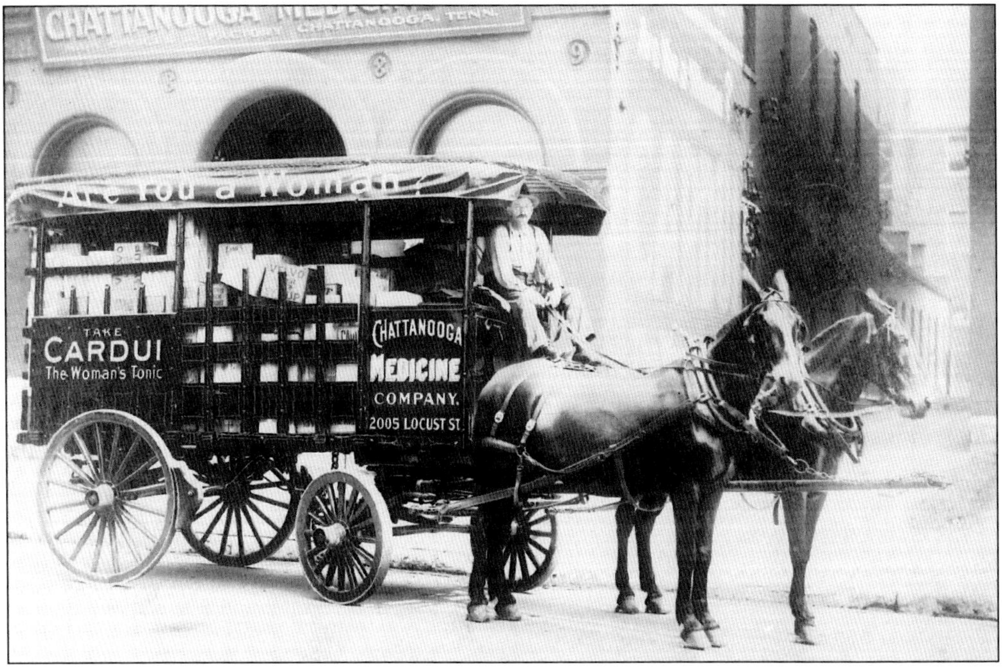

"Are You a Woman?" asks the sign on the canopy of this Chattanooga Medicine delivery wagon. If so, "Take Cardui, The Woman's Tonic," it advises. Ten percent of the Cardui formula was alcohol, which was, according to the company's advertisements, intended "as a solvent and preservative of the active medicinal ingredients."

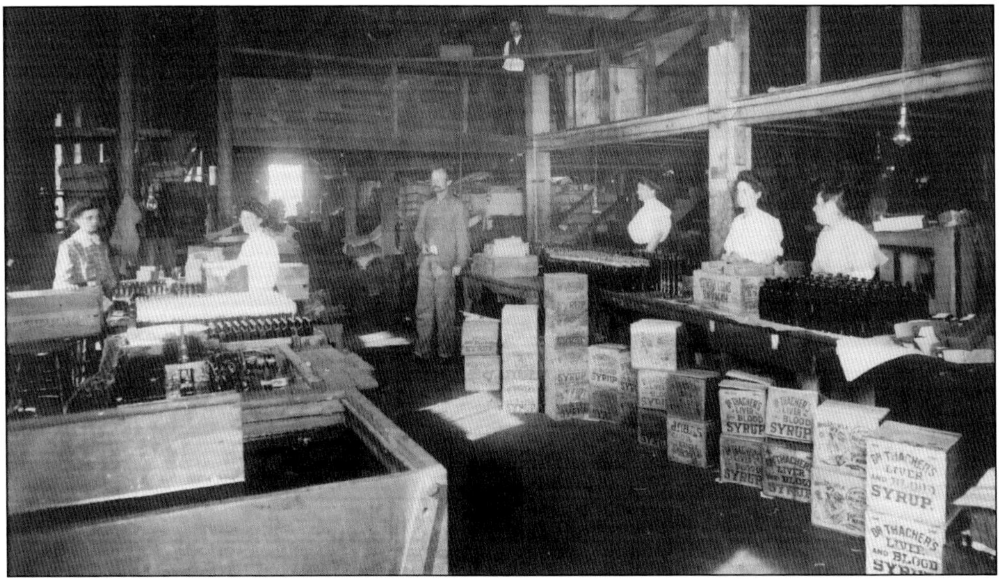

This photograph shows the interior of the Thacher Medicine Company. Dr. H.S. Thacher was born in Maine. After the Civil War, he moved to Chattanooga and opened a drug business on Market Street. His Liver and Blood Syrup was well known across the South. In addition, he concocted a Worm Syrup, Diarrhea Mixture, "Stella-Vite" (another remedy for women's complaints), and other remedies. The Thacher Medicine Company was purchased by John T. Lupton in 1910. It was sold to Allied Drug in 1924.

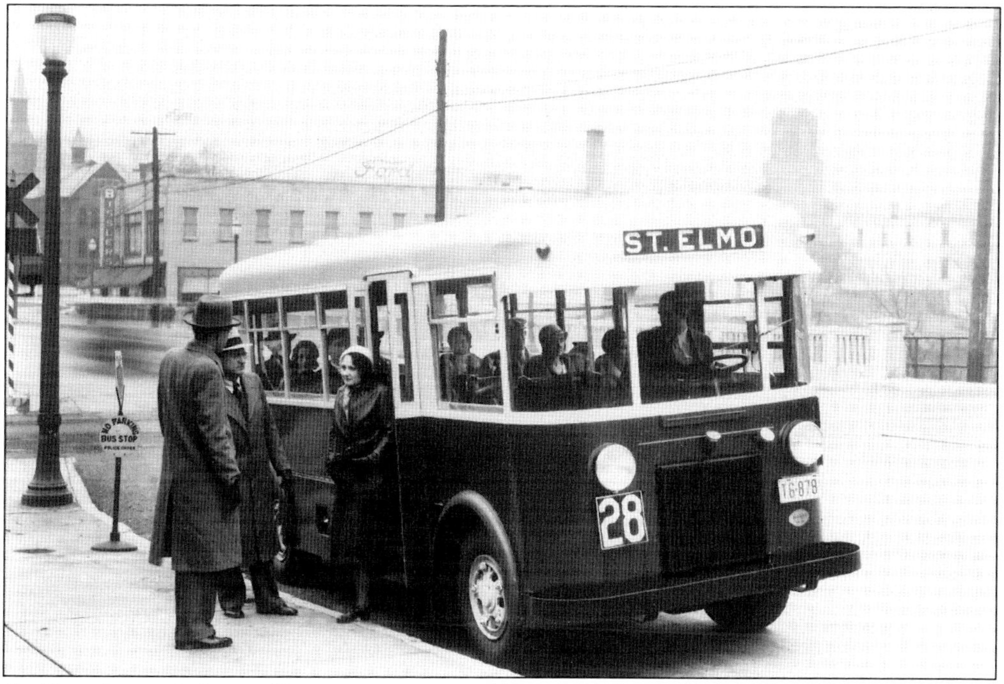

St. Elmo bus #28 drops off passengers on a cold winter's day in 1932. The Chattanooga Area Regional Transportation Authority (CARTA) currently operates the regional bus lines and Incline #2. St. Elmo, the oldest suburb of Chattanooga, was annexed in 1929. The community was named after a novel written by Augusta Jane Evans Wilson in 1866. Part of the story takes place at the base of Lookout Mountain, where St. Elmo developed.

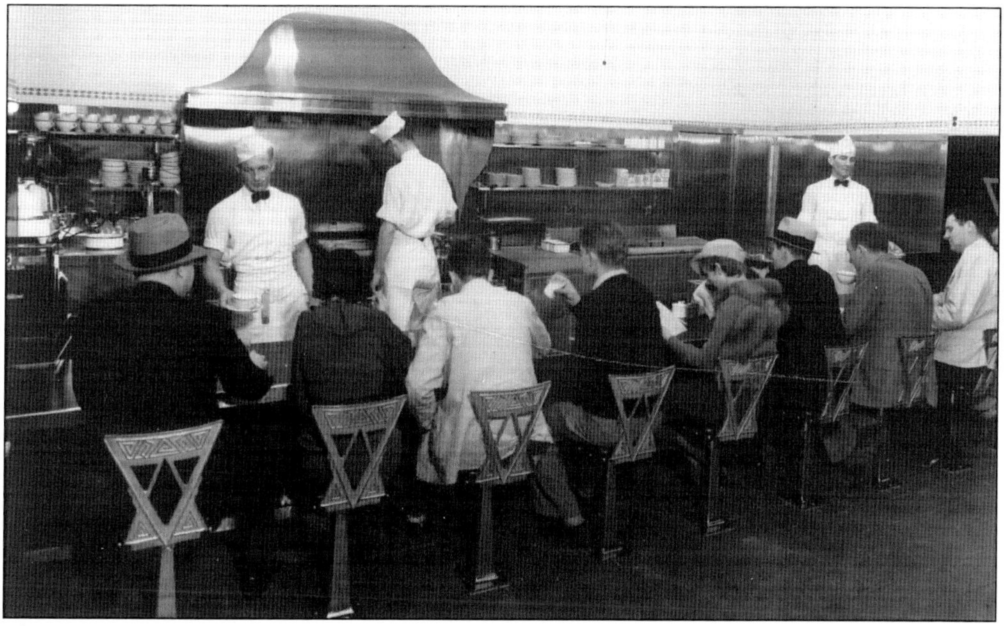

This restaurant, at 1012 Market Street, took its name from the distinctive backs on the chairs inside. The Triangle Grill was a popular stop for breakfast and lunch when this photograph was taken in 1935. In 1942, there were fifteen restaurants on Market Street.

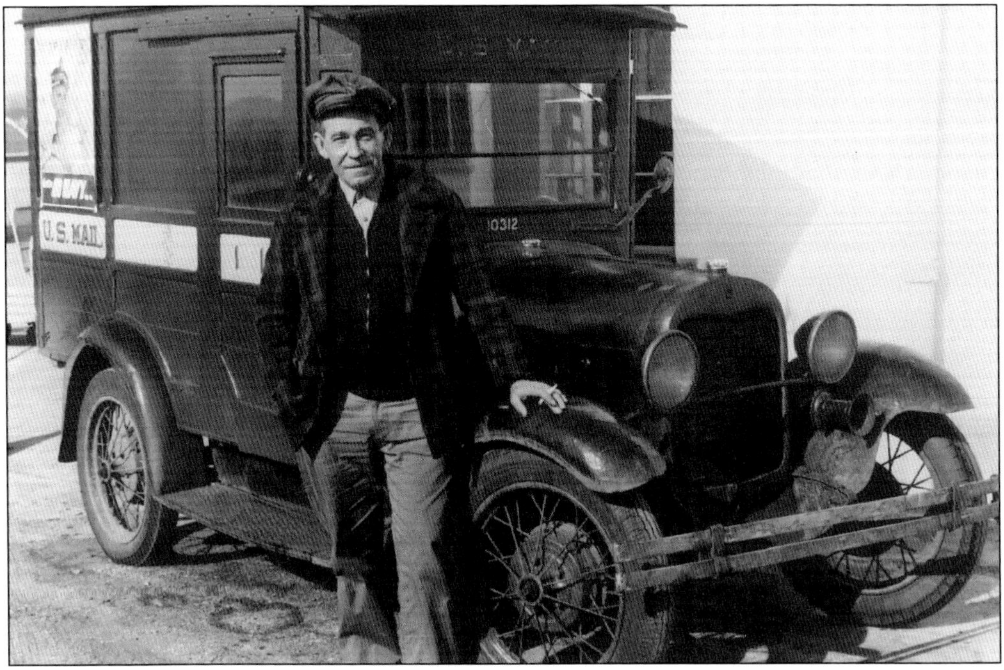

A postal worker stands in front of a 1920s mail truck. The first postmaster in Chattanooga was John P. Long, a founder and prominent businessman of the city. By 1925, the postal service included a main office and nine branches across the city, and offered free delivery and rural service.

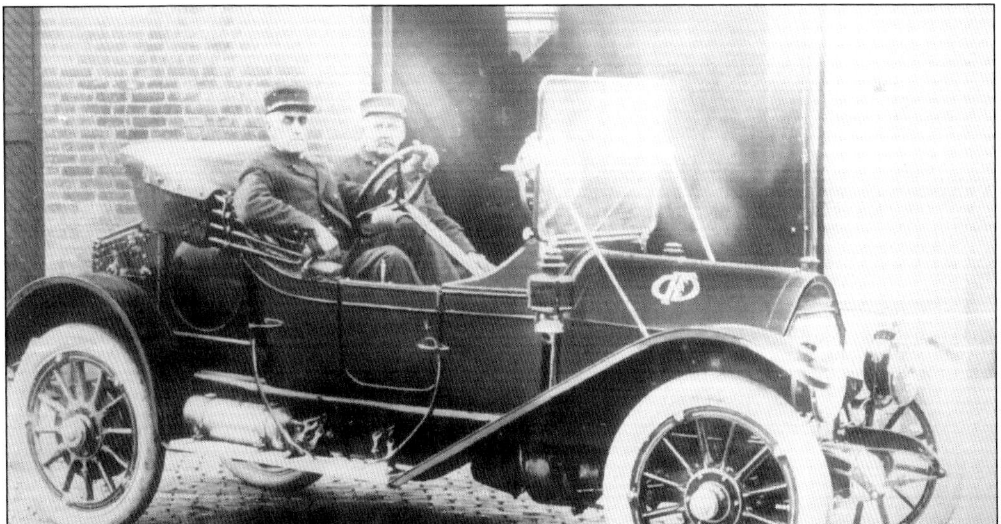

Fire Chief Alfond and Assistant Chief Hollingsworth of Anderson, IN, proudly pose in a roadster made for the Cincinnati Fire Department by the Nyberg Automobile Company of Chattanooga. Henry Nyberg started manufacturing his cars in Anderson. In 1911, he convinced several Chattanooga investors to start a Chattanooga branch of the company. Unfortunately, the company went bankrupt after producing only a few hundred cars. Other ventures were more successful: for example, in 1916, Ernest W. Holmes, Sr., began building the world's first tow trucks in Chattanooga.

Seven

Edification

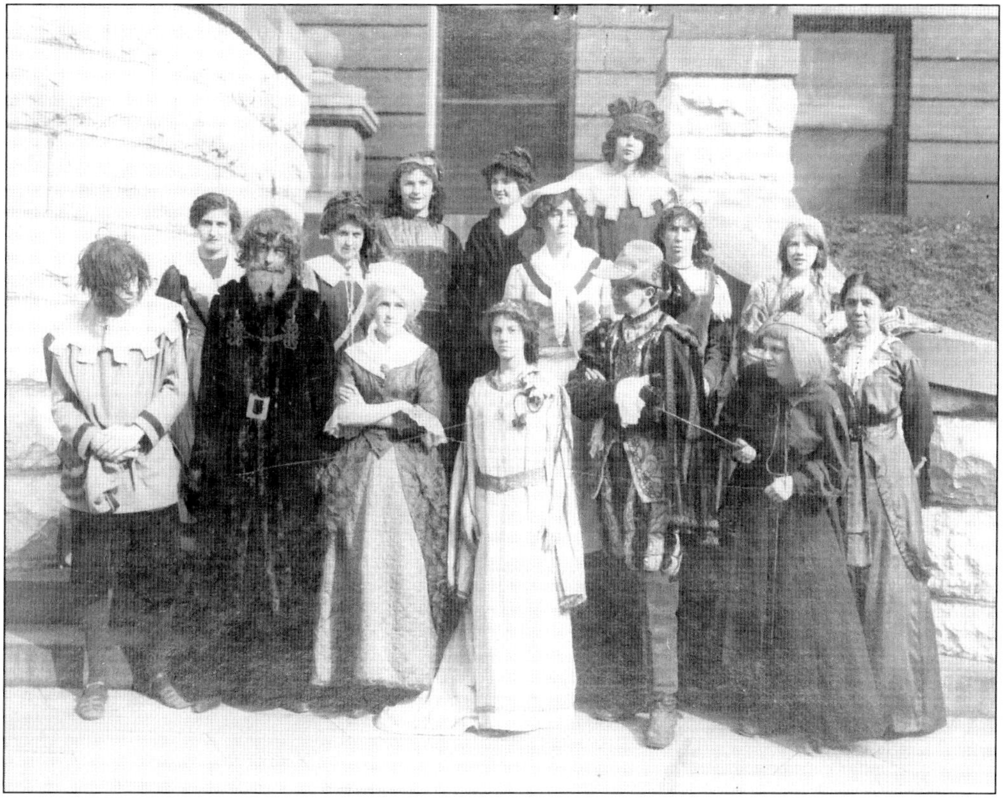

There are few discernible patterns in history, but one pattern that seems to hold true is that a generation that is touched by the fire of war will be followed by a generation interested in the pursuit of the finer things in life such as art, music, literature, and education. Such was the case in Chattanooga and Hamilton County after the Civil War: the public school system was developed; universities were established; libraries, opera houses, and theaters were built; and the culture of the outside world was brought into the city. In addition, civic-minded leaders in Chattanooga worked to repair the physical and social damage caused by the Civil War.

These students of the Chattanooga High School class of 1914 are dressed in costumes made for the school play. They are, from left to right: (front row) Fred Painter, E.M. Counts, Larine Pruitt, Mary Sue Holt, Bradley Dunlap, Josephine Swick, and Lucy Holtzclaw (advisor); (second row) Gertrude Shaw, Marian Wills, ? Thompson, Sena Blair, unknown, William Miller, and Louise White; (top row) Dan Forin.

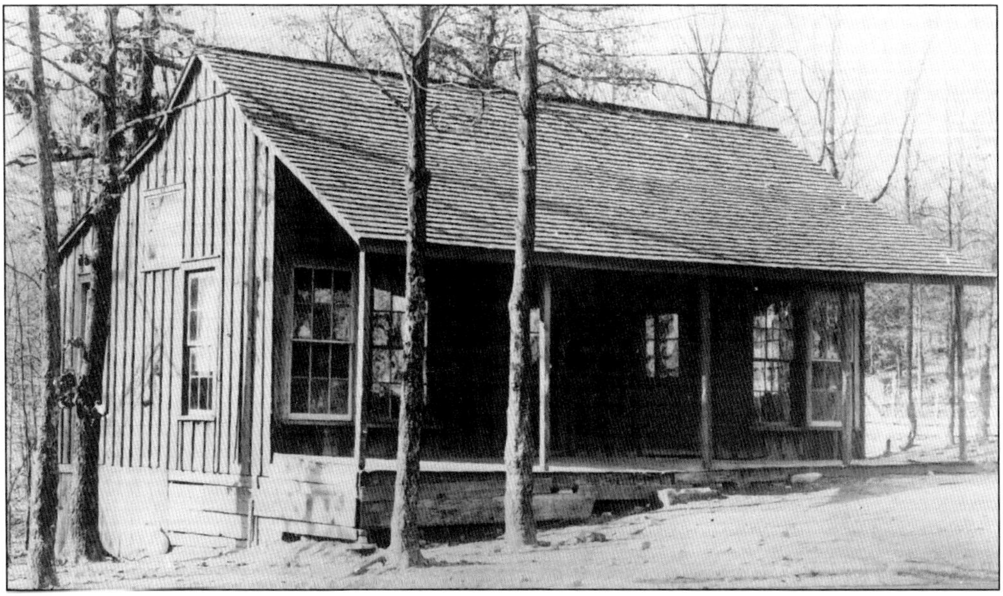

Prior to the Civil War, most of the schools in Hamilton County were private institutions. A county school system was established just after the war, and in 1872 the City of Chattanooga passed an ordinance creating the public school system. Most of the county schools were one-room, one-teacher institutions like the Lookout Mountain School that was established in 1878 (shown above). Progress in education was relatively slow, however: by 1885, the school year was still only five months.

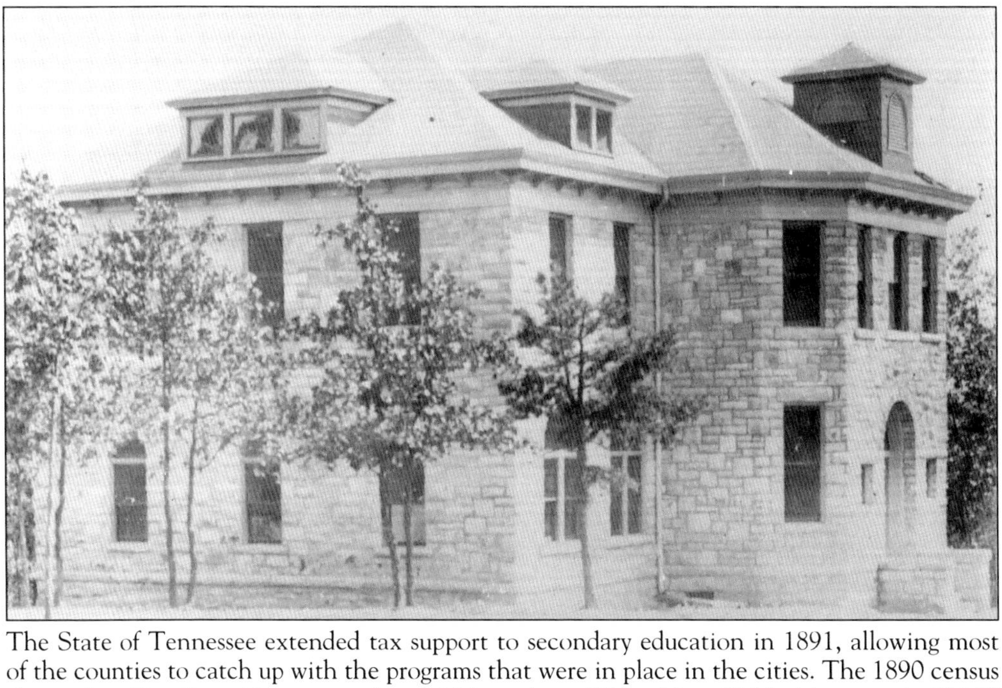

The State of Tennessee extended tax support to secondary education in 1891, allowing most of the counties to catch up with the programs that were in place in the cities. The 1890 census shows that Hamilton County employed 164 teachers (115 white; 49 black) to teach 10,160 students (7,106 white; 3,054 black). A new building for the Lookout Mountain Public High School was built in 1900.

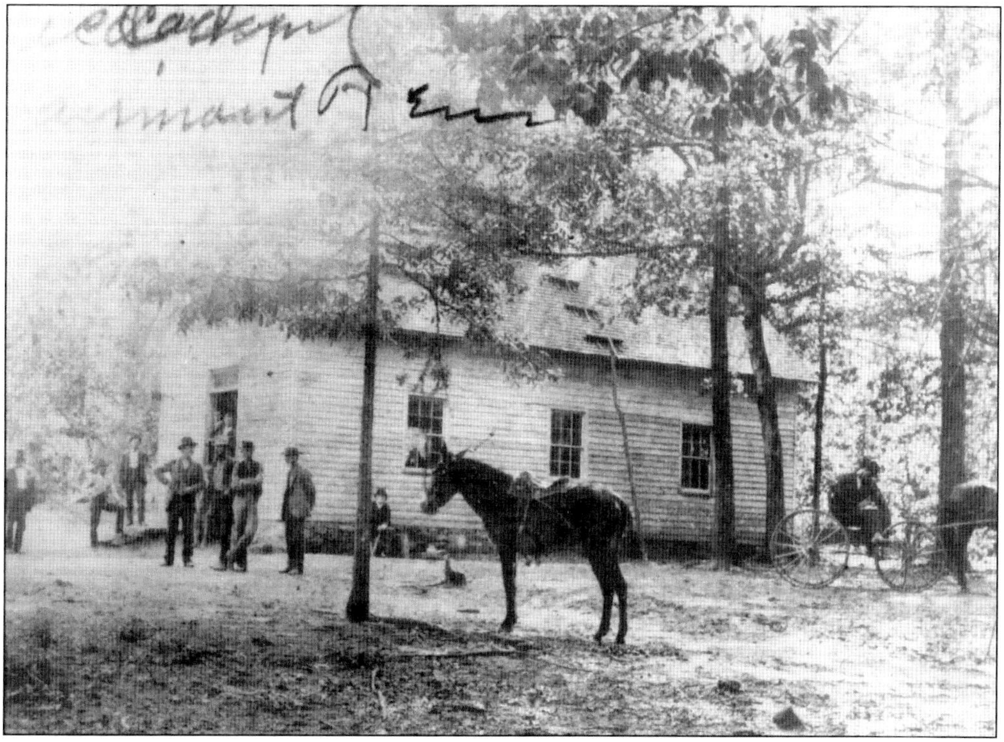

Soon after this 1910 photograph was taken, Fairmount Academy on Signal Mountain was consolidated with Oakwood School in a new building on Fairmount Road. The academy had become part of the public school system between 1875 and 1880. The academy building served as a community center and election polling station until it burned in 1946.

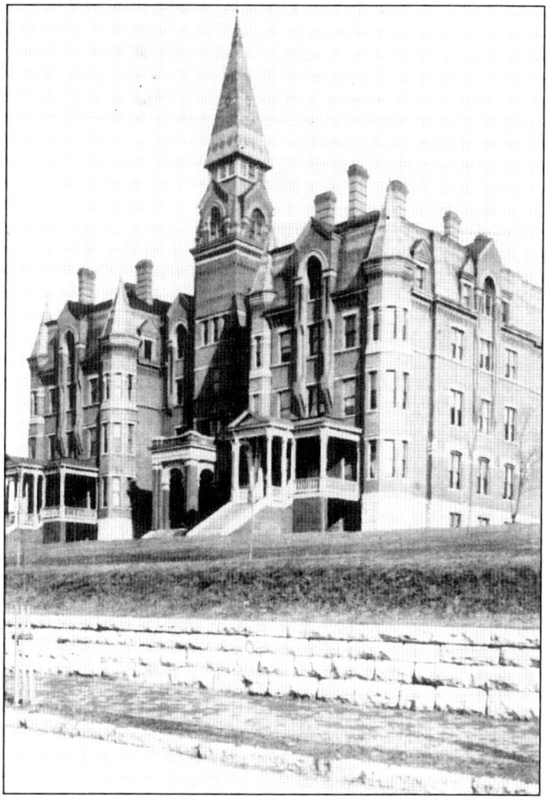

Chattanooga University opened its doors to students in 1886. At various points in its long history entitled the College of Chattanooga and Grant University, it is now part of the University of Tennessee system. University Hall, nicknamed "Old Main," was built on McCallie Avenue at a cost of $40,000. The building housed the entire university, including dorm rooms, classrooms, a library, an apartment for faculty, offices, a kitchen, a mess hall, and a chapel. It was torn down in 1917 to make way for expansion.

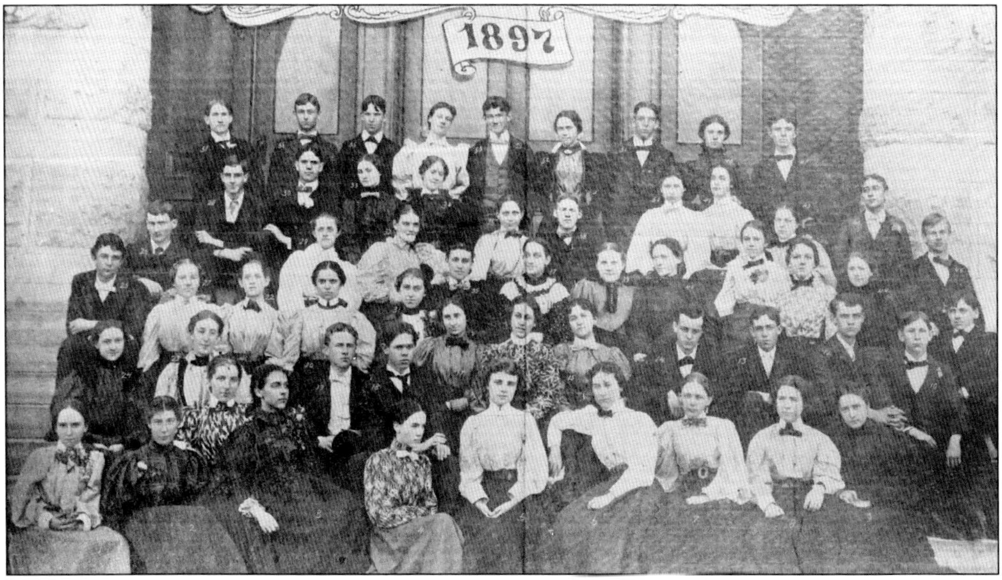

Chattanooga High School was established in 1874 at the old McMillin home on Eighth Street. Professor H.D. Wyatt served as the first superintendent with Mr. W.D. Underhill and Miss Hattie Ackerman as teachers. The school had an enrollment of thirty-five students at its inception. A brick building large enough for five hundred students was later built on the site. Wyatt served the school until his death in 1917. Miss Ackerman died while nursing the sick during the 1878 yellow fever epidemic.

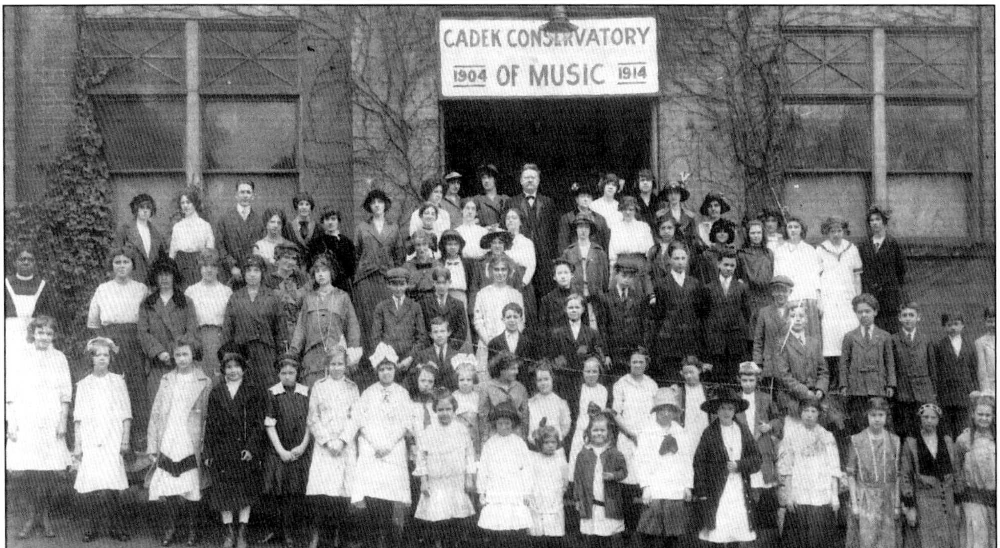

Several important private schools were founded in Chattanooga near the turn of the century. Notre Dame (1886), Baylor School (1893), McCallie School (1905), and the Girls Preparatory School (1906) are still in operation today. The Cadek Conservatory was founded by Joseph Cadek in 1904. Cadek, a gifted violinist, was born in Prague, Bohemia (now the Czech Republic). He migrated to America in 1892 and settled in Chattanooga because the mountains reminded him of his homeland. In 1935, Cadek Conservatory merged with the University of Chattanooga.

Teachers at the Cedar Hill School posed for the photographer on the front steps of the school in the 1910s. In 1907, a county board of education replaced the old system of having directors for each district school, signifying the development of a more professional school system. However, illiteracy was still a major problem in Chattanooga and in Hamilton County. The 1900 census, for example, reported that 7,331 citizens of the county over the age of ten were unable to read or write.

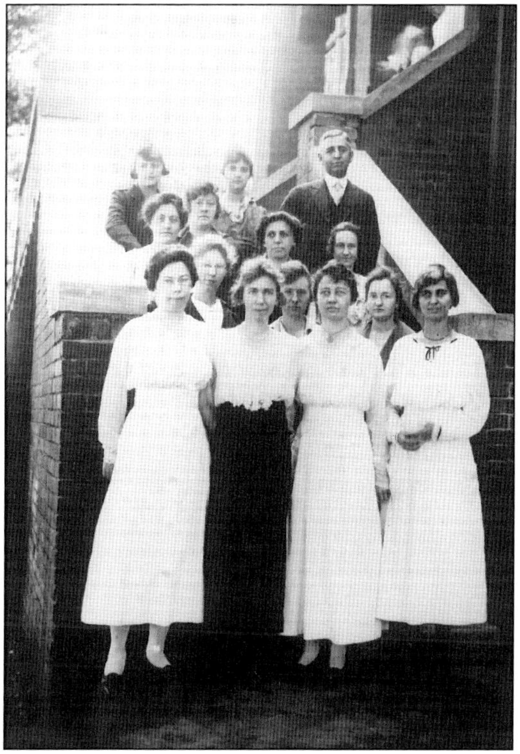

By the time these students from the Missionary Ridge School were posing for class pictures during the 1950s, illiteracy had virtually been eliminated in Hamilton County. In 1950, there were seventy-six public schools in Chattanooga and Hamilton County, and more than thirty-eight thousand students were enrolled. A plan for the gradual desegregation of the Chattanooga school system was handed down by United States District Judge Frank Wilson in 1962.

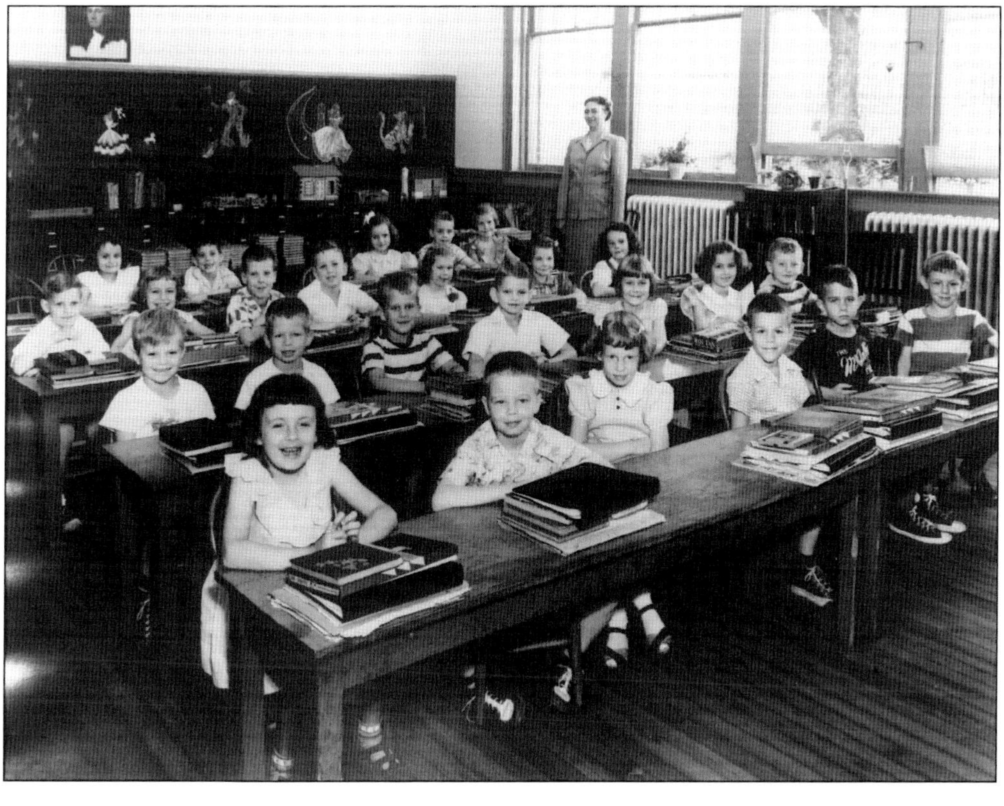

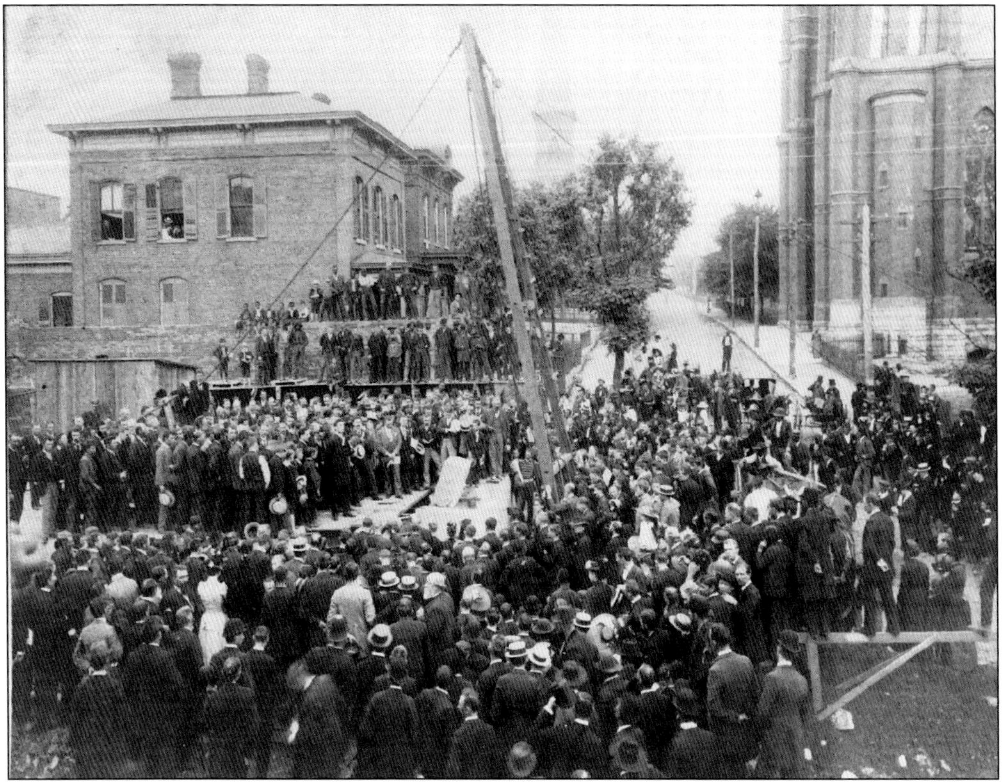

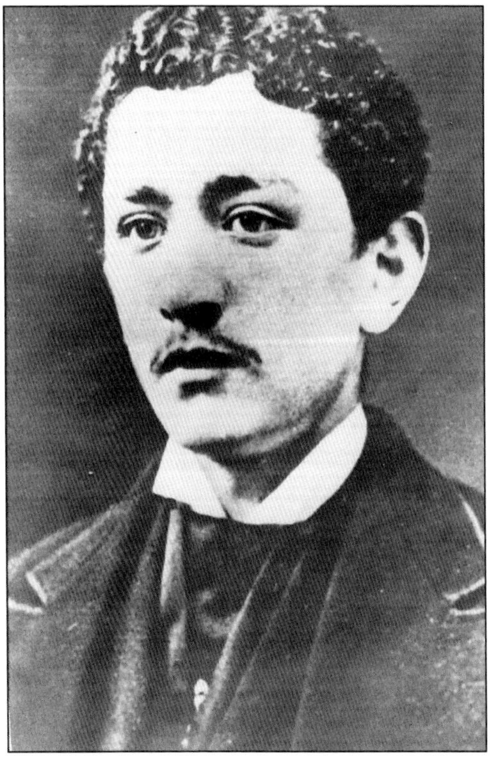

The Chattanooga Times was originally published from a one-room brick building on the corner of Eighth and Cherry Streets. Several hundred people attended the cornerstone laying ceremonies for the newspaper's new headquarters, the six-story Dome Building on Georgia Avenue. The building was dedicated on December 8, 1892, before a crowd of ten thousand spectators.

At the age of twenty, Adolph S. Ochs was a young printer with big dreams. In 1878, he purchased *The Chattanooga Times* with $250 (which he had borrowed) and began operations with $37.50 in capital. He soon became a tireless promoter, using the newspaper to muster support for local projects such as the public library, road improvements, the fireman's memorial, hospitals, and the promotion of tourism.

Lapsley Green Walker succeeded Colonel J.E. MacGowan in 1903 as the second editor-in-chief of *The Chattanooga Times*. A graduate of Princeton, Walker had set up a law practice in Rogersville before coming to Chattanooga in 1882 to serve as editor of the *Chattanooga Democrat*. In 1883, he switched to the *Times* as a proofreader and then moved up to the city desk before taking the top spot.

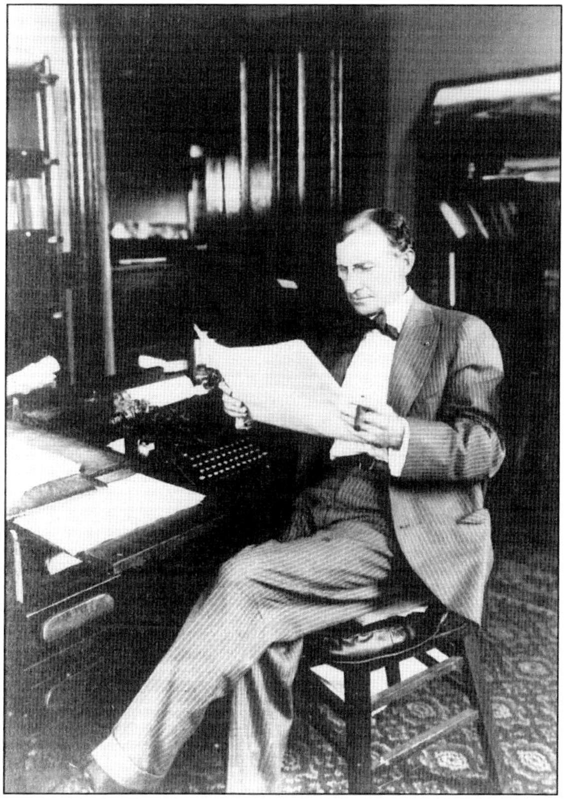

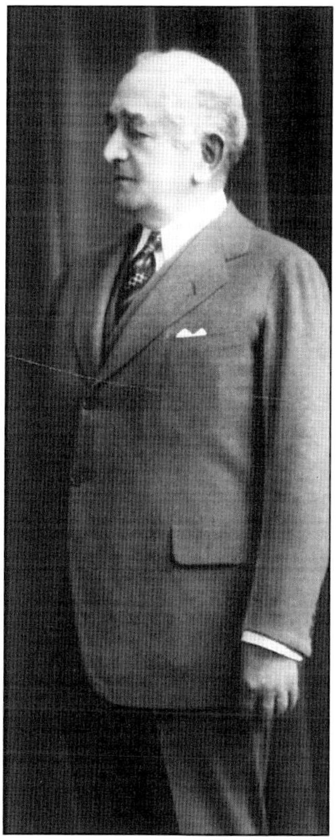

In 1896, Adolph Ochs purchased the *New York Times*. He continued to publish his Chattanooga newspaper, however, leaving his brother, George Washington Ochs, in charge, and continued to make contributions to the people of Chattanooga. A few months after his death in 1935, 2,700 acres of land on Lookout Mountain were purchased by a foundation created by Ochs in 1921 to save such areas for public use and presented to the National Park Service. In 1940 the observatory museum at Point Park was named in his honor.

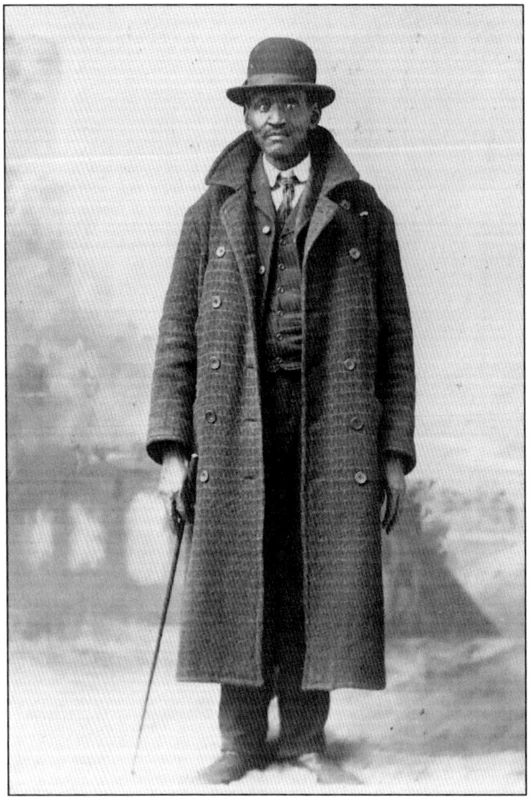

Randolph Miller was a former slave who had come to Chattanooga with Sherman's army in 1864. He learned the newspaper business while working at *The Chattanooga Times*. In 1898, he started his own newspaper, the *Blade*, probably with the quiet support of Adolph Ochs. Miller was well known in the white and black communities for his flamboyant style: his personal trademark was a silk hat. He also followed a strong set of values which he preached in his editorials.

"They have taken our part of the library; they have moved our school to the frog pond; they have passed the Jim Crow law; they have knocked us out of the jury box; they have played the devil generally; and what in thunder more will they do no one knows."

Miller was relentless in his condemnation of racial segregation and civil rights restrictions. In response to a 1905 law segregating public transportation, he and other leaders launched a boycott of Chattanooga streetcars. Although unsuccessful, the attempt predated by over fifty years the Montgomery bus boycott led by Dr. Martin Luther King, Jr. The *Blade* went out of business after twelve years of publication.

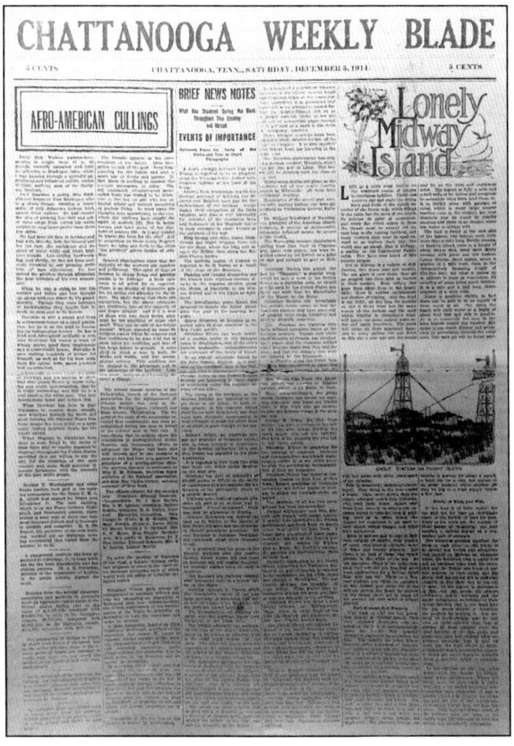

CHATTANOOGA WEEKLY BLADE

5 CENTS | CHATTANOOGA, TENN., SATURDAY, DECEMBER 5, 1914 | 5 CENTS

AFRO-AMERICAN CULLINGS

BRIEF NEWS NOTES

EVENTS OF IMPORTANCE

Lonely Midway Island

Emma Bell Miles wrote stories and painted watercolors of nature and life on Signal Mountain. Included among her works are several books, the most popular being *The Spirit of the Mountains* (1905) and *Our Southern Birds* (1919). Despite some literary success in her lifetime, she remained poor and died a young woman in 1919. The Chattanooga Regional History Museum has a substantial collection of her drawings and watercolors.

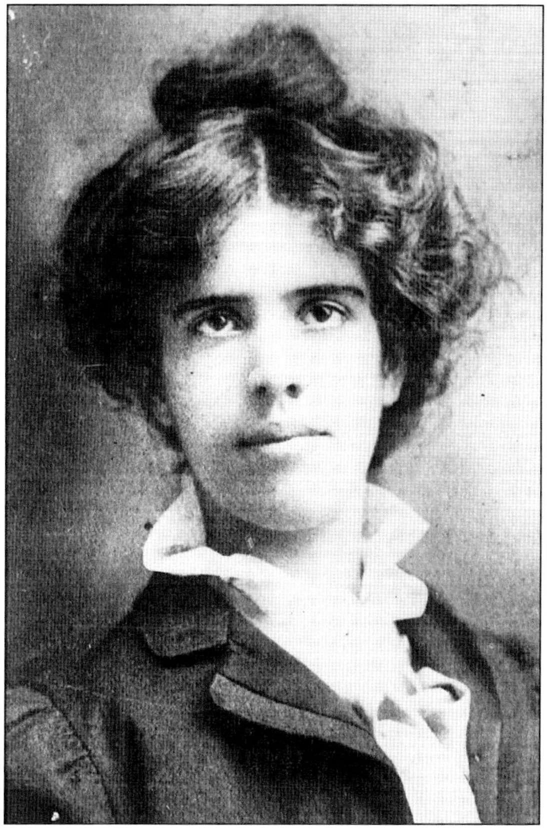

William H. McGee was an artist and craftsman who quietly devoted his life to making violins in the rural isolation of Sand Mountain. In his workshop he aged and cured the variety of woods needed to make a violin and covered each handmade instrument with a special varnish. McGee created violins for prominent local musicians who recognized him as a master of his craft.

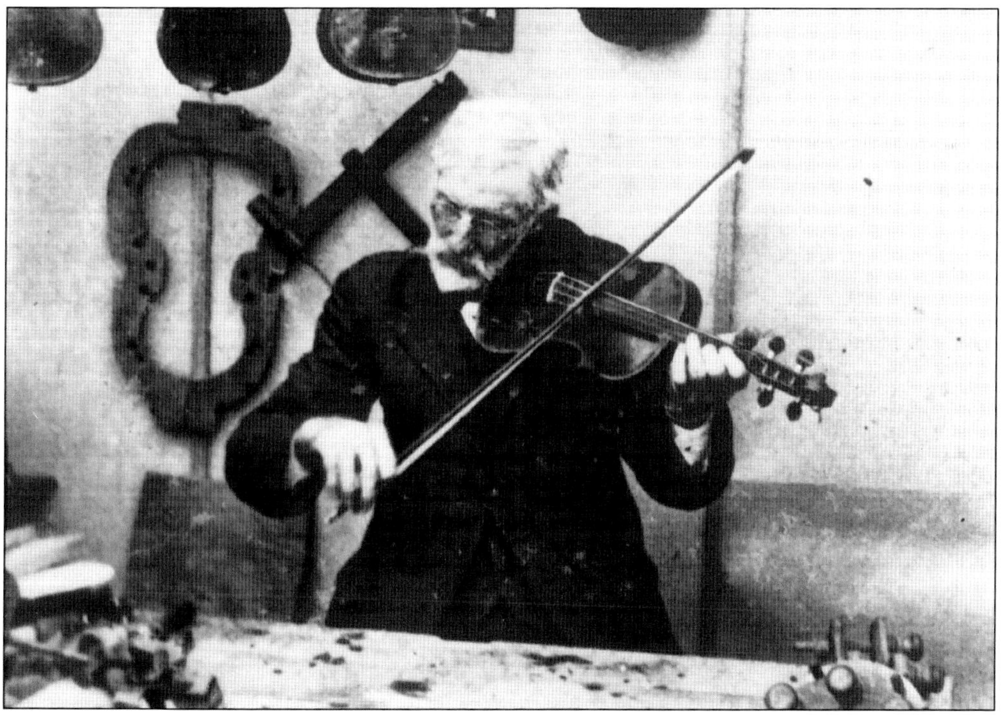

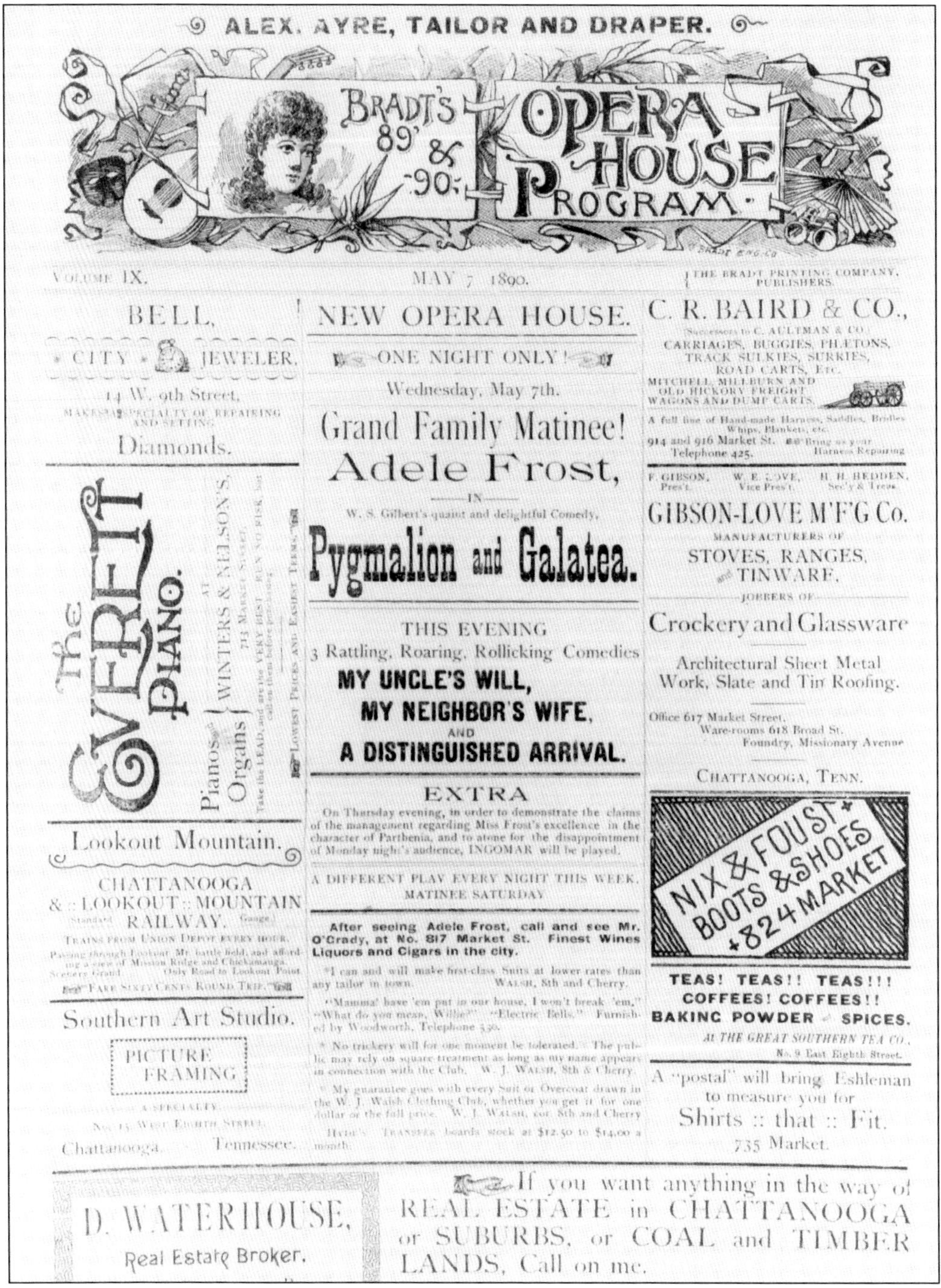

In 1886, Adolph Ochs started a fund to transform the old James Hall on Sixth and Market Streets into an Opera House. Forty prominent citizens contributed $1,000 each to begin the renovations. The opening night in October of that year proved quite interesting: several members of the audience walked out after a female in the production walked on stage in tights. Chattanoogans soon became more tolerant of stage productions. Under the management of Paul R. Albert, the Opera House reached its golden age in the 1890s.

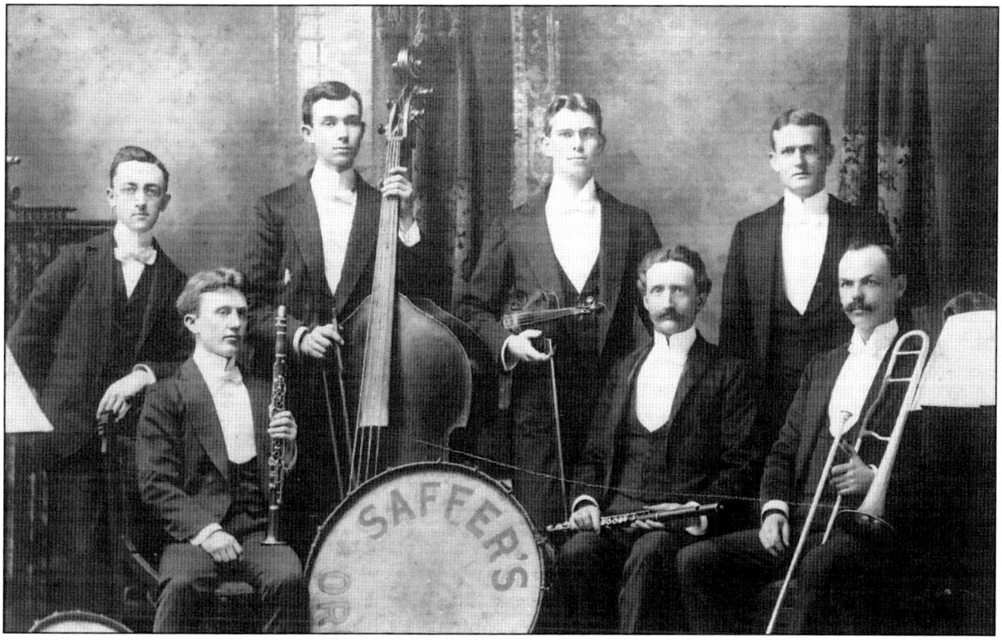

Saffer's Orchestra posed for this picture at the Lookout Inn in 1900. The Saffer brothers had come to the United States from Germany before the Civil War. Trained as coopers, they supplied both armies with barrels and continued making barrels for local distillers after the war. From there, it was natural to switch to the saloon business. Several members of the family were very talented musicians. The members of the orchestra in this photograph are, from left to right: Charles Park, Thomas Thorbahn, Frank Saffer, George Saffer, Louis Pahmeyer, George Gault, and Will F. Stewart.

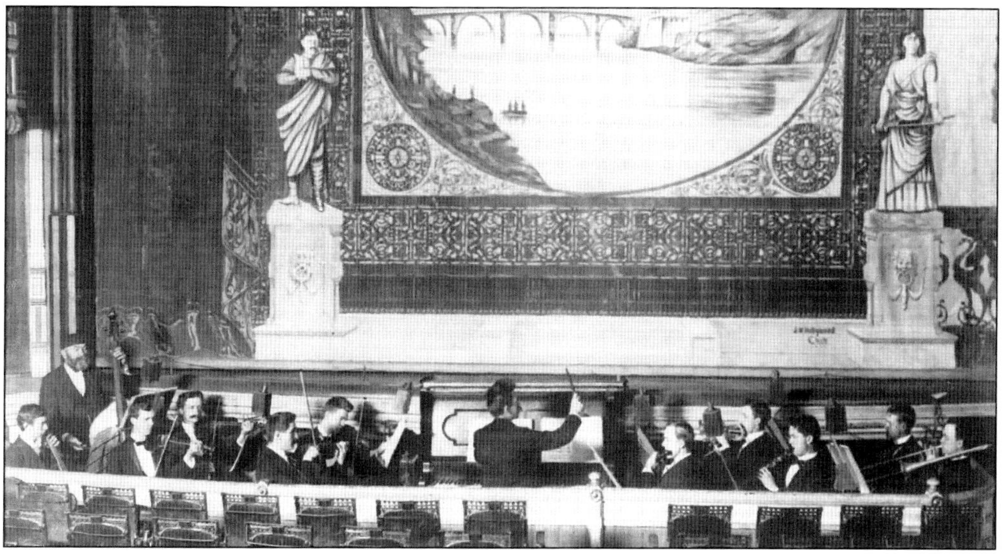

After its heyday in the 1890s, the Opera House was taken over by new management and renamed the Lyric Theater. A less sophisticated program of vaudeville acts and silent films was the main fare of the Lyric. This photograph, taken in 1900, shows members of the orchestra practicing in the pit. Louis Pahmeyer, a member of Saffer's Orchestra (pictured above), also played in the Lyric Orchestra. He is seated fourth from the left.

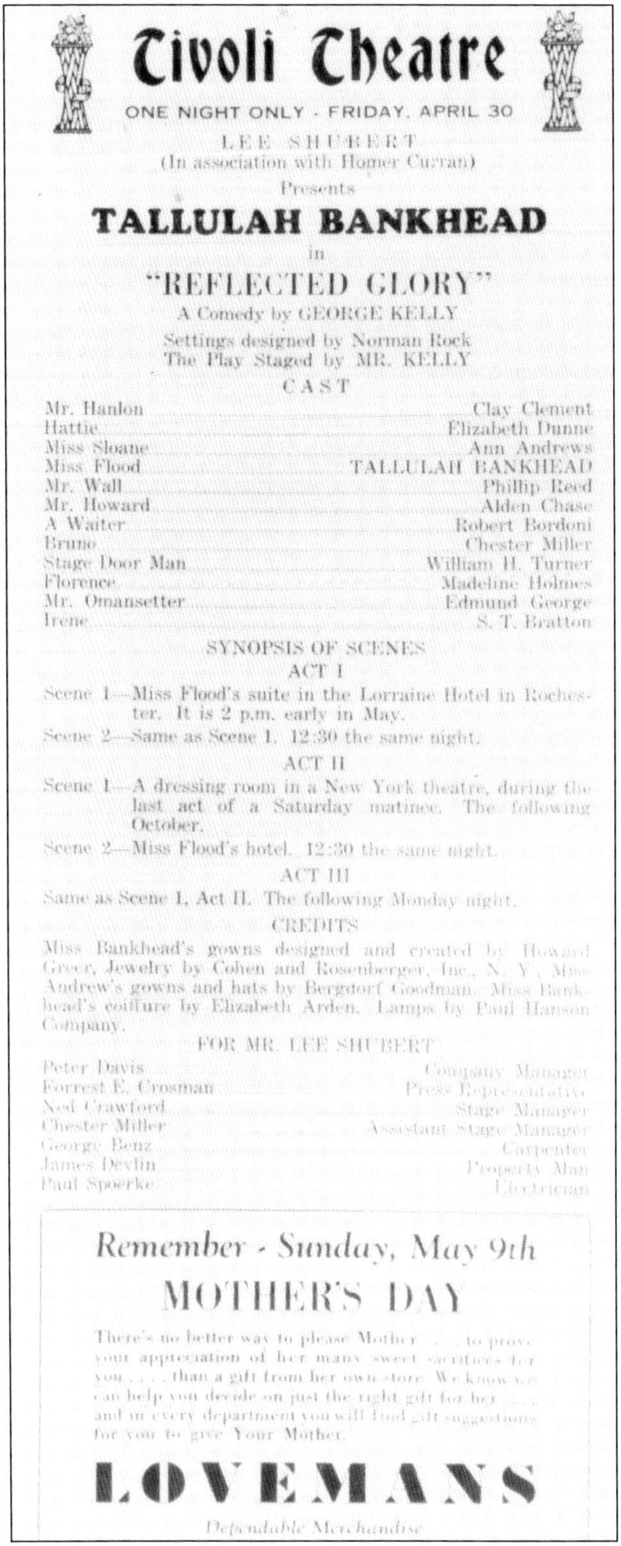

Tivoli Theatre

ONE NIGHT ONLY - FRIDAY, APRIL 30

LEE SHUBERT
(In association with Homer Curran)
Presents

TALLULAH BANKHEAD

in

"REFLECTED GLORY"

A Comedy by GEORGE KELLY

Settings designed by Norman Rock
The Play Staged by MR. KELLY

CAST

Mr. Hanlon	Clay Clement
Hattie	Elizabeth Dunne
Miss Sloane	Ann Andrews
Miss Flood	TALLULAH BANKHEAD
Mr. Wall	Phillip Reed
Mr. Howard	Alden Chase
A Waiter	Robert Bordoni
Bruno	Chester Miller
Stage Door Man	William H. Turner
Florence	Madeline Holmes
Mr. Omansetter	Edmund George
Irene	S. T. Bratton

SYNOPSIS OF SCENES

ACT I

Scene 1—Miss Flood's suite in the Lorraine Hotel in Rochester. It is 2 p.m. early in May.

Scene 2—Same as Scene 1. 12:30 the same night.

ACT II

Scene 1—A dressing room in a New York theatre, during the last act of a Saturday matinee. The following October.

Scene 2—Miss Flood's hotel. 12:30 the same night.

ACT III

Same as Scene I, Act II. The following Monday night.

CREDITS

Miss Bankhead's gowns designed and created by Howard Greer, Jewelry by Cohen and Rosenberger, Inc., N. Y., Miss Andrew's gowns and hats by Bergdorf Goodman. Miss Bankhead's coiffure by Elizabeth Arden. Lamps by Paul Hansen Company.

FOR MR. LEE SHUBERT

Peter Davis	Company Manager
Forrest E. Crosman	Press Representative
Ned Crawford	Stage Manager
Chester Miller	Assistant Stage Manager
George Benz	Carpenter
James Devlin	Property Man
Paul Spoerke	Electrician

The grandest of all the Chattanooga theaters was the Tivoli. Built at a cost of $750,000, this majestic theater opened in March 1921. The first program featured *The Kid*, a Charlie Chaplin film. With a full orchestra and a pipe organ costing $30,000, the Tivoli became one of the finest entertainment centers in the South. The City of Chattanooga bought the property in 1976. It has been added to the National Register of Historic Places and it underwent a complete restoration in the early 1990s.

Eight

Sports and Leisure

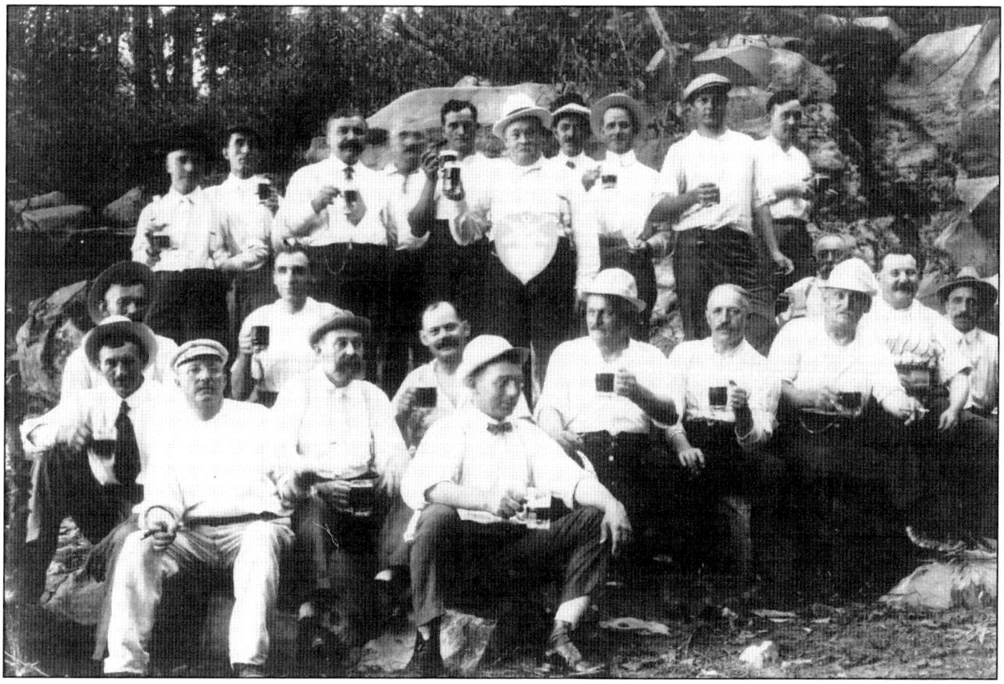

A group of unidentified men raise their beers in a toast at an outdoor event. Perhaps they were members of the German Turner Club or patrons of the popular Rathskeller Restaurant located in the Turner Hall on Cherry Street.

With the increase in labor-saving machinery at work and in the home and with the concurrent decrease in the number of hours people were expected to work each week, Chattanoogans found themselves with more leisure time. The streetcar and the automobile made it possible for citizens to enjoy the outdoors on the weekend: it was now easy to take a trip to a park, a county fair, or a baseball or football game. By the turn of the century, Chattanoogans had begun to develop a rich sports heritage.

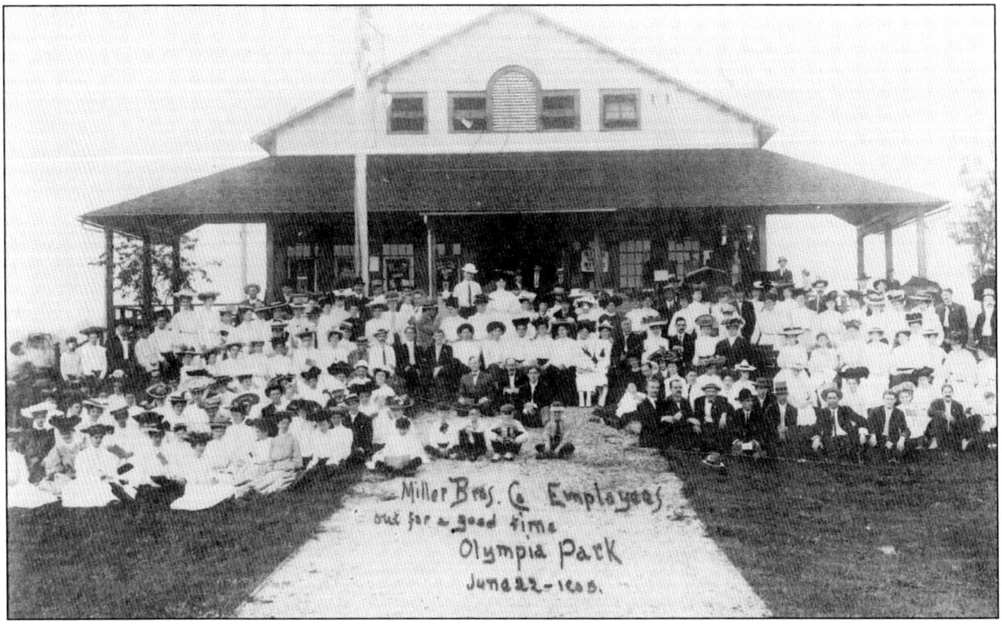

Employees of the Miller Brothers department store enjoy a company picnic at Olympia Park in 1905. Olympia Park, on McCallie Avenue, had opened in 1902. Built by the Chattanooga Electric Railway Company, the park had a theater, a race track, and many other attractions. More than one thousand people watched a production of *The Mountain Waif* at the theater's opening.

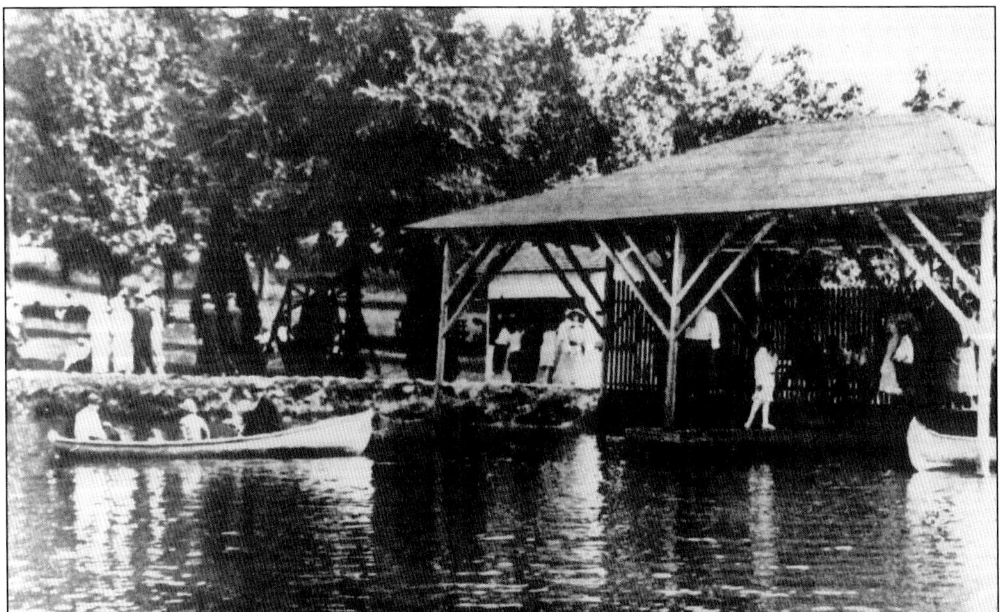

Another popular stop along the "Belt Line" (operated by the Union Railway Company) was East Lake Park. The park, located southeast of town near Rossville, GA, was built by Charles James as part of his Mission Ridge Land Company development. On July 4, 1896, James gave the lake to the city. The community of East Lake was annexed by Chattanooga in 1925.

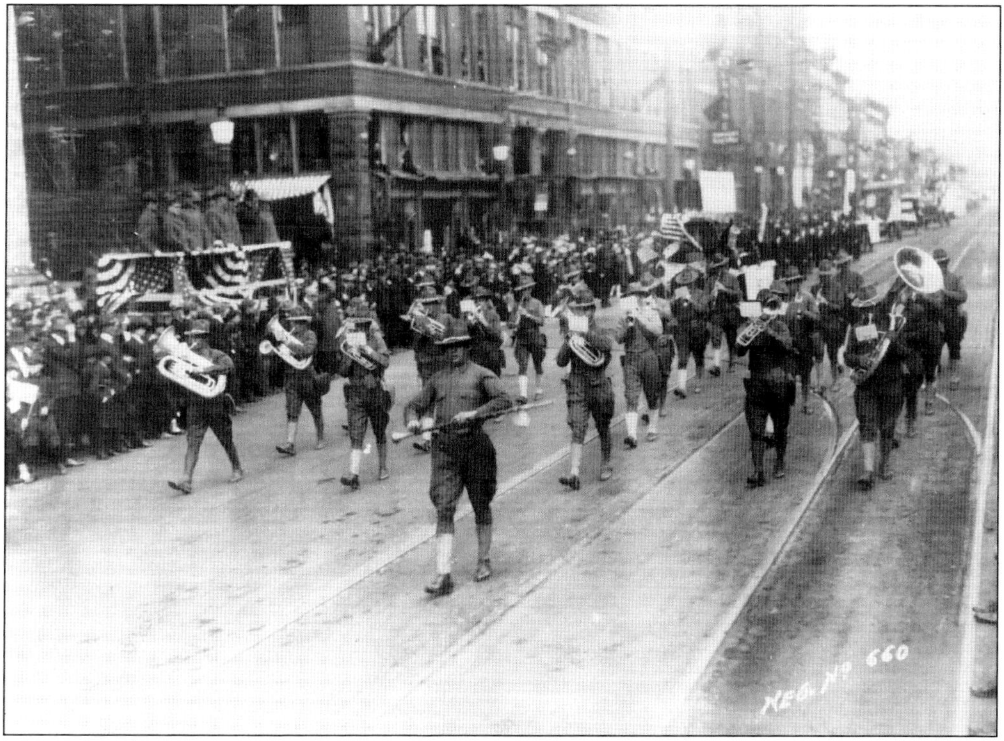

There is nothing like a good military parade to stir up patriotic feelings. This photograph shows the third Liberty Loan Parade, held on Market Street on April 6, 1918. City officials and military leaders stand on a review platform at the left. Although parades are held less frequently nowadays, the Armed Forces Day parade is still a popular annual event in Chattanooga.

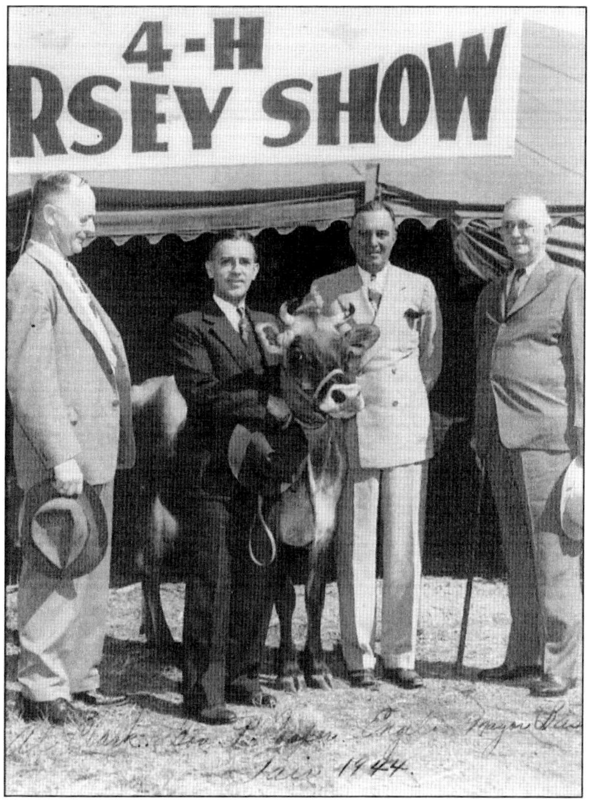

County fairs were and are popular events in east Tennessee. At this 4-H show in 1944 are, from left to right: Al Clark, Prentice Cooper (governor of Tennessee), Joe Engel (president of the Chattanooga Lookouts baseball team), and E.D. Bass (mayor of Chattanooga) admire a prize-winning cow.

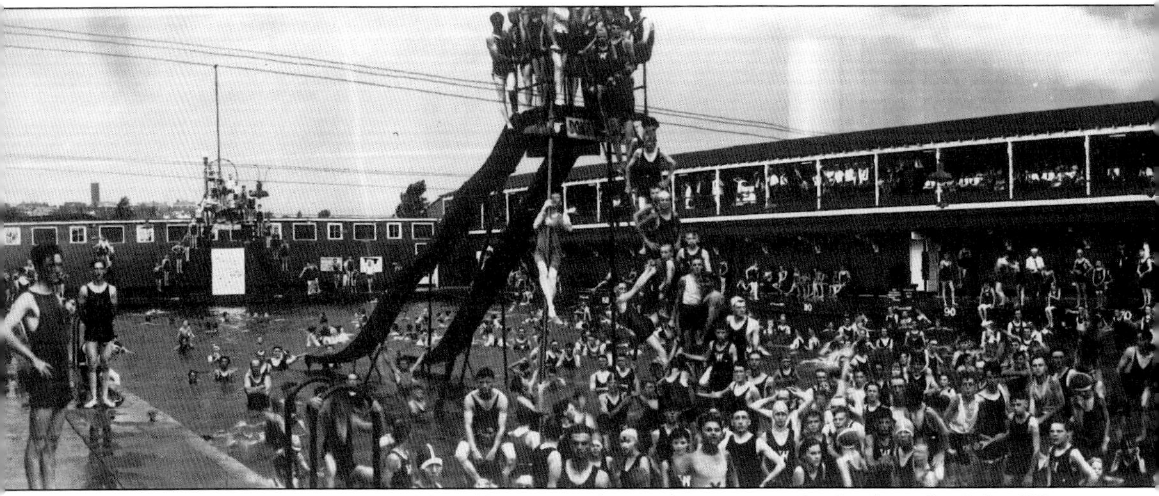

"Sanitary Pool, Ask the Health Officer," proclaims the sign on the back wall of the Warner Park Natatorium in this 1924 photograph. In 1912, Olympia Park was bought by the City of Chattanooga and renamed Warner Park. A natatorium, or swimming pool, was soon built.

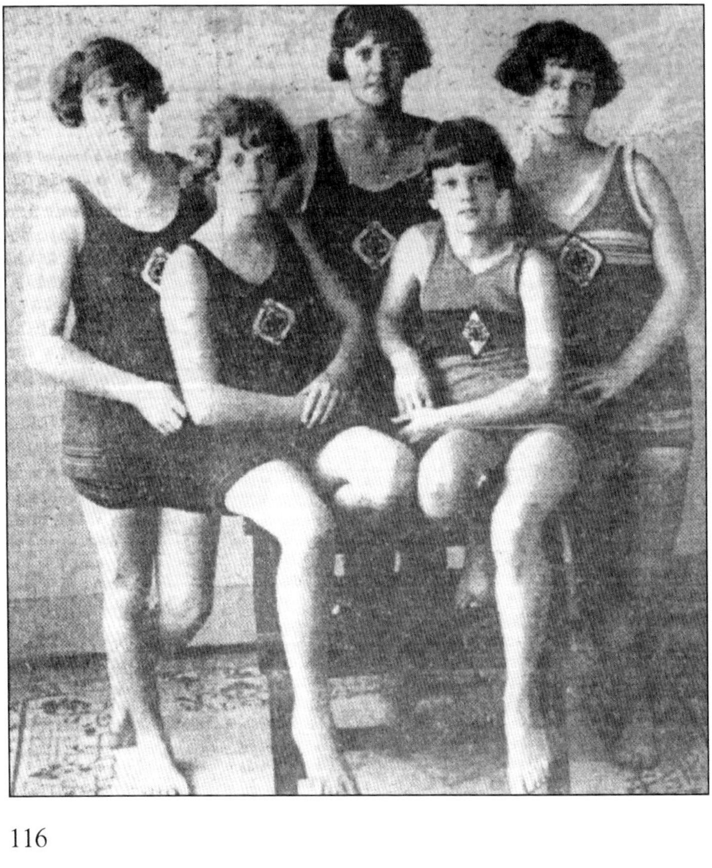

The Elberfeld sisters (Ruth, Edith, Dorothy, Miriam, and Nan) comprised a team that became famous throughout the South during the 1920s, where they played colleges and leading amateur teams. Excelling in swimming, diving, horseback riding, golf, gymnastics, and tennis, they gave boxing and wrestling exhibitions prior to basketball games. All later became physical education instructors, coaches, or playground supervisors.

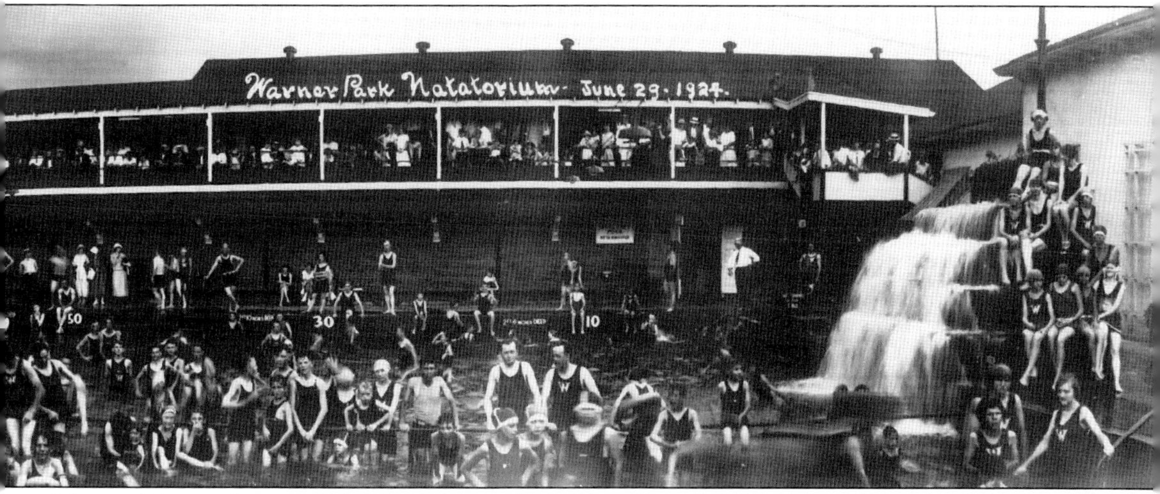

The pool featured a waterfall, water slides, a high diving board, and an observation platform for parents and other spectators. Swimmers without suits could rent a black suit with a large "W" on the front at the park.

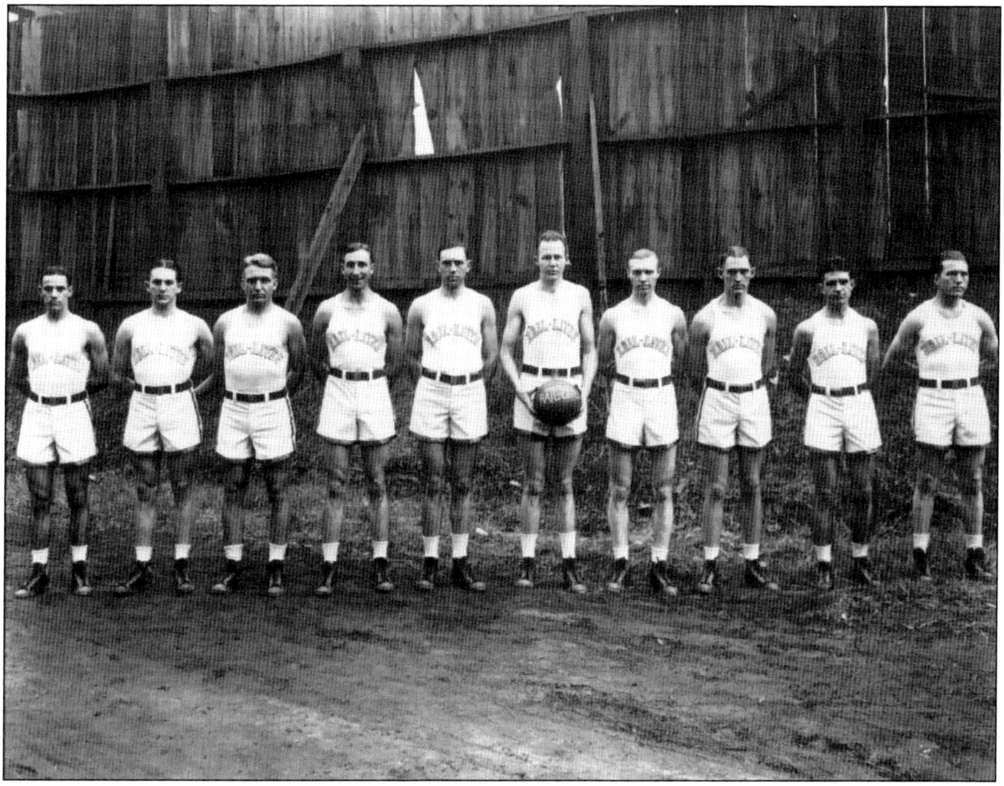

The members of the 1922 Rail-Lites semi-pro basketball team were all employees of the Chattanooga Railway and Light Company. The team played other company-supported teams across the South, often in front of large crowds. In the summer, most of the players played semi-pro baseball. In this photograph, team members are, from left to right: Shep Lauter, George Benjamin, Kenneth Keegan, Arthur Cooper, Humpy Philips, Bill Redd, Harry Cate, Miller Pruett, Tommy Hadete, and Roy Morphen.

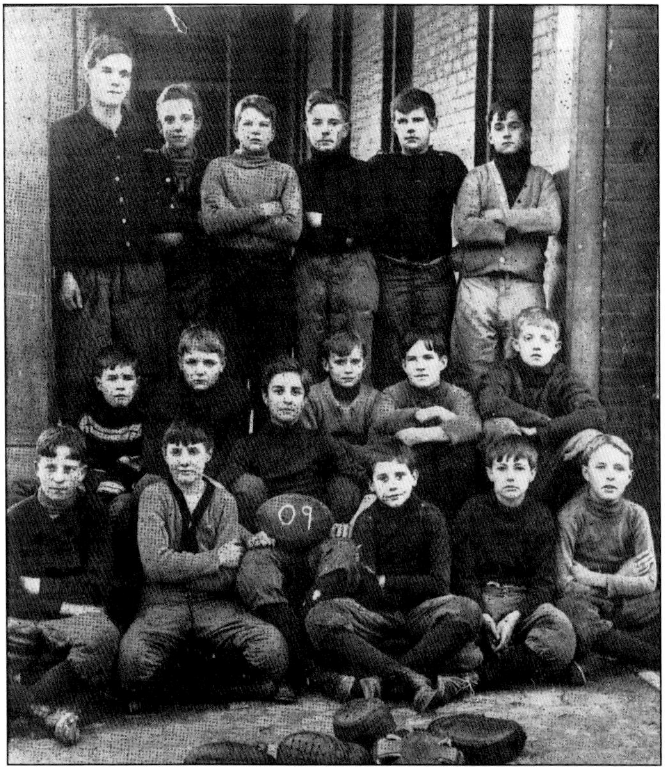

Football became a popular spectator sport in Chattanooga around the turn of the century, and local schools soon began competing for the city championship. Several private schools began rivalries which continue to this day. The first football game between the McCallie and Baylor Schools was played before a large crowd at Chamberlain Field in 1908. The game ended in a 0–0 tie.

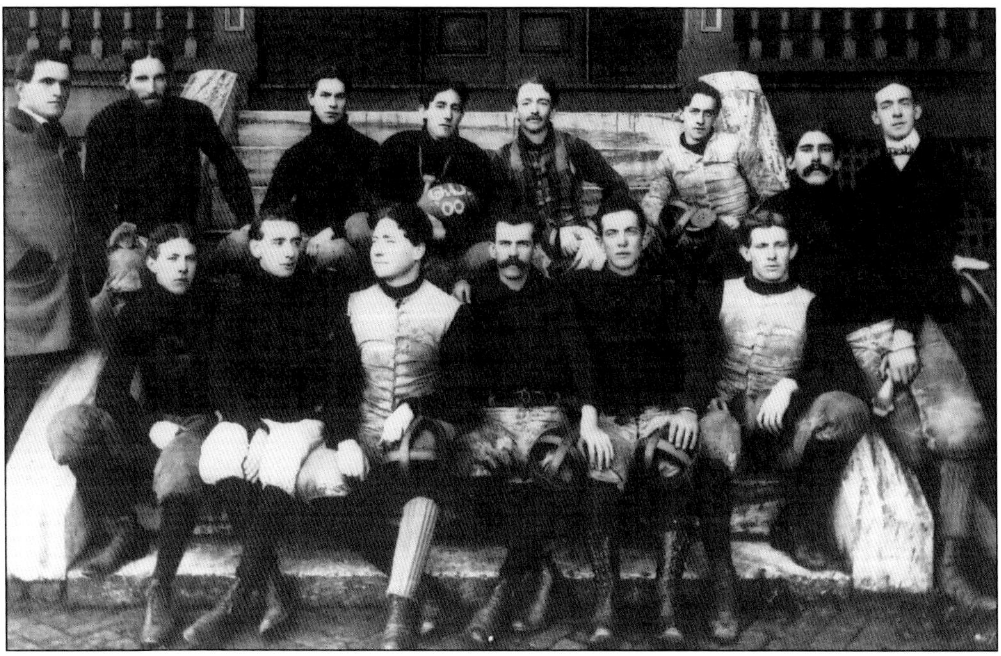

Members of the Grant University football team in a 1900 photograph. Football was played at Olympia Park or at the old Southern League baseball field. The only real competition for the university team at this time was the Chattanooga Athletic Club. The first real schedule of games was played in 1905. Dr. Walter Hullihen, a professor of Greek and Latin, was the coach.

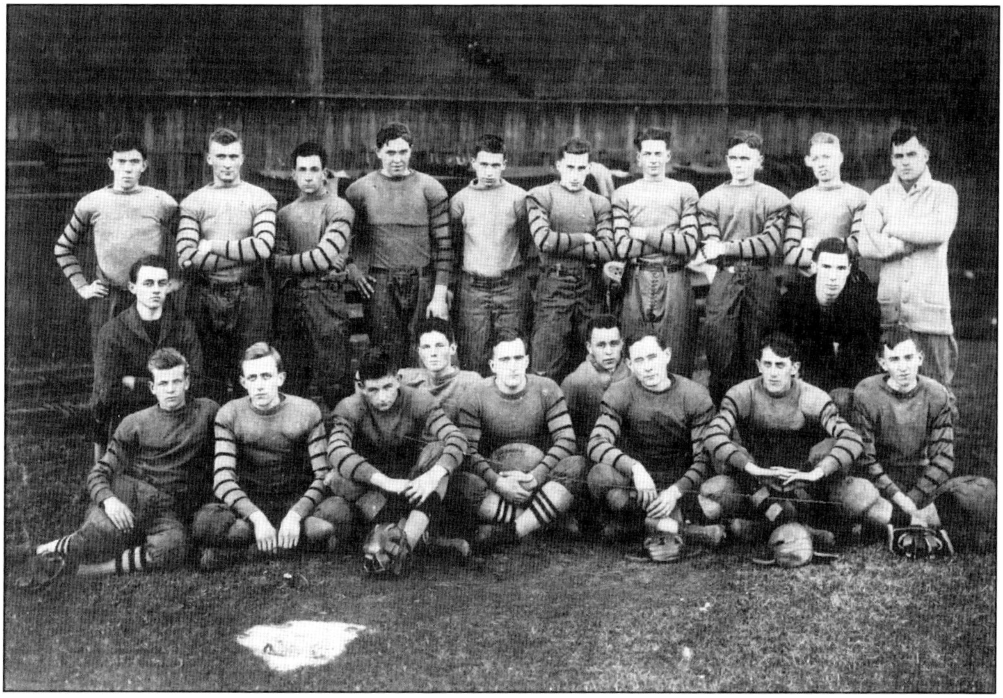

This 1920s University of Chattanooga football team poses at home plate. The 1919 *Moccasin* (the university's yearbook) reported that UC "suffered the worst football season in some years . . . the first team played was composed of ex-college stars and outweighed the University twenty pounds to the man. The second game's enormous score was due to "breaks," a muddy field, and two serious injuries, while the third game was snatched from UC's hand long after the game should have been called on account of darkness."

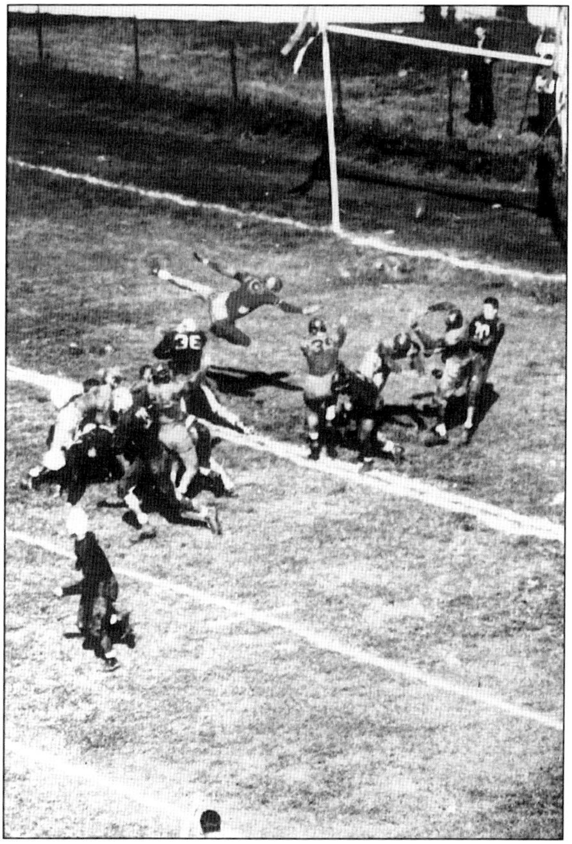

Some of the most exciting years in the history of football at the University of Chattanooga occurred in the 1930s when the school was a member of the Dixie Conference. In this photograph, the team blocks a kick at the goal line at Chamberlain Field. One member of the team, Robert Klein (shown here in the air after blocking the kick), was named to the Little All-American team, an honor that has been shared by eighteen other Moccasins.

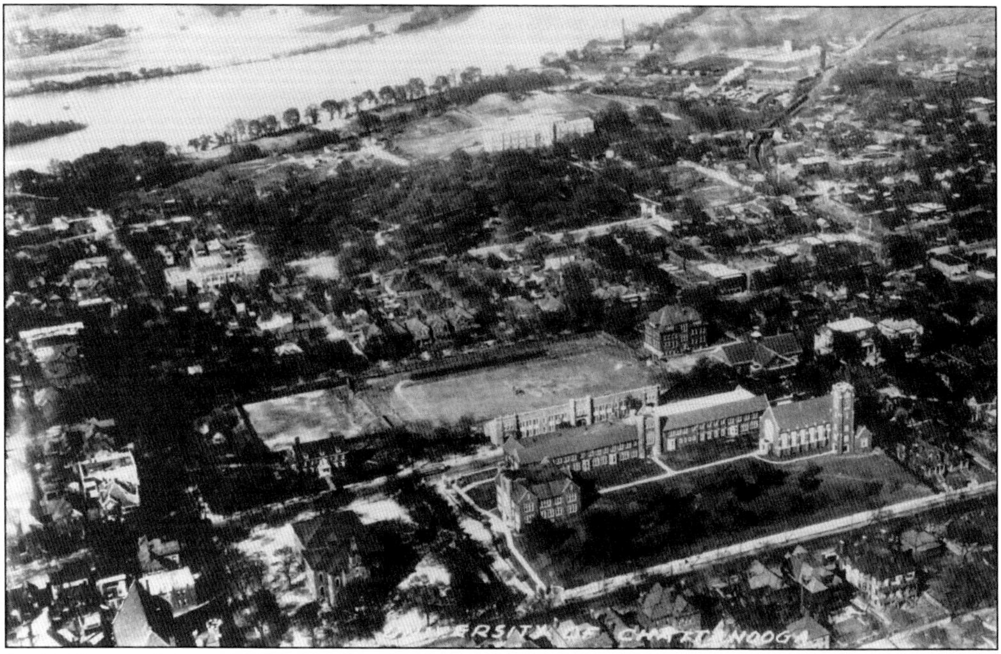

In 1908, an athletic field, complete with stands for spectators, was built at the University of Chattanooga. It was named Chamberlain Field, in honor of Captain Hiram S. Chamberlain, president of the university's board of trustees. To the left of the newer university buildings is the Central High School Building, which at the time this photograph was taken was being used as an elementary school.

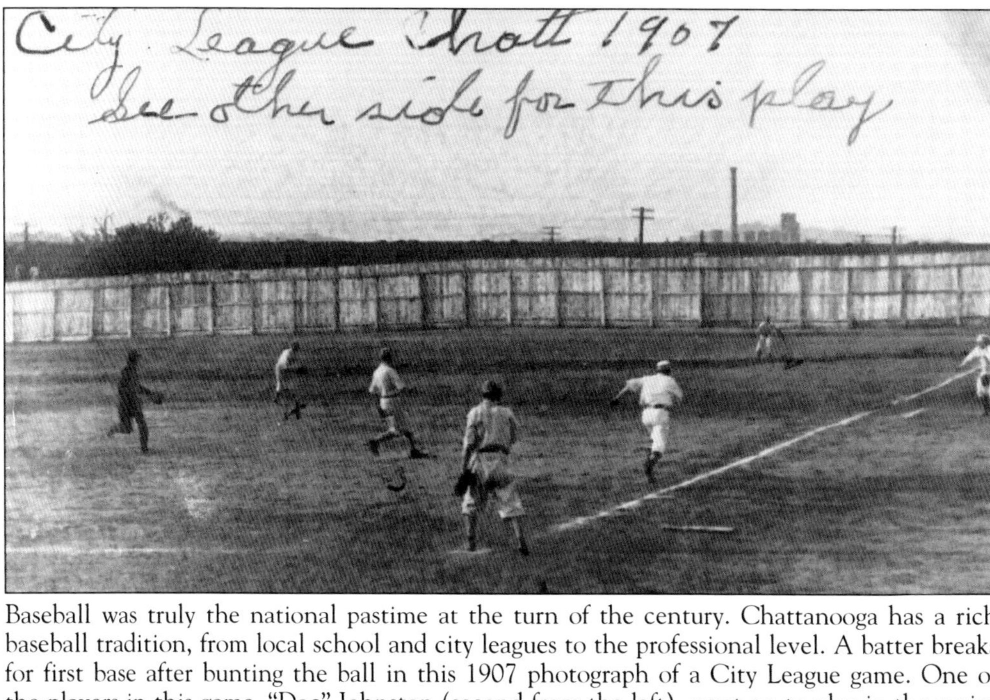

Baseball was truly the national pastime at the turn of the century. Chattanooga has a rich baseball tradition, from local school and city leagues to the professional level. A batter breaks for first base after bunting the ball in this 1907 photograph of a City League game. One of the players in this game, "Doc" Johnston (second from the left), went on to play in the major leagues for eleven years.

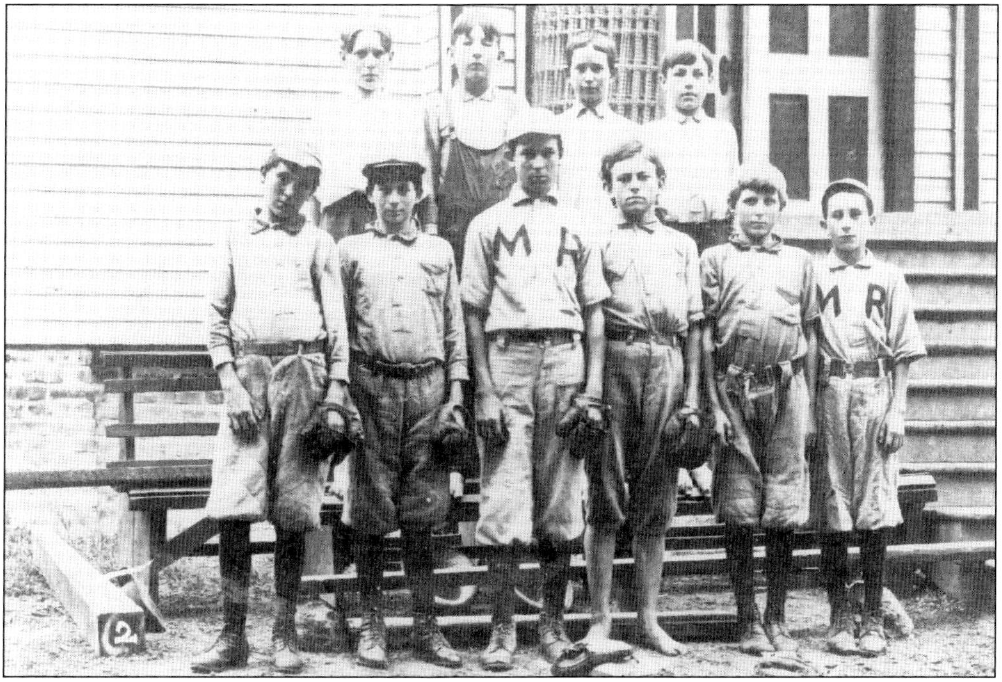

This photograph was labeled "Uncle Ed's School Team at Mission Ridge." Ed Carroll, a teacher at Missionary Ridge Elementary School, was probably the coach of this team. Two of the boys have "MR" painted on their shirts. One player better watch his toes!

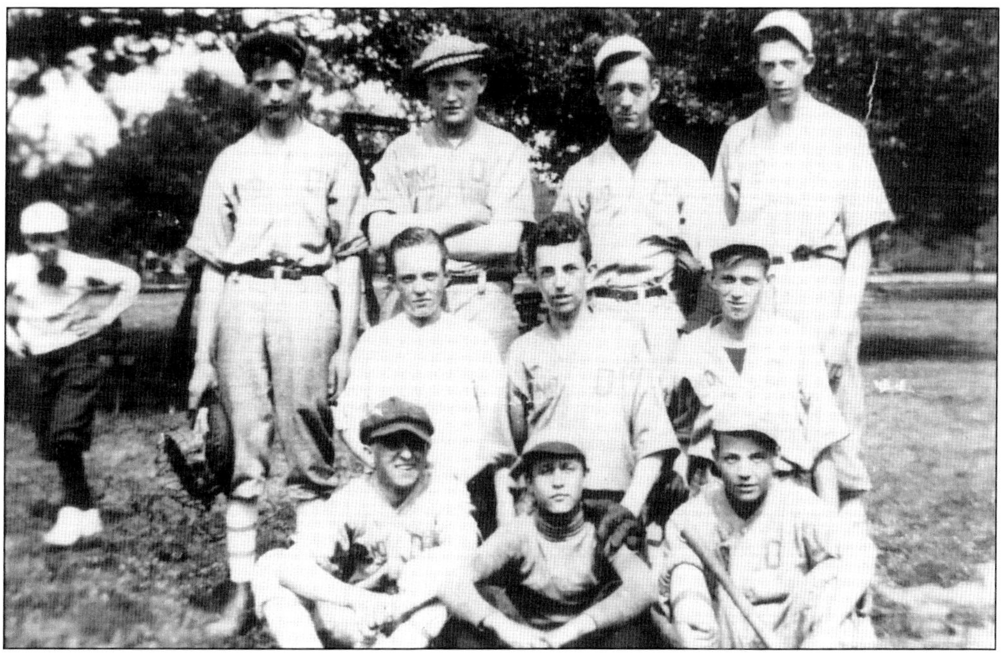

The Second District School baseball team posed for this photograph in 1914. These boys probably followed the sports pages for the daily scores from the three professional leagues (National, American, and Federal) and copied the batting styles of their favorite ballplayers: Ty Cobb, Tris Speaker, and Joe Jackson, amongst others.

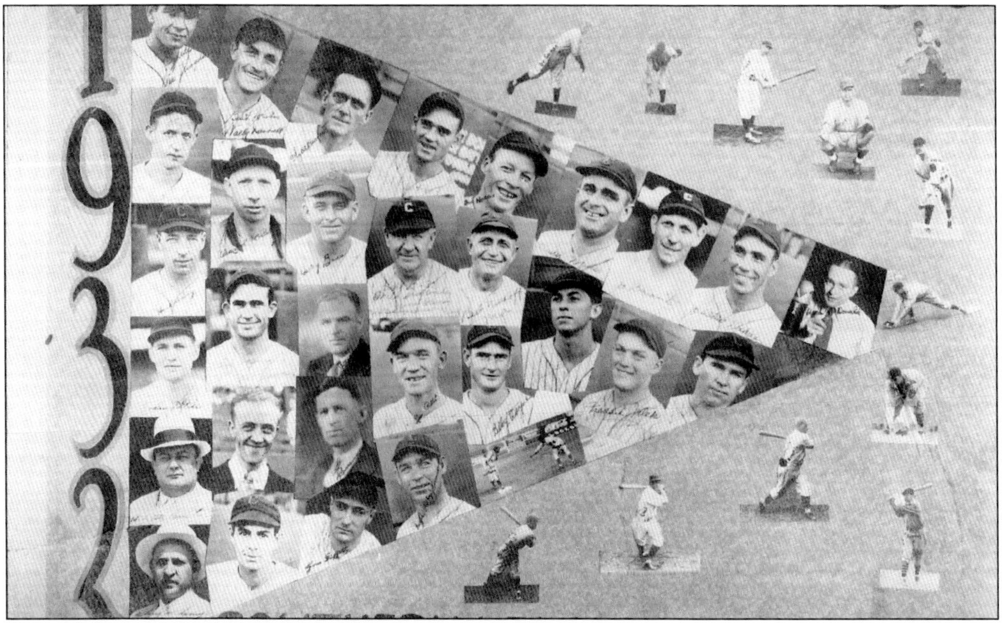

The first Southern League (minor league baseball) was organized in 1885. The Chattanooga representative in the league was an all-Irish team managed by Ted Sullivan. In 1901, Chattanooga became a charter member of the Southern Association but dropped out in 1903. Six years later, O.B. Andrews obtained a South Atlantic (Sally) League franchise. That year the team won the championship and was given the name "Chattanooga Lookouts" as a result of a fan contest. The team rejoined the Southern Association in 1910, but did not win another championship until 1932.

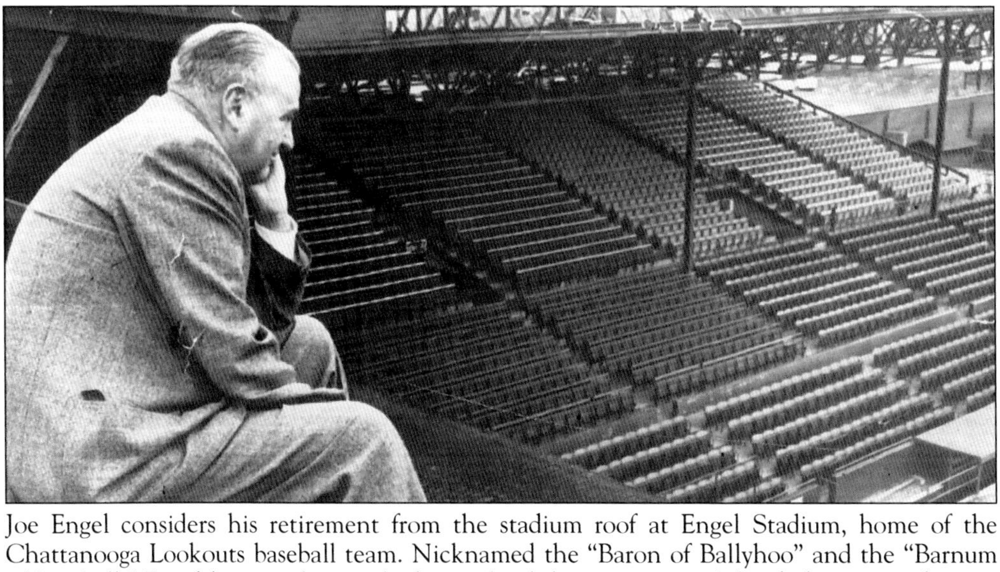

Joe Engel considers his retirement from the stadium roof at Engel Stadium, home of the Chattanooga Lookouts baseball team. Nicknamed the "Baron of Ballyhoo" and the "Barnum of Baseball," Engel became famous for his outlandish promotions. A borderline major leaguer for a few years (1912–1920), Engel worked as a scout in the Washington Senators organization before coming to Chattanooga in 1929. In his first year as the president of the club, he increased attendance at the ballpark from 78,000 to 172,000; an amazing feat considering it was the first full year of the Depression.

In 1931, the great New York Yankees team came to Chattanooga for an exhibition game. Joe Engel grabbed headlines across the country when he hired a girl, Jackie Mitchell, to pitch against the most feared lineup in baseball. Mitchell struck out Babe Ruth (shown above), Lou Gehrig, and Tony Lazzeri.

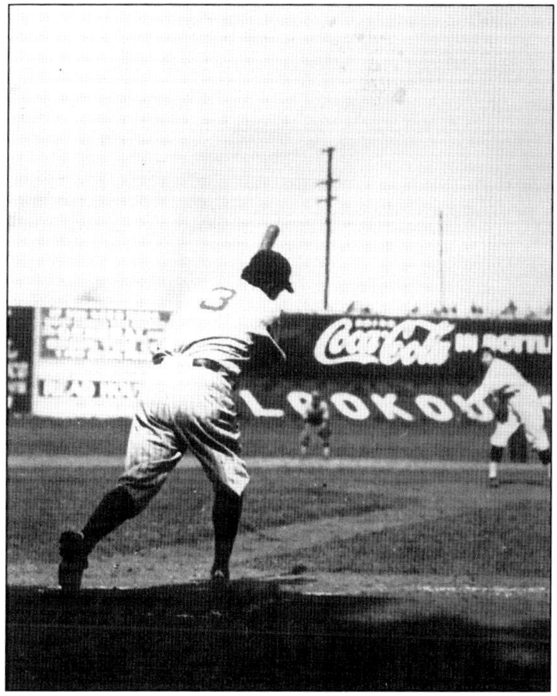

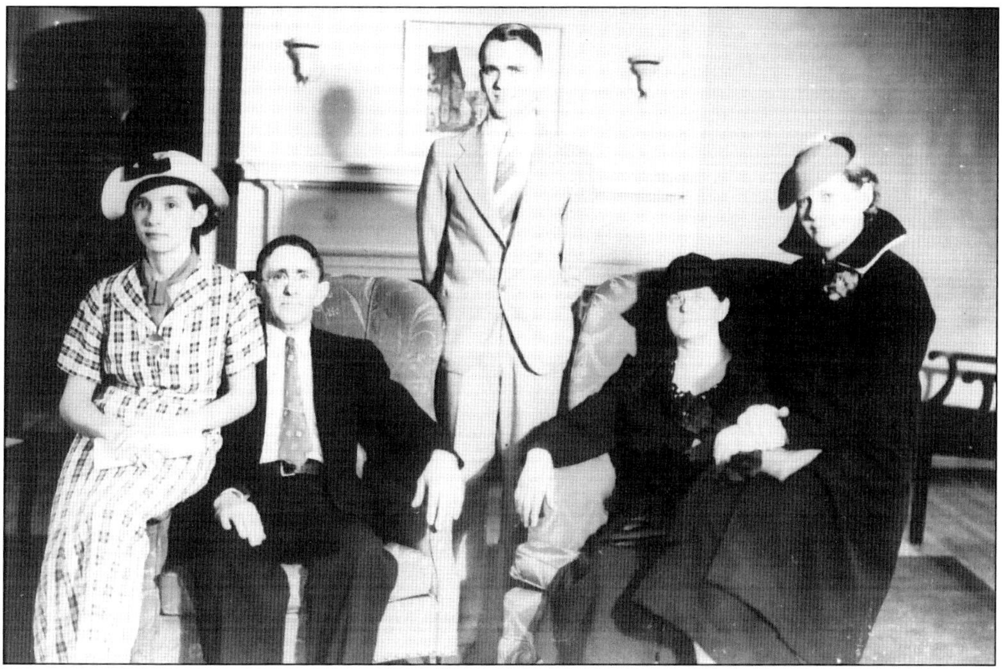

In 1936, lights were installed at Engel Stadium. In one of the most bizarre promotions in baseball history, Engel gave away a house and lot. Because the game attracted a crowd of 24,839 (the largest in stadium history) much of the crowd watched the game from the outfield. Engel's secretary, Eleanor Sandlin, secretly froze the baseballs before the game so that not too many would be hit into the overflow. The family pictured above was the proud winner of the $15,000 home.

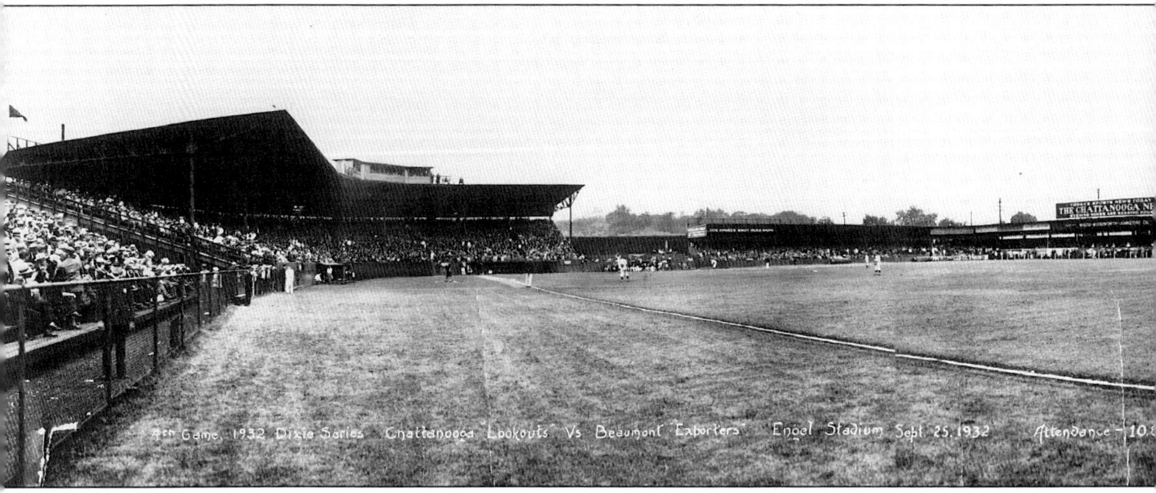

When it was built in 1930, Engel Stadium was considered the most modern minor league ballpark in the country. This panoramic photograph was taken just before the fourth game of the 1932 Dixie Series. Attendance on this day was 10,849, and the Lookouts beat the Beaumont "Exporters" for the championship. The panorama below shows a night game during which a lucky family in the crowd (see p. 123) won a house and lot. This game set an all-time attendance record. However, at the height of the Depression, attendance dwindled, causing the owner to

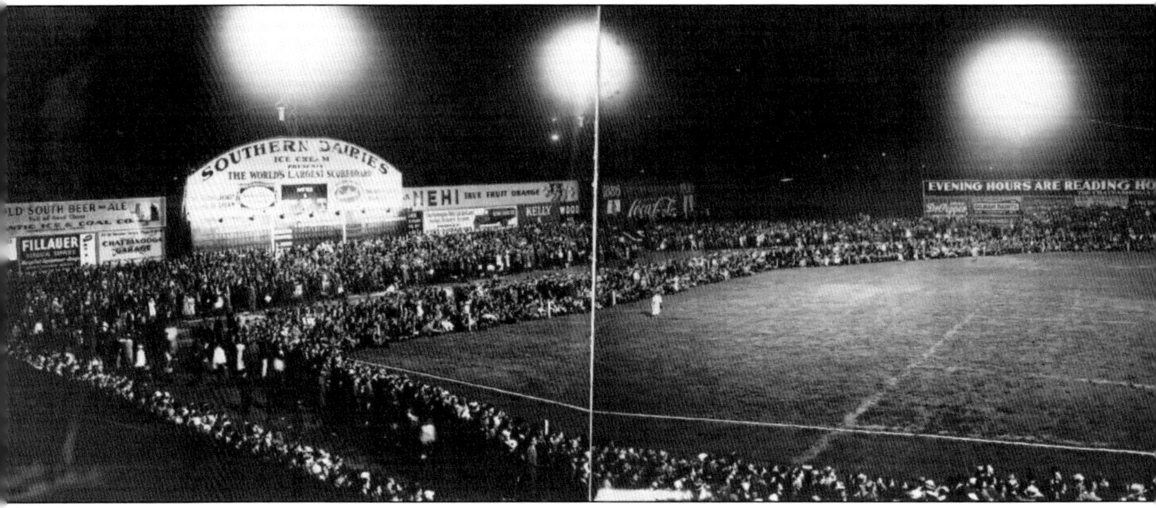

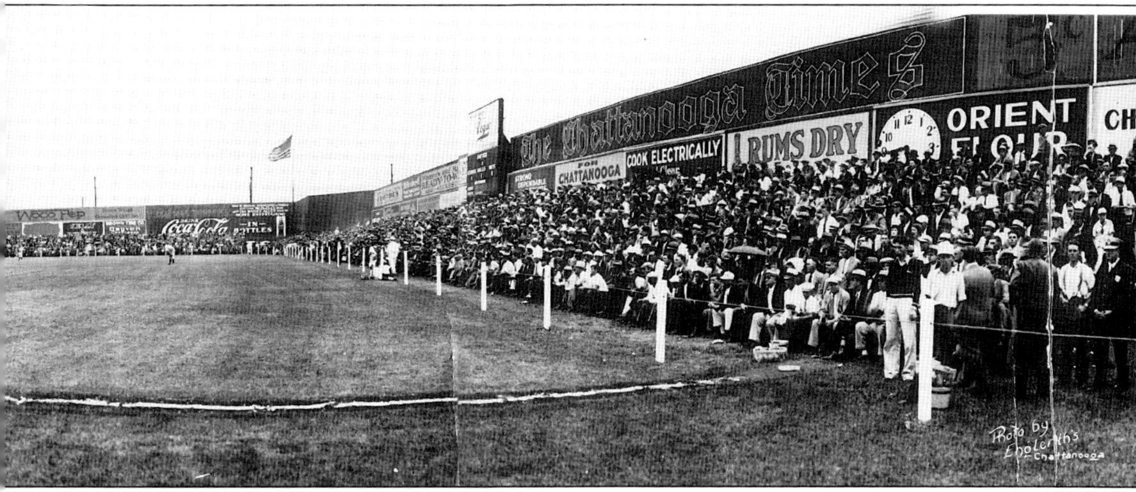

sell shares of the team to the public. During World War II the franchise shifted to Montgomery, AL, for half a season before returning to Chattanooga. After the Southern Association folded in the early 1960s, the Lookouts rejoined the Sally League (renamed the Southern League) but soon folded themselves. For ten years there was no minor league baseball in Chattanooga. Finally, in 1976, another attempt was made to operate a franchise in Chattanooga. Today, the AA Chattanooga Lookouts are affiliated with the Cincinnati Reds.

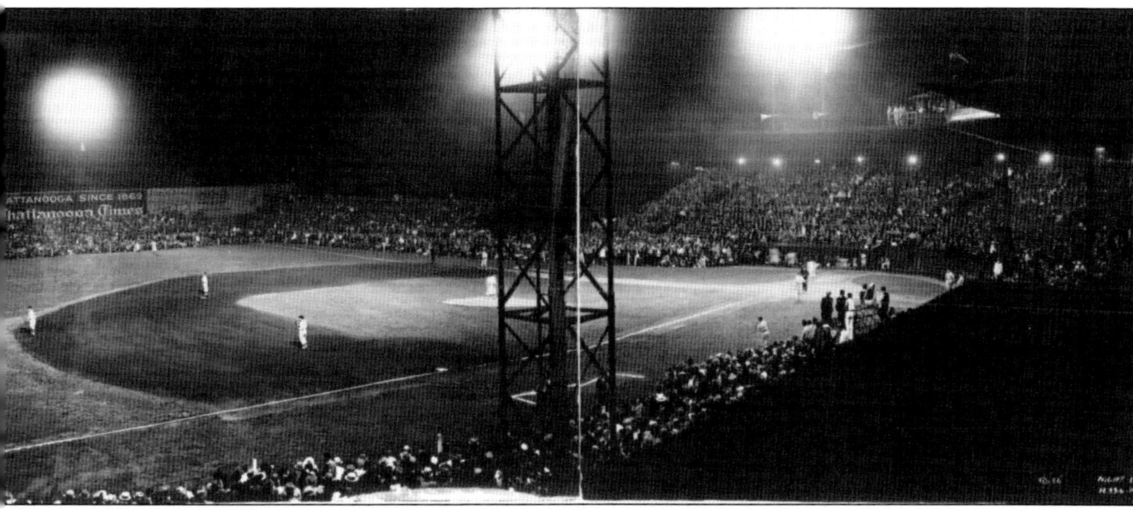

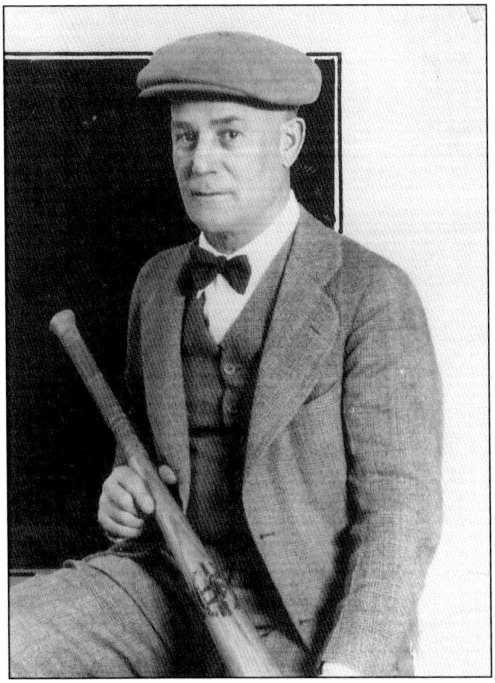

Norman Arthur "Kid" Elberfeld played professional baseball for fourteen seasons. Also known as the "Tabasco Kid," Elberfeld played most of his career with the New York Highlanders (renamed the Yankees). Elberfeld managed successful baseball schools after his retirement from the playing field. He managed the Lookouts for three different terms and made his home in Chattanooga until his death in 1944.

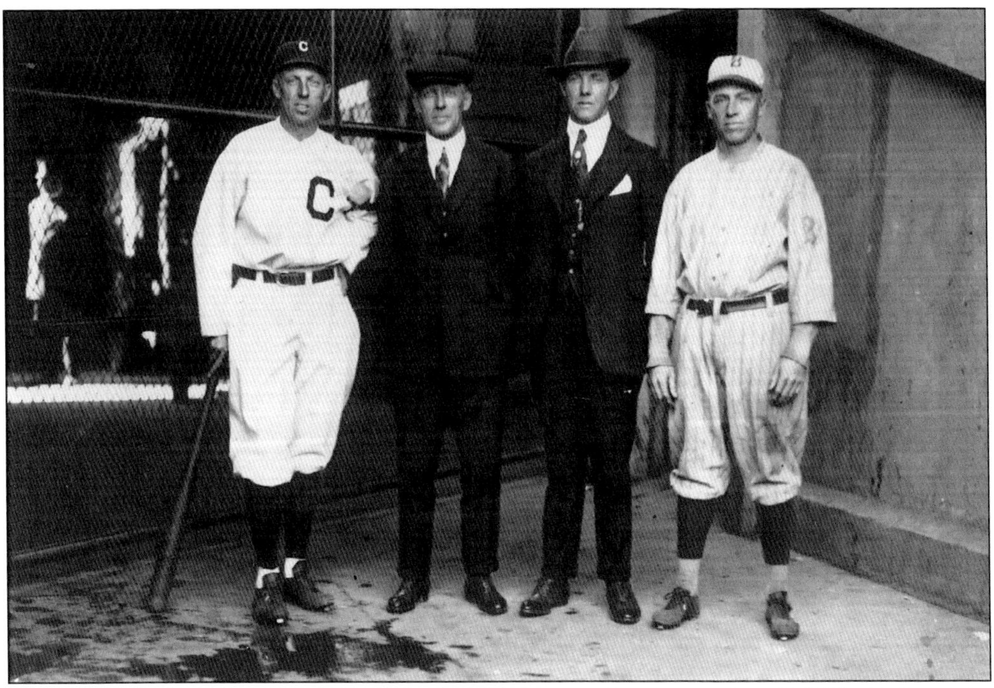

Two natives of the Chattanooga region played against each other in the 1920 World Series. In fact, they were brothers. Wheeler "Doc" Johnston (left), the first baseman for the Cleveland Indians, and James Johnston (right), the second basemen for the Brooklyn Robins, were born in Cleveland, TN, but played ball in Chattanooga as boys. They both got three hits in the series won by the Indians. Both men had fine careers in the majors (Jimmy had a lifetime batting average of .294) and died in Chattanooga in the 1960s.

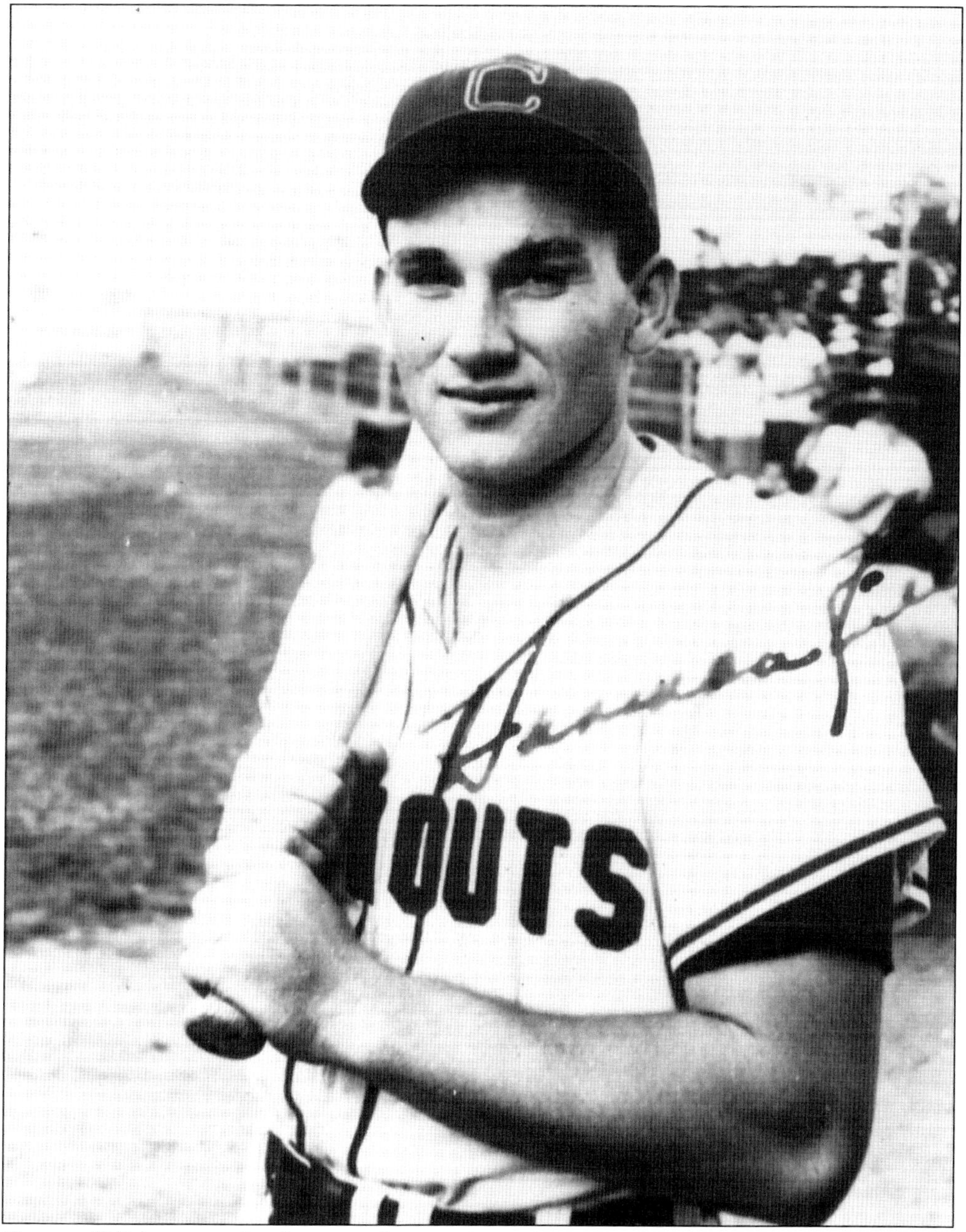

Harmon Killebrew in a Lookouts uniform in the 1950s. Several Hall of Fame baseball players have come through Chattanooga as either players or managers. This list includes: Kiki Cuyler, Burleigh Grimes, Rogers Hornsby, Ferguson Jenkins, and Harmon Killebrew. Clark Griffith, owner of the Chattanooga Lookouts for many years, was inducted into the Hall of Fame in 1946. In addition, Satchel Paige played for the Chattanooga Black Lookouts in 1926 and 1927, and Willie Mays played for the Chattanooga Choo-Choos, a black semi-pro team, in 1947.

Acknowledgments

A special debt of gratitude is reserved for David Estabrook, Donna Ettkin, Mary Jane Blake, the rest of the Chattanooga Regional History Museum staff, and the Bridgeview Black and White Photo Lab.

Bibliography

Armstrong, Zella. *The History of Hamilton County and Chattanooga, Tennessee*. Chattanooga, Tennessee: Lookout Publishing Company, 1931.

Govan, Gilbert E. and James W. Livingood. *The Chattanooga County, 1541–1951*. New York: E.P. Dutton and Company Inc., 1952.

Livingood, James W. *Chattanooga, An Illustrated History*. Woodland Hills, California: Windsor Publications, Inc., 1980.

———. *Hamilton County, Tennessee*. Memphis, Tennessee: Memphis State University Press, 1981.

———. *The Chattanooga County: Gateway to History*. Chattanooga, Tennessee: Chattanooga Area Historical Association, 1995.

Walker, Robert Sparks. *Lookout, Story of a Mountain*. Kingsport, Tennessee: Southern Publishers, Inc., 1941.

Wilson, John. *Chattanooga's Story*. Chattanooga, Tennessee: *The Chattanooga News-Free Press*, 1980.

———. *Lookout*. Chattanooga, Tennessee: John Wilson, 1977.